Knight Prisoner

Thomas Malory Then and Now

In memory of
Tony Tanner, 1935–1998

Knight Prisoner

Thomas Malory Then and Now

T. J. LUSTIG

sussex
ACADEMIC
PRESS
Brighton • Chicago • Toronto

2 4 6 8 10 9 7 5 3 1

First published in 2013 by
SUSSEX ACADEMIC PRESS
PO Box 139
Eastbourne BN24 9BP

and in the United States of America by
SUSSEX ACADEMIC PRESS
Independent Publishers Group
814 North Franklin Street, Chicago, IL 60610

and in Canada by
SUSSEX ACADEMIC PRESS (CANADA)
8000 Bathurst Street, Unit 1, PO Box 30010, Vaughan, Ontario L4J 0C6

British Library Cataloguing in Publication Data
A CIP catalogue record for this book is available from the British Library.

Library of Congress Cataloging-in-Publication Data
Lustig, T. J., 1961–
Knight Prisoner : Thomas Malory Then and Now / T.J. Lustig.
    pages   cm
Includes bibliographical references and index.
ISBN 978-1-84519-605-9 (p/b : acid-free paper)
    1. Malory, Thomas, Sir, active 15th century. Morte d'Arthur. I. Title.
PR2045.L86 2013
823'.2–dc23

                                                          2013021492

Typeset and designed by Sussex Academic Press, Brighton & Eastbourne.
Printed by TJ International, Padstow, Cornwall.
This book is printed on acid-free paper.

Contents

Contents

List of Illustrations

Source details are provided *in situ* with the illustrations. The author and publishers apologize for any errors or omissions in the copyright information detailed and would be grateful to be notified of any corrections that should be incorporated in the next edition or reprint of this book.

Preface

The present book combines the traditional methods of biography and textual analysis with less conventional approaches to literary criticism. This combination may alienate those who prefer the 'critical' to the 'creative' as well as those whose preferences incline in the opposite direction. In the end, however, such distinctions don't take us very far. I would never suggest that scholarly work on the *Morte d'Arthur* precludes emotional or imaginative engagement. Nor would I accept that the insights of autobiographical writing are 'subjective' – at least in any pejorative sense. My quest in this book eventually takes me to Newbold Revel in Warwickshire. By the time I get there, I hope to have said something worthwhile about literary style and the equally mysterious nature of nationhood.

The first part of the book is devoted to the *Morte* itself. I discuss Malory's representation of spatial and temporal relationships and his depictions of physical violence and sexual desire. I do so by counter-pointing my account of the *Morte* with an analysis of my responses, aged 8, to Phyllis Briggs's *King Arthur and the Knights of the Round Table* – an abridgment which served as my introduction to Arthurian narrative. Briggs didn't simply transmit what one might call 'ideology' (although she sometimes did just that). My experience as a young reader sheds light on the ways in which understandings and misunderstandings about narrative develop as stories alter our deepest beliefs.

The second part of the book is more 'traditional' in that it is a study of Malory's life – what we know of it. Although I depend on previous scholarship I make a sustained effort to situate Malory within the complex network of loyalties and obligations known as the 'affinity system' during a period of national instability not seen since the Norman invasion. Reading the life into the work and the work into the life, I make new suggestions about Malory's relationship with Humphrey Stafford, 1st Duke of Buckingham. I also consider Malory's life in relation to that of Henry VI, seeing these two figures as an emblem of the national mind in the period after 1450.

Part III of the book addresses the afterlife of the *Morte* – its survival in twentieth and twentieth-first-century culture, often in the most unexpected of places (*The Wind in the Willows* is one example, *The Guns of Navarone* another). Much of this section focuses on the *Morte*'s effect on the work of Alfred Tennyson and T. S. Eliot. Among other things I claim to have identified which edition of Malory was read by Eliot at the age of 11 or 12 – the children's version which in 1934 the author of "The Waste Land" said had always been his favourite book. This section is a biography of a book rather than a traditional study of reception. But textual analysis is not abandoned: indeed, I make a more sustained argument for the structural centrality of Book X of the *Morte* – and of Malory's Sir Dinadan – than has previously been advanced.

Acknowledgements

I would like to thank those who read parts of this book in draft form: David Amigoni, James Hamilton-Paterson, Andrew Hewson, Simon Ross and John Schad. I am grateful to Judith Woolf for getting me to think about the *Morte d'Arthur* in 1981. Thanks are due to Maurice Tennant for his advice on early maps of Warwickshire. I am grateful to Catherine Fell, Andrew Hinett and Dot Jeffcott at Her Majesty's Prison Service College, Newbold Revel. I wish to record my thanks to those staff who gave so generously of their time, knowledge and expertise at Keele University Library (particularly Phil Johnson), Cambridge University Library (particularly Les Goodey and Don Manning), the English Faculty Library, Cambridge, the British Library and the John Rylands Library. For her advice on the use of the *Dictionary of National Biography* I am grateful to Alannah Tomkins. I would also like to thank Anthony Grahame, my editor at Sussex Academic Press and David Avital of Bloomsbury publishers. My gratitude to Maryse Tennant is beyond words. Above all – for many hours of support and for many years of friendship – I would like to thank Alan McIntosh.

Introduction

It was in York, some time in the October of 1981 – quite early one morning, I seem to remember. The day was cloudless and the air in the streets was imbued with the blueness above. It was here, in a bookshop on Micklegate, quite near the river – a bookshop which no longer exists – that I bought Sir Thomas Malory's *Le Morte d'Arthur*, in two volumes (£1.50 net UK price per volume), with an introduction by Sir John Rhys, a 1978 paperback reprint by J. M. Dent & Sons of the 1906 Everyman's Library Edition. Each of the two volumes had a green spine (much faded now) accompanied by Dent's fish and anchor design. Each had a cover with lettering in the same shade of green, together with the figure of Everyman. Inside both volumes, those famous lines:

> *EVERYMAN, I will go with thee,*
> *and be thy guide,*
> *In thy most need to go by thy side*

FIGURE 1 The J. M. Dent motif. Joseph Malaby Dent founded the company in 1888; it became J. M. Dent & Sons in 1909 when Hugh Dent joined the firm.

FIGURE 2 The Everyman motif. Under the editorship of Ernest Rhys, the Everyman's Library series started publication in 1906 with James Boswell's *Life of Dr Johnson*. Also published in 1906, *Le Morte d'Arthur* formed Volumes XLV and XLVI of the series, accompanying other first year authors such as Francis Bacon, Jane Austen, Samuel Taylor Coleridge and Alfred Tennyson.

The text of the Everyman *Morte* was taken by Rhys from F. J. Simmons's two-volume edition of *The Birth, Life and Acts of King Arthur* (1893–4).[1] Simmons preserved the structure of the first printed edition of the *Morte*, published by William Caxton at Westminster in 1485. But by modernizing Malory's English he made the *Morte* accessible to a new generation of readers. Rhys chose Simmons as his copy text because he wanted a Malory for Everyman. Unfortunately, Rhys's introduction isn't as reliable a guide to the *Morte* as one might wish: it claims that Malory was Welsh – something most contemporary scholars would reject out of hand. I nevertheless prefer the Everyman to the third edition of *The Works of Sir Thomas Malory*, which is now accepted by most (but not all) scholars as the standard text. *The Works of Sir Thomas Malory* is based on a manuscript of the *Morte* which was discovered at Winchester in 1934 and is, according to its first editor, "more complete and authentic" than Caxton. In spite of its shortcomings, however, I will always think of the Everyman edition as *my* Malory. I have kept it for 30 years; it was with me as I wrote; it is why I refer to *Le Morte d'Arthur* rather than *Le Morte Darthur*, to Launcelot rather than Lancelot, and to Guenever rather than Gwenyvere.[2]

I wanted to use the Everyman to reconstruct my first reading of the *Morte* in 1981. Unfortunately, the marks left by more recent visits have obscured my original annotations. Back then, being aware that Eliot mentioned Jessie Weston in his notes to "The Waste Land", I was fascinated by the figure of the Fisher King. Turning the pages of my Everyman, I see that I was also interested in Malory's references to magical potions and poisons. Just before that famous line in Book XXI which my Everyman placed in emboldened Gothic, like an inscription on a tombstone – "𝔥𝔦𝔠 𝔧𝔞𝔠𝔢𝔱 𝔄𝔯𝔱𝔥𝔲𝔯𝔲𝔰 𝔯𝔢𝔵, 𝔮𝔲𝔬𝔫𝔡𝔞𝔪 𝔯𝔢𝔵 𝔮𝔲𝔢 𝔣𝔲𝔱𝔲𝔯𝔲𝔰" – I placed quotation marks around Malory's last and more skeptical words on King Arthur:

> men say that he shall come again, and he shall win the holy cross. I will not say it shall be so, but rather I will say, here in this world he changed his life.

Regrettably, my Everyman reveals almost nothing about how I responded to the *Morte* some three decades ago. Those two volumes remain precious but neither is quite as magical as the book in which I first read about King Arthur. I follow the stair as it descends into the past, and now the light brightens. There is a garden with a pear tree and a wall of reddish brick. In the evening sunshine my parents are

FIGURE 3 The Dean & Son motif. Thomas Dean was publishing children's books prior to 1800; his son George became a partner in 1847. *King Arthur and the Knights of the Round Table*

PRINTED IN

DEAN &

4˙/43 Ludgate Hill

GREAT BRITAIN

SON Ltd.

LONDON E.C.4

TRADE MARK

was No. 12 in their Dean's Classics series and was preceded by *Treasure Island* (No. 5), *Little Women* (No. 6), *Black Beauty* (No. 8) and – more surprisingly – *Moby-Dick* (No. 7).

playing tennis on the lawn. In half an hour I will be in bed, straining to read another chapter of my book in the fading light.[3]

   It wasn't *Le Morte d'Arthur* which fascinated me as an 8-year old: what I read was *King Arthur and the Knights of the Round Table* – Malory's tale "retold" by Phyllis Briggs. This book had originally been published by Thames & Hudson in 1954, although my own copy was a Dean & Son reprint which came out three years later. The title page carried the publisher's address, together with a rather charming silhouette of 'Dean', as one supposes, and 'Son'. As a child, however, it was the jacket which caught my attention. In the foreground, a knight bestrode an armoured horse. He carried a lance from which fluttered a pennant bearing the title of the book. How strange that was! How could a knight display the title of a work in which he featured? The memory of that illustration never left me, though it altered over time. In my mind's eye I began to see a group of knights riding along a road which wound downhill towards the viewer. In the actual illustration, the knights are in the background, near the castle gate. Yet when at long last I discovered that cover illustration on a website, the image I had invented immediately resolved itself into the one I wondered about long ago.

FIGURE 4 Jacket design for *King Arthur and the Knights of the Round Table*, Phyllis Briggs's 1954 adaptation of the *Morte d'Arthur*.

I first read *King Arthur* in the summer of 1970 – five hundred years after Malory's death. I couldn't have known, then, that more than four decades later an older self would conjure up that boy reading his Arthur stories on a summer's evening. Illuminations and refractions: one's childhood as a medium for critical investigation. It sounds eccentric and even wayward. Yet Phyllis Briggs was herself a medium. And the same is true of Malory. The Arthurian legend didn't begin in his own head: he went to work on materials which had for centuries been crafted by other hands.[4]

My Dean & Son abridgement made me realize for the first time that narratives have shapes. The drawing of the sword from the anvil; the marriage of Arthur and Guenever: to me, this formed the first part of the story and culminated with the King's victory over the Emperor Lucius. Once the kingdom had been unified internally and fortified against external threat, the story turned to individual knightly adventures. This second section saw high summer come to Camelot, though now and then a cooler breeze produced a shiver. Then, in the third part of the story, there was the quest for the Grail. The fourth and final section began when the knights came home. The relationship between Launcelot and Guenever became the subject of gossip at court. Eventually, there was war both abroad and at home. On the last page of my Dean & Son abridgement, Arthur was mortally wounded by Mordred, Guenever entered a nunnery, and Launcelot died. In the hall at Camelot, the swords lay still. The "old order", as Briggs writes, was "gone for ever".[5]

Scholars have variously divided Malory's narrative into two, three, five or eight sections whilst others have emphasized its unity.[6] So I should treat my early sense that the story has four parts with caution, though it remains as strong now as it was then. Yet it was back then that I realized something else. Reading *King Arthur* involved more than feeling a shape: stories also had anxieties – things to which they kept returning. Arthur didn't just happen to become "rightful king of all England" and to rule over "Scotland and Wales". The whole story worried about 'England' – which appeared to include both Wales and Scotland. Like the cake we stirred in the autumn so that it would be ready for Christmas, it seemed to me that 'England' was made by mixing things together. Arthur's efforts were devoted to collecting and combining. The narrative moved this way and that: Camelot was located at Winchester, but the King held court across the land. There were references to places I knew: Carlisle and Cardiff, Westminster and Windsor. Other place names had no modern equivalents. And the adventures of the knights took place in forests which could not be found on any map.[7]

When Rome and Camelot made peace, the theme of England receded. It's scarcely present in the third part of the story: the knights who seek the Grail aren't moving through a nationally defined space. Yet the very absence of England somehow brings it to mind. And in the final stage of the narrative, the nation takes centre stage because its very existence is under threat. In the last chapter of Briggs's retelling, Mordred declares himself "rightful King of all England" – the very words which appeared at the start of the narrative. This verbal circle creates a satisfying if not a cheerful shape. As a child, however, I found another line in the same chapter more troubling. Launcelot is told to "go back to your own realms in France". I was astonished: Sir Launcelot was Arthur's greatest knight, but he didn't live in the same country as me.[8]

It's encouraging to think that an 8-year-old reader of an abridged Malory could see that the story was concerned with Englishness. The theme has been addressed in several studies. In *Forging Chivalric Communities*, for example, Kenneth Hodges suggests that the *Morte* explores "what it means to be English". For me as a child, the issue of nationality was connected to that of historicity. I didn't put it to myself in that way, of course, but although I lacked a critical vocabulary I knew that *King Arthur* wasn't realistic. This was not a problem: unlikely things also occurred in the Bible, and at school we were encouraged to think that this book was 'true'. If Jesus came back from the dead, why not Arthur? The victory over the Roman emperor was admittedly implausible, even to one whose knowledge of early British history was as limited as mine. But I desperately wanted Arthur to have been 'true' – if only long ago. I didn't know that Winston Churchill expressed the same sentiment, writing of King Arthur's reign that it is "all true, or it ought to be". I was not aware that "from Henry II onwards until at least Henry VIII" – the words are N. J. Higham's – "English kings, their courtiers and their apologists took the existence of . . . Arthur as a matter of fact which was beyond doubt".[9]

Historically speaking, Arthur is a figment. But the fact that he never existed is by no means the end of the story. For Arthur did exist in one sense – as a story. And the "*idea* of King Arthur", as Higham argues, tells us a great deal about "ethnicity . . . and nationality". It is, in fact, a "foundation myth". John Burrow agrees: legend, he suggests, is itself a "historical fact of a kind". And Malory's role is central, for he was the one who gave "classic shape to the legends of Arthur for English readers".[10]

The Arthur stories introduced ideas about Englishness. But, as I was aware even at the age of 8, this was not their only theme. The public and political story has a private and personal side. Arthur's knights fight – but they also love. In the *Morte*, traditions and cultures meet: history and romance, Britain and France, Geoffrey of Monmouth and Chrétien de Troyes. To the national theme must be added a sexual one, for the *Morte* is about nothing if it is not about desire. Arthur is conceived when Uther magically assumes the form of the Duke of Tintagil in order to sleep with Igraine. Mordred is born when Arthur lies with his sister Margawse. Briggs draws a veil over these events, but even in *King Arthur* the story hinges on love – its mysterious origins and unpredictable consequences – or on the absence of love. "I love Guinevere", Briggs's Arthur tells Merlin. There is the same line in Malory. But the King is marrying because the barons "say that the kingdom should have a fair queen" – a detail also found in the *Morte*. And though Guenever is as fair as fair can be, she does not appear to return even the measured emotion of the king. It's not until the appearance of Sir Launcelot that 'love' becomes more than a dynastic motive. And even then it's mainly evident by its absence: Launcelot's refusal to declare his love for the four queens in Book VI suggests that his feelings are engaged elsewhere. In the case of Launcelot and Guenever, love is a matter of secrecy and of shame: love drives lovers apart. As a child I was confused when Guenever commanded Launcelot to leave the court and then longed to have him back again. I had for the first time encountered the pains and pleasures of adult life. I was an 8-year-old boy, and I wanted to be Sir Launcelot.[11]

It took years; it took Malory as well as Briggs. Long after the discovery of form and theme, however, something else began to come through in my reading. It isn't just that themes are there, like shapes or flavours. It's that they are questions. What does it mean to love? To live in 'England'? What is the connection between what we are and what we want, between being and desiring? The *Morte* bridges the eras of script and print; it is medieval, but it is also modern. And one of the reasons Malory's tale survived is not just because it raised such questions but because it offered no easy answers. In keeping its problems to itself so gravely, so gracefully, the *Morte* preserved them for us.

Part I

The Work

CHAPTER
1

"Alas"

I'm supplementing my childhood thoughts, but to re-read *King Arthur and the Knights of the Round Table* is to remember things I had long forgotten: the churchyard in which appears a marble stone and a sword bearing in gold letters the legend: "Whoso pulleth out this sword from this stone . . . is rightful king of all England"; the scene in which, by fitting a fragment of metal into a chip along the blade of Sir Tristram's sword, the Queen of Ireland realizes that her mysterious guest killed her brother. I remember Excalibur, of course: what reader could forget the lake, and the arm "raised above the dimpled water"? I remember the scene in which Arthur's knights set out on their quest:

> In the cool grey morning light the knights marched out of the castle and along the streets to the minster. They were fully armed except for heads and shields, and the people lined up to see them pass. Flaxen-haired, brown-haired, dark-haired, their armour shining, the knights marched.

It was the last sentence which caught my eye. It has no parallel in Malory, though it might owe something to the characterising formulae one finds in earlier romances. But I didn't have any sense of a tradition when I read Briggs. I was simply drawn to the word 'flaxen' – and then my ear became involved. The rhythm: it was simple, solemn and 'beautiful', I thought (though at this very time I was having trouble spelling that word in weekly tests at school).[12]

It was just a little book: loved, lost and only recently recovered. The more I think about it, however, the more the memories come. But this evidence isn't just fragmentary: it is sometimes plain wrong. In Malory, the final battle between Arthur and Mordred is accidentally precipitated when a soldier raises his sword to kill an adder which has "stung" him on the foot. Re-reading *King Arthur*, I was convinced that Briggs would include this image. But it isn't there.[13]

As a child reading *King Arthur* I felt that the present was a reduced version of the past. 'Tournament': like 'flaxen', the word shone with the glory of another age. A tournament was like a cricket match, I thought, though in the Age of Camelot it would have been much more important. Those who attended tournaments were certainly more eminent. The names of the knights! They were better than anything I knew. There was Sir Bleoberis and Sir Blamore, Sir Hontzlake and Sir Launcelot of the Lake. I wondered if Bleoberis was a better knight than Blamore. I wondered what Launcelot had to do with lakes. As a child I loved the word 'Tintagel': it made me think of a castle floating angelically in the air. I adored Malory's archaic verbs of violence, which Briggs often preserved: to 'hew', to 'slay', to 'smite'. I still like the way in which Malory's knights are filled with 'wrath' or 'dolour', 'swoon' of their 'grievous' injuries, display 'prowess', express 'fealty' and perform acts of 'obeisance'. I'm intrigued, too, by the greeting customs at Camelot. When they meet after a period of separation, knights who are friends kiss each other 'an hundred times'. That's rather nice – though no longer characteristically English.[14]

I couldn't put my finger on it, but even at the time I knew there was something wrong with *King Arthur*. The narrative had a distinct shape but when it came to space – to the places through which the knights passed – matters weren't so clear. Years later, in a seminar on Spenser at York, my tutor, Bob Jones (a gaunt and charismatic Leavisite) observed that the opening scene of *The Faerie Queene* – the gentle knight "pricking on the plaine", the "lovely ladie" on an "Asse more white then snow", and finally the dwarf "That lasie seemed in being ever last" – resembled a painting from the age before perspective (he was perhaps thinking of *The Discarded Image*, in which C. S. Lewis suggested that, like the art of the period, medieval poetry was "deficient in perspective"). Until that seminar at York I wouldn't have been able to find words for something I had known since childhood. Narratives have form, but they aren't just lines. Stories have foregrounds and backgrounds, insides and outsides. When I read Arthur Ransome's *Swallows and Amazons* I could almost feel the wind on the lake. I knew the water was clear in the inlet on Wild Cat Island and turbid near Beckfoot, where a river ran slowly through the lilies. But there was none of this in Briggs. Ransome particularized; *King Arthur* generalized. The Walker children have 'adventures', but each journey they take is distinctive. In *King Arthur*, however – and still more so in the *Morte* – the knights seem always to be travelling in circles. Meadows and pavilions are repeatedly and uniformly 'fair'. Equally unspecific are the 'wild' valleys and 'deep' forests.[15]

One might see this curious spatiality as a feature of Malory's 'paratactic' style. In more homely terms, E. K. Chambers once suggested that the *Morte* resembles a tapestry, with streams, castles and "bright little figures in blue and white and red armour". For me at the time, reading Briggs was like watching the revolving background in a TV cartoon. All the castles were one castle; the knight's horse was always tied to the same tree. Bob Jones was right: like *The Faerie Queene*, the *Morte* is uninformed by the example of perspective, and more generally by a sense of space as something measurable – a sense which is now entirely natural to us. In Malory, space is oddly interior: we never seem to get out of doors. The *Morte*, as one critic complained in 1890, has "no seasons, no weather". No rain falls; there is no fog and no hail. Even the occasional references to snow are figurative ('as white as snow').[16]

There is, however, a more immediate reason for Malory's cursory approach to the representation of space. It can be glimpsed on the occasions when court and country meet. Malory suggests that Arthur's kingship is created by popular consent. When young Arthur draws the sword from the stone on New Year's Day, the lords do not want to be "overgoverned with a boy of no high blood born". They put off a decision until Candlemas, then till Easter, and then again until Pentecost. But when at this time Arthur repeats his deed before both lords and commons, it is the latter who proclaim that "We will have Arthur unto our king". "High blood" does of course run in Arthur's veins, though the circumstances of his birth are known only to Merlin. Yet the young king does little to enhance his reputation with the people from whom he derives his authority. In Book III, admittedly, he knights the son of Aries the cowherd. But one quickly smells a rat here: Aries himself points out that Tor is always "shooting or casting darts", having refused to work on the farm, and it transpires that Tor's father is actually King Pellinore. The son's love of sports is a sign of aristocratic blood: it's not in his nature to muck out the cowshed, and knighting him confirms that he belongs within the martial order. When such an act is performed by the King of England, however, it confers nationality as well as courtly status. Englishness is not so much a geographical concept as a hierarchical one: it's less a matter of place and habitation than of social level. And whilst it might include bastards, Englishness doesn't extend to peasants. A cowherd works the land; he can never be a citizen of it. Malory doesn't show the landscape in detail because his knights don't know it in that way. They have never ploughed a field; for them, 'England' is an arena for knightly enterprise.[17]

Malory is no more critical of feudalism's inequity than his knights, and this poses a problem which Briggs addresses. In the Tor episode, she puts a more egalitarian line into Arthur's mouth than anything in Malory. When a herald complains that Aries "smells of the cowhouse", Arthur affirms that a knight should "treat all men as brothers". The attempt to depict Arthur as a democrat continues in Briggs's account of the war with Lucius. In Malory, this is fought by "kings, princes, and noble knights". In Briggs the campaign involves smiths, armourers and carpenters. Nor does Briggs allow us to forget the "work of the women", for banners and pennants have to be sewn "with silk and wool and gold thread". Yet Briggs's efforts to show that Arthur's kingdom contains ordinary people sometimes misfire. In an early passage, she describes "common men" harvesting barley "in the fields about Camelot" – a bit of picturesque detail. Less easy to accept is her description of a "peasant" who "gaped and scratched his beard" as Arthur's wedding procession passes by. Elsewhere – as when Briggs introduces a "woefully ugly" dwarf who is not "a proper man" – the writing would no longer be considered acceptable.[18]

Space in the *Morte* obeys peculiar rules. Yet Malory's representation of individual people operates according to conventions which are equally strange. One can understand why Gareth isn't recognized when he arrives at Camelot: Malory makes it clear that Gawaine hasn't seen his younger brother for fifteen years. Given the rigid divisions of Arthurian England, it's not surprising that Lamorak fails to recognize Tristram when the latter dresses as a fisherman. But it's strange that Isoud can't recognize her lover when he appears before her as a "sick man". Tristram has "waxed lean" and become "poor of flesh" but is surely more or less the man he was. Yet the state of his clothes as well as his lack of a horse and servant mean that he is no longer recognized as a member of the courtly class – even by one who shared his bed. Culturally speaking, Tristram has fallen out of his former existence. Caring nothing for these niceties, Isoud's dog isn't fooled for a moment: "she leapt upon him and licked his . . . ears, and . . . smelled at his feet and at his hands, and on all parts of his body that she might come to". On his return to Ithaca, the travel-weary Odysseus enjoys a similar if less slobbery greeting from his dog Argus. In Homer and Malory, human senses cannot easily penetrate deceptive appearances: men are what they seem to be. Lacking the olfactory sensititivity of Isoud's dog, knights sometimes come to blows because they don't know who they are fighting. Misrecognition even occurs for the simple reason that a knight has lowered his visor. Smite first and ask questions later: it is standard operating procedure.

But the potential for making mistakes in these circumstances is so great that one wonders why nobody modifies the rules of engagement. "Alas", says Balan, having "put off the helm" of Balin and realized that he and his brother have inflicted fatal injuries on each other. "Alas", says Percivale, having discovered that his latest conquest is his friend Ector. "Alas", Gawaine declares equally ruefully when he realizes he has just "smitten" Uwaine "through the breast" so badly that "the spear came out on the other side".[19]

Yet the difficulty that Arthur's knights have in identifying each other cannot always be explained so easily: it sometimes seems to be the product of selective blindness. Gawaine identifies Launcelot by his "riding" even when the latter is disguised. Although he is wearing a magic ring to prevent him from being recognized, Gareth is known by his "hair". But Gareth cannot see that Dame Liones is the woman he fell in love with at Castle Perilous only two chapters earlier. Poor Gareth! Unable to recognize the one he loves, he will later be killed by one who loves but fails to recognize him. In Book XX, Launcelot kills Gareth and his brother, smiting each "upon the brainpans" as he rescues Guenever from death at the stake. The brothers are "unarmed and unware" – so without helmets – but in the red mist of combat, Launcelot "saw them not". Launcelot's involvement in this most tragic misrecognition – we've known since Book VII that "there was never no knight that Sir Gareth loved so well as he did Sir Launcelot" – isn't entirely surprising. Launcelot may be the most famous of Arthur's knights but he is also a master of disguise – as other knights discover to their mortification. "Alas", cries Sir Nerovens, having fallen "flatling" to his knees when he realizes his antagonist is none other than the mighty Sir Launcelot. "Alas . . . what have I done!" complains Tristram on learning he has spent four hours fighting "the man in the world that I love best". And when Launcelot and Percivale unknowingly come upon each other during the quest, the outcome is thoroughly predictable: "Alas", says Percivale, "what have I done?"[20]

Launcelot presumably knows that he is Launcelot even when he is disguised. But from the point of view of those with whom he fights, Launcelot only becomes Launcelot when he says that he is Launcelot. Precisely because Launcelot is Launcelot, other knights are reluctant to engage him in combat. In order to do what he does best and therefore become what he is, therefore, Launcelot must pretend to be somebody else, or at least make it appear that he is not the person he is.[21] Who then is Launcelot? He is and is not himself; he is the scattering of his seemings. He is a puzzle – a "man of mist", as Edwin Arlington Robinson's Gawaine puts it.[22]

We moderns see the body as a guarantee, the ground and housing of the self. But in Malory flesh is mere matter encased in armour. The body of the knight has limbs and bones and blood, but lacks defined internal organs and isn't apprehended as a system or sensorium. Emotions rage in breasts, but thoughts don't take place in heads. Just as all space is one space, so all flesh is one flesh, subject to the same blows, endlessly inflicted. Launcelot smites Tristram "so sore upon the shield that he bare horse and man to the earth". Then Bleoberis smites Palomides "so hard upon the shield that Sir Palomides and his white horse rustled to the earth". Then Ector smites Gareth "so hard that down he fell off his horse". And then Arthur smites Dinadan "quite from his saddle". After a while, Malory seems himself unsure how many knights have been borne down, confused by the elaboration of his own motif.[23]

Yet Malory isn't just interested in bumps and buffets: sometimes the body of the knight is penetrated to the core. By "misfortune" Bors smites Launcelot "through the shield into the side, and the spear brake, and the head left still in the side". The image is a little vague (which bit of "the side"?). When Lavaine pulls out the spearhead, however, Launcelot gives a "great shriek and a marvellous grisely groan, and the blood brast out nigh a pint at once". This is more specific: Launcelot clearly feels pain and the seriousness of his injury is measured by the loss of a quantified amount of blood, though one might wonder why the groan and not the wound is "grisely". Yet Launcelot's injury remains curiously schematic, and this is still more true of the injury which fascinated Malory most of all. Even as a child, the infliction of head wounds in *King Arthur* struck me as symptomatic although in fact, as I now see, there are only four instances: Lucius' head is "cleft . . . from crown to chin", Meliagrance dies of a blow which carves through "steel and bone and brain", Gawaine is injured by a "grievous blow upon the head" and, finally, Arthur is fatally injured by a blow on the head which "split the bone". In the *Morte* itself, head wounds proliferate almost pathologically, and are described with greater relish than anything in Briggs. During the Battle of the Eleven Kings Brastias smites a knight on the helm so hard "that it went to the teeth". In the next battle Pellinore strikes King Lot a "great stroke through the helm and head unto the brows". In the next, Kay takes out his opponent by smiting him "so hard on the helm that the stroke clave the helm and the head". In these scenes of nation building, those who can split a head from crown to chops enjoy complete and public triumph. Suitably enough, one of the most

14

emphatic of these victories belongs to Arthur. In Briggs, Lucius is only cleft from crown to chin. In the *Morte*, Arthur smites the Emperor with such vigour that the blow "cleft . . . from the summit of his head, and stinted not till it came to his breast". As the headline in the Camelot *Sun* might have read: "Gotcha!"[24]

2

Smiting and Cleaving

Modern readers might be puzzled by the way in which Malory presents the physical existence of his knights. Yet this isn't because we ourselves have an entirely perspicuous view of our bodies. As a child, I felt that my arms and legs had an obvious and tangible existence. Not every part of my body was equally self-evident, however. Although my nose and ears were present to my mind I could only see the former if I squinted whilst the latter remained invisible. Other parts of my body were still more problematic. My 'tummy' was an outside as well as an inside: it was an area of skin which could be tickled and also the organ which made sloshing sounds when I drank water. I sometimes thought the 'calf' referred to the front part of my lower leg and the 'shin' to the back. My 'navel' and 'nipples' were actual inversions of each other, one singular and the other plural, one concave and the other convex – though the structure of these features in no way explained why people found them funny.

Lucius is despatched in Book V of the *Morte* and the manner of his death is surely appropriate, for the head, as Edmund Reiss points out, is the "traditional seat of pride". Following Arthur's victory in Europe, however, head splitting becomes less consequential and also less symbolic, being instead presented as a spectacular demonstration of an individual knight's prowess. In Book VI Launcelot protects a "fair damosel" by cleaving the head of Sir Peris de Forest Sauvage "unto the throat". Shortly afterwards, having come upon a "foul churl", Launcelot splits him "unto the paps". He rounds off these achievements by taking on two giants. The head of the first is shortly "clave . . . asunder". The second runs away, but "Launcelot after him with all his might, and . . . clave him to the navel".[25]

Launcelot's status as the "best knight of the world" is evident from the injuries which he inflicts. When it comes to cleaving, nobody else gets as far as the navel or paps, though Gawaine and Arthur carve their victims to the "breast" whilst Balin and Gareth reach the "shoulders". But Pellinore only gets to King Lot's "brows" and Uwaine to Sir

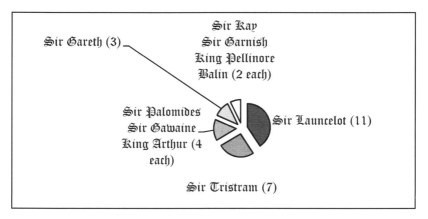

FIGURE 5 Arthur's top ten knights.

Edward's "canel bone".[26] Yet Launcelot's superiority is not simply a matter of wound depth: his sword cuts deeper but also more frequently than that of any other knight. The figure above gives beheading and cleaving totals for Arthur's Top Ten knights (in descending order read clockwise from noon).

One wouldn't expect the saintly Sir Percivale or the perfect Sir Galahad to make much showing here, though in an unusually blood-thirsty moment the latter does at one point chop off somebody's arm. It's more startling that Arthur and even the insignificant Sir Garnish make it into the premier league; surprising, too, that Lamorak's tournament successes aren't always matched in actual combat. The scores nevertheless speak for themselves: Launcelot is top dog, and his superiority is still more obvious if we count only cleavings (which would come above beheadings in any self-respecting knight's *curriculum vitae*). Launcelot chalks up an impressive seven; Arthur and Gawaine manage two apiece, Gareth just one. Tristram and Palomides make it into the premier league on the basis of beheadings, though Tristram's first major achievement involves smiting Sir Marhaus "through the brain-pan". It's true that Palomides almost decapitates Launcelot's horse, but this is poor sportsmanship (he is, after all, a Saracen). And the distribution of these deeds throughout the narrative offers still more telling evidence of Launcelot's supremacy. Gawaine clocks up his full score of head wounds before Launcelot enters the field. Launcelot's victories in Book VI (four cleavings and two beheadings in just seven chapters) are so impressive that when other champions appear – Gareth in Book VII, Tristram in Book VIII, Palomides in Book X – they never measure up. This is particularly true in the case

17

of Gareth, whose figures are questionable because (odd as it sounds) one of his victims survives decapitation on two occasions owing to the administration of an "ointment" (one more efficacious than Savlon, presumably). When in Book XII Launcelot beheads a boar (excluded from my figures), he has already levelled with Tristram, who has clearly peaked too soon. Isoud's lover isn't to blame, though: the manager's job is to manage, and Malory takes Tristram off at half time, allowing Launcelot another nine books in which to add to his tally.[27]

Numerous scenes in the *Morte* are indeed, as P. J. C. Field acknowledges, "unintentionally hilarious". As I child, I probably took *King Arthur* too seriously. But I remember thinking that the scenes of violence were also – well – *funny*. I didn't know that Mark Twain had been there long before me. When informed that "Sir Uwaine smote Sir Marhaus that his spear brast in pieces . . . and Sir Marhaus smote him so sore that horse and man he bore to the earth", Hank Morgan, the Connecticut Yankee, responds that the "archaics" "suffer in the matter of variety". In fact, as he continues:

> the fights are all alike: a couple of people come together with great random . . . and a spear is brast, and one party brake his shield and the other one goes down . . . and brake his neck, and then the next candidate comes randoming in, and brast *his* spear . . . and down *he* goes . . . till the material is all used up . . . and as a *picture* of living, raging, roaring battle, sho! why, it's pale and noiseless – just ghosts scuffling in a fog.

The "archaics" aren't always incapable of picturing "living" battle. In the *Orkneyinga Saga* (*c.* 1200), Earl Einar pursues Halfdan Long-Leg, who has fled following his defeat in battle. When Halfdan is captured, Einar has "his ribs cut from the spine with a sword and the lungs pulled out through the slits in his back". The line is more brutal in its specificity than anything in Malory. Moreover, even in translation, the prose of the saga has a matter-of-factness which suggests that the teller is close to what he tells. In the *Morte*, by contrast, events take place at a distance and the wounds are as formulaic as the conflicts in which they are inflicted.[28]

Malory's knights struggle to draw out the new order from the old, and in a sense their head-splitting is parturitive. It doesn't work, as we discover. What the knights do individually to others is in the end done to them collectively: the split heads return in the form of a divided state. There isn't a single cleaving between Books XIII and XVI of the *Morte*.

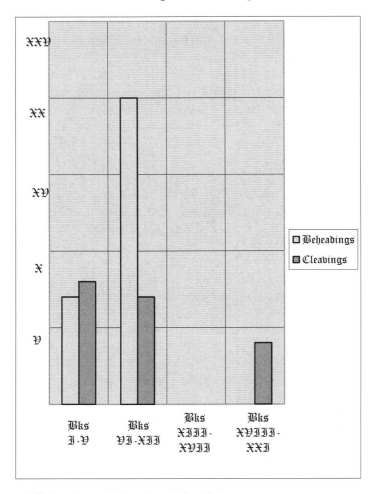

FIGURE 6 Beheadings and cleavings in the *Morte*.

There's an increasing sense that this activity, though conclusive for the combatants and entertaining for the spectators, is rather vulgar. In a civilized society one doesn't brain people. The figure above gives beheading and cleaving totals for each of the narrative's main parts.

A few qualifications are again in order. The graph doesn't represent absolute levels of violence in Arthurian society, and the victims of the set-pieces are far outnumbered by the nameless dead left behind by the *Morte*'s numerous crazed tyrants. Gorings and piercings are not recorded; nor are severed limbs; nor is the instance in which Arthur nimbly severs a giant's "genytours". We can nevertheless see a trend: violence peaks in the second part of the narrative and seems to stop altogether when the quest for the Grail begins. This is a time of signs and portents, of dreams and visions. Chambers are filled with "summer light" – more than this, with a "sunbeam more clearer by seven times" than the light of any earthly day. It tantalizes Launcelot: he seems almost to want to wash himself in the light and yet, as a hermit tells him, "ye shall have no power to see it no more than a blind man should see a bright sword". But Launcelot cannot help himself. By the "water of Mortoise", in a vision, he witnesses a "great clereness"; there is then a journey by sea, a castle guarded by lions, a voice, a door which opens – and a room "bright as all the torches of the world". It's too much for Launcelot: burnt by the brilliance, he lies "still as a dead man" for twenty-four days and nights.[29]

The pursuit of the Holy Grail is no walk in the park. "They shall die many in the quest": Arthur's prediction to Gawaine proves accurate, for only a "remnant" of the knights "come home". Still, these deaths are rarely dramatized by Malory: Galahad's is the most notable, and his is a transcendence of the spirit rather than a defeat of the body. Dinadan's is the most significant, as I will argue in Chapter 19. But Malory gets this out of the way in Book X, before the quest begins. Male-on-male violence structures the *Morte*. But if one notices only this one misses something else. A number of critics suggest that Arthurian society is defined by the penalties it imposes for acts of violence against women. As early as Book II, Arthur reprimands Balin, who has just "lightly . . . smote off" the head of the Lady of the Lake right in front of him: "Alas, for shame! . . . ye have shamed me and all my court". A similar reaction has percolated down to the knightly body when in Book III Gawaine smites off the head of another lady (apparently this is a "misadventure" – she "fell over him" whilst emerging from her chamber). "Alas", cries Gaheris, "that is foully and shamefully done". At the end of Book III, Arthur codifies his new regime in an oath which his knights renew each year at Pentecost and which commits them "always to do ladies, damosels, and gentlewomen succour". Sir Pedivere plainly isn't offering succour when he "swapped off his lady's head" (he suspects her of having an affair with her "cousin germain", though she denies it). But we shortly see the authority of the new order: Pedivere yields to Launcelot and is instructed to carry the body (and head) of his wife to Winchester, where Guenever requires him to journey to Rome (along the way, rather disgustingly, Pedivere is compelled to take his wife to bed) and confess his "foul deeds" to the Pope. This penitential journey is evidently successful, for Pedivere becomes "an holy man".[30]

It's true that the *Morte* contains three subsequent instances of female decapitation. In each case, however, there are mitigating circumstances. Tristram beheads Sir Breunor's wife with an "awk [backhand] stroke", but with justification. Breunor maintains an "old custom" at his castle: whenever a knight and his lady turn up, he reserves the right to behead the female visitor if she is less beautiful than his wife. Breunor is also magnanimously prepared to let his own wife be decapitated if the lady of the visiting knight turns out to be the fairest. When Tristram and La Beale Isoud arrive, however, Breunor sees his folly – Isoud is nothing if not drop-dead gorgeous – and "repenteth" of his custom. But Tristram's point is not that the custom is stupid as that it is "shameful": he chops off the wife's head in order to provoke the husband. Two hours later, Breunor finds himself "grovelling" on the ground; then Tristram "unlaced his helm and struck off his head". It is the last act of the old order and the first of the new.[31]

It's true that the King himself beheads Annowre in Book IX. But fair's fair: she tries to do the same to him. The other instance of female decapitation in the *Morte* is more troubling. In Book X, Gaheris beheads his mother for sleeping with Lamorak, whose father, King Pellinore, killed her husband, King Lot. Gaheris is not reproached for this deed. And Malory doesn't forget either Gaheris's deliberate act of female decapitation or Gawaine's earlier and accidental one. In the short term, however, matricide in Orkney has little effect in England. On the surface (as fig. 6 demonstrated) Arthurian society is more peaceful. The tournament at Lonazep in Book X of the *Morte* is the high point of Arthurian England. The nation-defining battles have been fought and won, and it's time to bring together knights from Scotland and Ireland, from Wales and Cornwall, from "the country of Gore, and Surluse, and of Listinoise, and they of Northumberland". Chambers's image of a tapestry springs to mind: a stream; pavilions and pennants; knights in Union Jack-coloured armour. But Gaheris's murder of his mother has exposed the enmity between clan Lot and the Pellinore family. It has shown that the old order, with its culture of violence against women, hasn't been superseded. The tiles of the Arthurian mosaic are brought together only to shatter on impact. And Camelot's collapse isn't simply the result of violence done by the 'bad' upon the 'good': when the old order triumphs again, it holds all England in its thrall. In Book XIX, Launcelot smites Sir Meliagrance "such a buffet that the stroke carved the head in two parts". We haven't seen so spectacular a head wound since Launcelot decapitated the boar in Book XII. Arthur's first knight has always scrupulously observed the gender policy at Camelot and is even now giving "succour" to Guenever. Launcelot is nevertheless returning to the shameful violence of the past, and his attempt to protect the Queen and preserve courtly order

21

produces the very foulness which that order abhors. In the final books of the *Morte*, Launcelot will go on to cleave Gareth and Gaheris to their "brainpans". He also gives Gawaine the head wound which eventually kills him. The only other head cleaver still in business is Mordred, and his is the *coup de grâce* for Arthurian England.[32]

CHAPTER

3

Achieving

The *Morte* is a fascinating but enigmatic work. "We are told how things happen", Terence McCarthy writes, "but never why". The landscapes are obscurely internal and not at all 'outside'; 'insides' on the other hand – the contents of bodies – are conceived of in a strangely distant way. Roads go round in dreamlike spirals; heads are subjected to outlandish injuries. Words, actions, objects: the narrative endlessly recombines the same few elements. "Now turn we": for P. J. C. Field, this repeated intervention is part of Malory's "unwearying factual style". To me it comes across as a desperate attempt to keep his story in order. In reality, however, Malory isn't always in control: at the end of Book XIX, he cuts to the "morte of King Arthur" because, as he claims, "I have lost the very matter of Le Chevaler de Chariot".[33]

Elsewhere in the *Morte*, incidents which one would expect to see depicted are left out without a word of explanation. Lamorak, Tristram and Percivale are all important characters, but we hear about their deaths only belatedly. And Malory surely loses the "very matter" of Book X, though the problem here is less a dearth than an excess of materials. At 88 chapters, Book X is longer than Books XI to XVI combined. And one can't lay the blame for this unequal division on Caxton: everything in Book X is made of the same stuff, but the narrative goes round and round like a carousel, a whirl of incidents without apparent form. In the *Morte d'Arthur*, as E. K. Chambers once observed, Malory had a chance to tell "two of the world's dozen great love stories". He managed Launcelot and Guenever rather well, but the tale of Tristram and Isoud was "hidden in . . . overgrowth": Malory "bungled his structural problem".[34]

Even as a child, I was aware of the opacities in *King Arthur* – aware, too, that in many cases the text's indirections contributed to its overall effect. In one sense, my abridgement is still more mystifying than the *Morte* itself. Retelling the tale, as the jacket puts it, for "modern boys and girls", Briggs chose not to explain Arthur's relationship to Mordred. At the start of the final book, Malory puts the case directly:

the Bishop of Canterbury informs Mordred that Arthur "begat you upon his own sister". And this is merely a reminder, for in Book I Merlin tells the young Arthur that he has unwittingly slept with his sister and "on her ye have gotten a child that shall destroy you". Briggs's Mordred is just a wicked man. In Malory, he looms throughout the narrative. His very name – one hears both 'murder' and 'dread' – is ominous. In the concluding chapter of Book I, Arthur scours the kingdom for "all the children born on May-day" and these, as Malory tells us, "were put in a ship to the sea". It's understandable that Briggs omits this curious echo of the Massacre of the Innocents (one which seems to have been Malory's own invention), for it establishes a rather baffling parallel between Mordred and Christ. Perhaps it is an inversion: Jesus is at the centre of the New Testament whilst Mordred seems peripheral to the *Morte*. We catch glimpses of his unpromising development in Books VI and IX; in Book X he murders Lamorak and is described as a "false knight". Yet the effect of these sporadic appearances is very marked. When Mordred takes on a larger role in Book XVIII we feel that he has waited and watched. Malory knows that narratives can be shaped by what they leave out. He may not be in control of every episode, but his handling of Mordred is masterly.[35]

As I've suggested, Malory's manipulation of the reader's memory – one's persisting sense of figures in the margin of the *Morte* – is highly effective. We see it again in the case of Morgan le Fay. She's there at the beginning, a "third sister . . . put to school in a nunnery" who becomes a "clerk of necromancy". As a child reading Briggs, I could see that there was something odd about Morgan. Briggs preserved the scene in which Launcelot is forced to choose between Morgan and three other queens and proclaims that he would rather "die here with honour than love one of you!" After that incident, however, Briggs doesn't mention Morgan until the final page, when a funeral barge carries Arthur away. Morgan's more frequent appearances in the *Morte* deepen the mystery. We know she plots against Arthur. But how should one account for Morgan's appearance at the end of the narrative? In Book XXI, she takes the dying King's head in her lap and speaks to him: "Ah, dear brother, why have ye tarried so long from me? alas, this wound on your head hath caught over-much cold". Geraldine Heng is surely right to describe these words as "gentle" and "chiding" and to suggest that Morgan should at this point be seen as "a protectress" rather than "a mortal enemy". And the beneficent Morgan is no lapse on Malory's part. Like some vortex curving down into the immemorial elements of story, she is both good and bad, a mysterious and primal mixture.[36]

The *Morte* never breaks but it sometimes creaks. As a child I would have had no sense that Galahad was vulnerable to mockery. I wasn't aware of *The Once and Future King*, in which T. H. White relates how the young Galahad is abused by Gawaine as a "lily laddie", a "catamite" and, worst of all, "an Englishman". I simply knew that Galahad was good; he floated into the narrative like an angel. When Briggs's Galahad takes his place in the Siege Perilous, the old man who accompanies him tells the court that the young knight "has come to be among you". The line has no parallel in Malory, but the wording is satisfying in its precision: Galahad can be 'among' Arthur's knights but could never be 'with' or 'of' this company. Galahad was almost transparent, I thought, as if he was made from sunshine. It did not surprise me that Galahad didn't smite or cleave: he was a Christian, and *they* turned the other cheek, observing rules which reversed the ones of the playground. This holy perversity partly explained why, during the quest, Galahad occasionally abandoned his fellow knights without a word, riding away until he disappeared from view. I could accept that Galahad, like Jesus, had to die. When he was good he was better than anybody else; when he became perfect, he was beyond any human best: there was no place left for him on earth.[37]

The presentation of Galahad's death doesn't trouble me now. Only a couple of pages after Galahad dies in Sarras, however, Malory informs us that the tournament on Lady Day is attended by Galahad the "haut prince". A "great multitude of angels" have only just carried the saintly one to heaven and now he's out jousting. Briggs irons out this wrinkle in the narrative, though I suspect it wouldn't have bothered me as a child: if Jesus rose from the dead, why not Galahad? The odd thing is that after their respective revivals, the protagonists of both narratives do little except appear and then pass out of sight. Galahad; Jesus: visitors on the earth, they gleam and are gone.[38]

Galahad's reappearance is irritating if one values consistency. But this isn't an isolated error on Malory's part. When Launcelot heals the festering wounds of Sir Urre in Book XIX, the "Duke Galahad, the haut prince" is once more in attendance. So is Percivale, whose death was also recounted in Book XVII and who, though good by earthly standards, has never been presented as resurrection material. How, then, if Bors buried him in Sarras, does Percivale reach Arthur's court at Carlisle? Malory could have excluded Galahad and Percivale from the list of those who attempt to cure Urre. Instead he reminds the reader – when the knights are right there in front of us! – that Galahad and Percivale "died in the quest of the Sangreal". Urre's healing must therefore have occurred earlier, though it is only now apparent that Malory is moving great blocks of material around. Yet it's not just that Malory tries to clarify things and fails; he often doesn't see that there is anything to explain. At the start of the quest he doesn't tell us that he is passing over important events in order to deal with a later period of time. Nor, after the healing of Urre, does he note that the quest is about to begin. The result is a curious though not unpleasant sense of disorientation: in the *Morte*, time as well as space goes round and round.[39]

It's narrow-minded to demand of Malory a strict consistency. At the same time, he surely doesn't want us to think that *all* the incidents which follow the healing of Urre take place before the quest. In that case Arthur would die before his knights depart in pursuit of the Grail. There must therefore be a junction, though Malory doesn't seem aware that this point exists. Earlier in the narrative, the Urre incident might have been given as it occurred in the actual sequence of events. But it's hard to see where it would come. It must take place between Galahad's arrival at Camelot and the start of the quest. But this happens at the beginning of Book XIII, when Galahad takes his place in the Siege Perilous and draws the sword from the stone (the scene oddly loops back to Arthur's initial proof of his kingship). There doesn't seem to be anywhere here for the healing to occur. Furthermore, if Galahad's assumption of the Siege Perilous is an indication that he is the one "by whom the Sangreal shall be achieved" it becomes hard to understand how, by healing Urre, Launcelot can demonstrate that he is the "best knight of the world". We already know that Launcelot's son is destined to be "much better" than him. So when does Galahad become "better" and when does Launcelot cease to be "best"? Malory doesn't provide the time or space in which these questions might be answered.[40]

Galahad's reappearance after his own death creates an eddy in the *Morte*'s timeflow. Yet his initial appearance is almost as enigmatic. At Corbin castle Launcelot lies with Elaine, the daughter of King Pelles; in Book XI she is "delivered of a fair child, and they christened him Galahad". Less than thirty pages later, Galahad is "fifteen winter old". Since Malory has spent most of the intervening time describing the period during which Launcelot runs "wild wood" (i.e. mad) for two years, Galahad appears to go from high chair to haut prince in no time – as in life, perhaps (time flies, and Launcelot would probably be a distant if not an indifferent father). But if this is simply time's worldly whirl, what is it that drives Malory to refer in Book X – before Galahad's birth has been mentioned – to "Sir Galahalt, the haut prince"? Malory might respond that he is talking about Gala*halt* not Gala*had*, though it's odd that there are two "haut" princes with virtually identical names. But why at an earlier point mention "Sir Galahad, the haut prince, the which was Sir Breunor's son"? This is needlessly confusing, as are the unexplained references to Galihud, Galihodin and Gahalantine. Who on earth are they? Malory doesn't tell us. I'm not sure he knows.[41]

It's hardly surprising, then, that in the view of C. S. Lewis, Malory "hardly knows what he is doing". There is indeed something 'wrong' with the story of King Arthur, though even at the age of 8 I could see this wasn't just because storytelling had in that distant time been hammered out rough and ready, like horseshoes in a smithy. There's beauty in the most ordinary elements of Malory's prose. 'And then . . . and then': it is like a pulse. The repeated 'on the morns' create, in Field's words, an "almost hypnotic" effect. After a while, one's attention begins to focus on something else, something both central and unutterable. Something may well have been wrong with *King Arthur*, but for the first time I was beginning to take pleasure in writing which evaded comprehension.[42]

I've said that I began to develop a sense of narrative form whilst reading Briggs. To my mind stories were made of impalpable stuff. They were lighter than air, yet nevertheless possessed a shape. They had corners and passageways and could lead one quickly through open expanses of fast-paced action; they could slow, almost to a halt, in a forest of detail. In the case of *King Arthur*, everything hinged on the quest for the Grail. It all led up to this: the Grail was the radiant centre, the object of the story. When the quest was over, it was the beginning of the end. As I more gradually became aware, however, the structure of the narrative could be experienced in other ways. The Grail didn't just represent journey's end: to reach out for it was to find that it eluded one's grasp. The story of the quest was less a culmination than a way of manufacturing more story stuff to put off the inevitable end. Guenever and Arthur; Arthur and Launcelot; Launcelot and Guenever: each pairing conjures up the complicating presence of a third figure. Launcelot and Guenever: it starts and stops, starts again and stops, then starts again. The quest is a device to gain control over something which cannot be mastered. Nobody can control it – least of all Launcelot.

By slowing down the flow of time, the quest contributes to our understanding of those who participate in it. Launcelot's involvement is particularly illuminating. As a child, I was struck by the way in which Launcelot became more interesting as triumph eluded him. When a lady on a white horse informs Arthur's greatest knight that "a greater one stands before you", Launcelot responds that "I knew right well I was never the best". To me, the dignity of this remark was hugely impressive: Launcelot became better by not being the best. I'm not sure I understood what exactly was wrong with Launcelot, though. If I had known he was Galahad's father – another detail which Briggs suppresses – I might have wondered how Galahad came to be so pure. Why wasn't Launcelot's earthliness passed down to Galahad?[43]

I partly understood that "forbidden love" made Launcelot unable to "achieve" the Grail. "Achieve": the wording – as when Galahad talks about having "achieved" an adventure – implies something conclusive, but it is misleading. When I read Briggs it seemed to me that the Grail was a trophy, like the World Cup. The object of the quest was to find the Grail and bring it back for all to see. But if so, the quest is unnecessary: Arthur's court has already experienced a "vision of the Holy Grail". I wondered if 'achieving' involved removing the "cloth of white samite" which conceals the Grail. I liked the idea of 'samite', which was evidently something finer than drip-dry polyester. But without knowledge of the sacraments the meaning of 'achieving' remained obscure. Had I been reading Malory instead of Briggs, I might have been still more mystified. The author of the *Morte* seems, as Vinaver puts it, to have had "little use for the doctrine of grace": as a result, his knights' encounters with the Grail can seem arbitrary. Some knights see the Grail even before the quest: Bors is "fed with the Sangreal"; Percivale and Ector are "made whole by the coming of the Sangreal"; Launcelot too is said to have "seen" the Grail and to have been "healed and recovered" through its agency. Galahad is only a babe in arms when it is foretold that he will "achieve the Sangreal". But when this prophecy is uttered this vessel is in the room.[44]

It was all, as Malory sometimes says and Briggs repeats, 'passing strange'. Even as he witnesses a knight being healed by kissing the "holy vessel of the Sangreal", Launcelot fails again. Poor Launcelot: he comes close, but he never achieves. On one occasion, the appearance of the Grail finds him "half sleeping and half waking". He can hear the conversation between a nearby knight and his squire: to them, however, his lethargy is the consequence of "deadly sin". And when Launcelot comes closer – comes closest of all, in the castle by the sea – he encounters a voice which commands him to "enter not". Previously, Launcelot was caught midway between sleep and waking; now, smitten with a breath which makes him fall to the ground, he hovers between life and death for four and twenty days and nights – a punishment for the "four and twenty years that he had been a sinner".[45]

4

Kissing and Clipping

I never forgot Arthur's knights – "flaxen-haired, brown-haired, dark-haired" – setting out from Camelot, although I can see no reason for this memory to have persisted. Yet I think I understand what Briggs is trying to do. She wants to make the story vivid, and to do this she must amplify as well as abridge. "Soon came Merlin unto the king": this is how Malory sets up the scene in which Uther is persuaded to entrust the young Arthur to the care of Ector. In Briggs, Uther sits in a "tapes-tried chamber" where "the cold east wind sifted in through the unglazed windows and harried the flames up the stone chimney". Malory's Arthur simply grasps the sword in the stone and "pulled it out". In Briggs, frost "twinkled on the steel" and the sun "blazed upon the golden letters".[46]

There's nothing wrong with a bit of scene-painting, of course: I don't object when Briggs refers to a "thick forest of scented pines", which is more evocative than Malory's cursory reference to a "little-leaved" wood. And one can see why Briggs includes horsy details: she also wrote *Son of Black Beauty* (1954) and *Pickles the Pony* (1959). Accordingly we see King Pellinore's horse "curveting and stepping high, his plumes waving and tossing". In the equivalent passage in Malory (indeed, throughout the *Morte*) the horses are taken for granted. Yet Briggs's equestrian elaborations sometimes pall: on one occasion, we are told that Galahad's horse "pressed its velvet nose against his outstretched hand, for" – as Briggs informs us – "children and animals knew Sir Galahad for a holy knight". And sometimes, we leave the world of Thomas Malory altogether and enter that of Beatrix Potter. When Arthur fights Pellinore, we are told that the "frightened red squirrels ran scolding away".[47]

The story of Arthur can stand a good deal of bashing about without coming to much harm. But Briggs would have been truer to Malory if she had been more austere. The knights of the *Morte* are mostly names, phenomena, patterns of behaviour. Malory shows them to his readers; he doesn't tell us – as Briggs does – that Gawaine is a case of "vaulting pride" or that Percivale is a "dreamer". He doesn't mention – as Briggs does – the "swell and curve" of Launcelot's muscles. Reading this passage at the age of 8 I could only sigh with envy.[48]

Malory's portraits are no sharper than his landscapes. After a while, however, the reader notices a certain amount of individuation. Kay is useless at jousting and keeps falling off his horse; he is also foul-tempered and sharp-tongued. Palomides loves Tristram as a fellow-knight but hates him as a rival lover and spends all his time obsessively pursuing a "questing beast" with a serpent's head and "buttocks like a lion". Dinadan is a "good knight, but . . . a scoffer and a japer". On one occasion he serves fish to Galahalt, who only eats meat: Malory tells us that Guenever and the haut prince "laughed . . . that they might not sit at their table". It's hilarious. But Dinadan's scoffing has a sharper edge than his japing: he's the only knight at Camelot who complains about his injuries; he's also the only one who refuses to do battle for a fair lady, telling Isoud that "the joy of love is too short, and the sorrow . . . dureth over long".[49]

Malory's attention to "individual behaviour" is indeed, as Terence McCarthy writes, "tantalisingly brief". But it's not entirely absent. Percivale is pure and strong but a bit dim. Bors is only so-so as a warrior, but remains steadfast to the end. Rattled along by the narrative, most of the lesser knights are as indistinguishable as potatoes in a sack. In the case of Arthur, Guenever and Launcelot, however, Malory conveys a sense of men and women ageing and eventually renouncing the urgings of the flesh. Even Launcelot is at last exhausted by his passion and wants only to pray. Nevertheless, Guenever is more of a condition than a character and Arthur is almost a blank. The most substantial character in *Le Morte d'Arthur*, then, is Launcelot. This isn't because he's different in any way. Launcelot embodies the chivalric code more completely than any other knight except Galahad, and this makes his violations of that code all the more striking. But his perceptions aren't unusual, and his unparalleled exploits don't make him what he is. Launcelot is a character not through action but reaction.[50]

A hero does but a character is: with Malory this knowledge was instinctive. In the *Morte*, accordingly, it's never a matter of where Launcelot gets to – wild valleys, deep forests – but of where he already is. Launcelot is possessed by a force which is in him but not of him. It animates him, but he cannot control it. When Launcelot begins to "resort unto Queen Guenever again", forgetting "the perfection that he had made in the quest", the Queen is faced with the first accusation against her. Launcelot defeats Sir Mador to "prove" Guenever's inno-cence and there is "great joy and mirths" at Camelot. A relieved Arthur and Guenever even kiss each other "heartily". But the crisis breaks out again: on this occasion Launcelot must divide Meliagrance's head in two before "noblesse and joy" can be felt once more. Then for a third time the murmurings begin, and this time they cannot be silenced. Yet even after Agravaine and Mordred accuse the Queen, there is a period during which catastrophe might still be averted. The point of no return comes only when Launcelot kills Gaheris and Gareth – Gaheris, who cut off his mother's head, and Gareth, who loved Launcelot "so well". Gawaine (another decapitator) previously refused to act when Launcelot killed two of his sons and his brother Agravaine in fair fight. But the death of Gawaine's remaining brothers – unarmed – cannot be overlooked. From now until the hour of his death, Gawaine is possessed by a hunger for vengeance. Arthur knows the truth about Guenever, but he also knows that to take the fight to Launcelot is to pull the keystone from the arch. Yet Gawaine is implacable: he will have Launcelot's life or die. In falling, one stone topples the next. The King's absence gives Mordred the opportunity he has waited for, and Arthur must now do battle for his own kingdom. "Alas, that ever this war began": the King's lament is the more poignant for its restraint. But no "soft salves" can help his knights now: "on the morn", as Malory tells us, "they made them ready to do battle".[51]

As we have seen, Launcelot isn't just an action hero. His cleaving rate puts every other member of the Round Table to shame, but it's being and not doing which counts in his case. Launcelot's is a position, a situation, a problem. It is both spiritual and sexual. It's also general: Malory has been preoccupied with the vagaries of desire even before Launcelot becomes central to the story. Tor's mother, the cowherd's "fair housewife", tells the King that when as a maid she "went to milk kine, there met with her a stern knight, and half by force he had my maidenhead". "Half by force": there is, as Terence McCarthy observes, a "world of meaning in that phrase". In the new dispensation, however, rape – like the decapitation of women – belongs to the past. When Gawaine sleeps with Sir Pelleas's love, the Lady Ettard, he breaks his promise to "do my true part that ye shall not fail to have the love of her". When Pelleas finds the lovers asleep together his heart "wellnigh brast for sorrow". But Ettard hasn't been taken "half by force". This meeting of bodies is entirely consensual, and the picture Malory creates – he writes of "either clipping other in arms" – is rather touching. At this stage, love's story works out well: Gawaine has a two-night stand and (after the initial shock) Pelleas "loved no more Ettard". Instead, he meets the Lady of the Lake, and Malory tells us that these two "loved together during their life days". It is a relationship which, in the view of Kenneth Hodges, is unique in Malory. In these early days, the delights of love outweigh the dangers. Men and women kiss and 'make joy' of each other. Malory sees the fun of it and wants us to see it too. When Launcelot rescues a "fair lady" from a room which by enchantment is "hot as any stew", she is "naked as a needle". Three pages later, Malory tells us how Elaine of Corbin "skipped" from her bed "all naked" to tell Launcelot that she is carrying his child. Elaine doesn't desire Launcelot because she is a victim of enchantment; magic simply ensures that he responds.[52]

Nevertheless, the cost of loving is rising. Even in the case of Gawaine and Pelleas one can see the potential for conflict if the conventions governing sexual intercourse tolerate contact as promiscuous as those governing knightly combat. When one knight cleaves another's skull, things are settled once and for all. But clipping is different because the effects of desire outlive desire. Launcelot sleeps again with Elaine of Corbin and is then driven mad by Guenever's jealousy and his own guilt. Later on, a second Elaine is equally "hot" in her love for Launcelot. On this occasion, Launcelot rejection is practical but brutal: he tells Elaine of Astolat that when she marries a "good knight" he'll give her "a thousand pound yearly". McCarthy suggests that Launcelot's offer displays "generosity and concern" rather than "showy vulgarity". But even if he is no Jeffrey Archer, Launcelot's offer makes the situation worse. Elaine isn't interested in a payoff: she loves Launcelot; she can't help herself. And she's not alone. Women find Launcelot irresistible, and he sometimes takes advantage of this. He's only human: he makes mistakes; he breaks hearts. But – conveniently, perhaps – Launcelot is always shown to be more acted upon than acting. In Malory's world, the lady has the erotic initiative.[53] It's true that there is an instance of rape. Since the victim is only a "housewife", however, and Arthur's knights protect "ladies, damosels, and gentlewomen" exclusively, this incident doesn't really count for Malory. When affairs of the heart are carried on between courtly equals, the women in the *Morte* almost always have the right, if not to propose, then to dispose. Guenever has it most of all, although – for reasons which continue to intrigue the critics – Malory shrinks from royal revelations. In Book XIX, he is clear that Launcelot "went unto bed with the queen" and "took his pleasance" until dawn. But in Book XX Malory refers merely to Launcelot and the Queen being "abed or at other manner of disports, me list not hereof make no mention".[54]

Launcelot's greatest problem is that he loves the "bobaunce and pride of the world". Guenever herself remarks on Launcelot's "pride and bobaunce". 'Bobaunce': the glossary in my Everyman *Morte* gives 'pomp' and 'bombast' as synonyms. The trait first emerges in Book XV. Some knights on black horses are defending their castle from some knights on white horses and Launcelot joins the fray "to help . . . the weaker party". But then he feels that strange paralysis which came over him when he saw the Grail in Book XIII. A "recluse" diagnoses the problem: Launcelot has leagued himself with sinners and fought "good men" for "bobaunce and pride". Yet Launcelot can't help himself, and this is what makes him interesting. He wants to live in the realm of the spirit, but the light burns too brightly, the door slams in his face. The world calls out to him, and he answers. And the Queen is by nature unable to forgive her lover's nature. In their final meeting, she repeats the earlier accusation: convinced that her lover will "turn to the world again", Guenever refuses Launcelot a last kiss.[55]

As it happens, Guenever is wrong. Launcelot does not "turn to the world": in fact, he becomes a monk. He still has a few years left, but at this point Launcelot's story – the story of the *Morte* – is essentially over. Monks sing mass, ring bells and "read in books". Launcelot was never a bookworm, so this looks like a living death. But this brooding pool of a man – he is true at last to his family name – was once a frothing torrent. When he was younger, Launcelot repented and felt shame for his sin. But he always went back to his old ways, renouncing perfection for the sake of pleasure. Launcelot lived. He loved. And he showed off. When Launcelot returns from the quest and forgets his promise, he and the Queen "loved together more hotter than they did toforehand". This is better than ringing bells or reading books. But it's also worse – far worse. It is desire beyond reason; it opens a gulf between the public and the private self. Launcelot's "privy thoughts" are continually set "privily on the queen". He even takes "privy draughts" with her although, as Beverly Kennedy points out, we needn't see this as a euphemism. Such privacies nevertheless generate publicity, and Launcelot identifies so completely with the Round Table that he finds himself at war with his inmost urges. He feels shame at his worldliness and, when the gap between his better and worse selves becomes apparent, he weeps. Alone of all the court, Launcelot is able to heal Sir Urre. Malory tells us that "kings and knights . . . gave thankings and lovings unto God". Feeling that he does not deserve this praise, however, Launcelot bursts into tears like "a child that had been beaten". It's a moment of psychological penetration on the part of Malory which is as deep as it is rare. It's the moment when Launcelot's remarkably extended youth comes to an end: in Malory, only old men weep like children.[56]

The line about Launcelot's tears is indeed, as Mark Lambert writes, the "most moving" one in the Urre scene – itself the "most purely Malorian episode" in the *Morte*. Launcelot's tears engage our attention because they are shed for an "order which is about to end". They also communicate a grief which has private as well as public dimensions. Love unseats Launcelot more unerringly than the most skilfully levelled lance. It makes him lurk in bushes and furtively climb ladders. He jumps from windows for love, "and there with thorns he was all to scratched in his visage and his body". This is the pattern: Launcelot's love casts him 'outside' and here, scrambling across ditches and through hedges, maddened in the wilderness, he comes to know the world as intimately as any churl. Launcelot's love pierces him more deeply than a spear in the side. It is a boar with its "arse to a tree" whose tusks "rove him on the brawn of the thigh". It is a wound which heals only to "brast both within and without". Launcelot is so consumed with desire for Guenever that when he tears out a bar from the window of her chamber and cuts the "brawn of his hands throughout to the bone" he doesn't even bother to treat the wound.[57]

Unlike the other fair ladies who minister to his injuries, Guenever wants Launcelot too much to care for him – or herself. When Meliagrance finds the sheets of the Queen's bed "bebled with . . . blood" he instantly concludes that one of Guenever's wounded knights has "lain by her". Even when he wins, Launcelot loses: loses his blood in a strange deflowering; loses his integrity, his status at court, and eventually his masculinity. Even at his best, as in the healing of Urre, Launcelot is compared to a child. Elsewhere, he becomes an almost absurd figure. At one point, he is shot in the buttock by a huntress and loses his manners: "Lady or damosel . . . in evil time bear ye a bow; the devil made you a shooter".[58]

As a child reading Briggs, I knew that reading involved rules. I could accept the forms of combat because this was how things were – or how they might have been in days gone by. But the rules surrounding love were new and strange to my 8-year-old self. By the end of the 1960s I had acquired some of the prejudices that were usual for boys of my class and generation. I can now, with a flush of embarrassment, picture myself telling an aunt that women shouldn't work for a living. I didn't really believe this, but I was content to repeat what I thought was the approved view. After all, as I thought, a woman's life would be nicer if she could stay at home all day.

It's only with hindsight that I can see how much the Arthur stories shaped my attitudes to women. On the face of it, Briggs is considerably more enlightened than Malory. I've mentioned the passage in the *Morte* when Arthur's knights swear "to do ladies, damosels, and gentlewomen succour". In Briggs, the oath requires the knights to protect and honour "all womenkind". I've also pointed out that in *King Arthur*, victory over Lucius depends on the "work of the women". For a twenty-first-century readership, however, Briggs's stance on the relation between the sexes elsewhere seems antique. At one point, Guenever plans a dinner party to show that "I do not care" about Launcelot's absence. This captures the Queen's haughtiness whilst firmly placing her in a traditional domestic context: even a Queen works out the menu "just as any housewife would do".[59]

When I read *King Arthur*, 'gender' had appeared on my horizon; 'sexuality', however, remained a mystery. Briggs was writing for children and couldn't include clipping or naked skipping. Yet desire still cast its shadow. Briggs may have wanted to confine herself to stories – as the jacket puts it – of "knights in shining armour who rode out to do battle against the enemies of peace and justice". But without the love of Launcelot and Guenever there would be no story. It's here, therefore, that Briggs's task becomes particularly delicate. In the *Morte*, Malory is clear that, from their first meeting, Launcelot "loved the queen". Guenever reciprocates by holding Launcelot "in great favour above all other knights". In Briggs, Launcelot is similarly held "in great honour" by Guenever and by Arthur. Briggs doesn't bite the bullet until Chapter 22, when she informs us that Guenever has "loved Sir Launcelot" for years and that he "loved her in return". Condemnation follows immediately: Guenever knows that it is "wrong of her not to fight this love"; in "giving way" to his love, Launcelot stains "the shining glory of his knighthood". As a child, I found this mystifying. What were Launcelot and the Queen getting up to? Briggs told me only that they "met secretly". *Not in front of the children*: in the 1960s this was still the received wisdom when it came to marital breakdown.[60]

I knew that what happened between Launcelot and Guenever was "wrong" but was too young to pick up the hint that the King's need to secure the succession comes before his feelings for Guenever (Arthur's lack of warmth is more evident in Malory). It was something else that bothered me. My Dean & Son abridgement was surely about King Arthur – and the knights of the Round Table. That was the title, after all. So why wasn't Arthur in the middle of the picture? He began to disappear the moment he ascended the throne and after the early encounter with Lucius did no fighting until the final battle with Mordred. Did Arthur love Guenever? Did she love him back? Did the King know about Launcelot and Guenever, and what did he think? I had no answer to these questions, which continue to preoccupy Malory's critics.[61]

Arthur's royalty veils his character. And it isn't just Briggs who makes the King seem distant. In Book XX of the *Morte*, Arthur admits that he is sorrier for the deaths of Gareth and Gaheris than he would have been for the loss of Guenever: "such a fellowship of knights shall never be together in no company", but "queens I might have enow". Though he is "sorry", Briggs's Arthur doesn't discriminate so unromantically between his feelings for his knights and for his queen. Arthur feels "great unhappiness" when told of Guenever's infidelity. But he does not display anger or jealousy. For me at the time, it was once again 'passing strange'. In the end, I decided that Arthur was simply very nice; he liked Launcelot so much that he let him go off with Guenever.[62]

As an 8-year-old reader, I found Arthur puzzling. But Guenever was even more enigmatic. It was baffling that she ordered Sir Launcelot to go away and then wanted him back. When Elaine of Astolat dies of unrequited love in Malory, the Queen rebukes Launcelot for not showing this damsel more "bounty". Briggs follows her source at this point, having Guenever say with a curled lip that Launcelot could have shown Elaine "some gentleness". In the *Morte*, however, Guenever's mood swings are more pronounced: Malory has the Queen "nigh out of her mind for wrath" when Launcelot wears Elaine's token.[63]

It's embarrassing but true: *King Arthur* had as much influence on my attitude to the opposite sex as the women's movement. Indeed – bizarrely – I came to feminism through the medium of Thomas Malory. I distinctly remember thinking as a university student that feminists were like Guenever in that they were always 'waxing wroth' with men. I also found myself wondering whether the best way to get a girlfriend was to be like Launcelot – passionate but flawed. I may have been a perverse or incompetent reader, but I found the image of a vitiated masculinity extremely appealing. It's sobering to reflect that archaic attitudes to gender persisted well into the twentieth century. One would expect them in the work of a fifteenth-century writer. McCarthy points out that Guenever is "quite simply, absent" at crucial points in the *Morte*. Elizabeth Archibald also notices that Guenever is "not . . . heard very often". When Launcelot returns the Queen to Arthur, for example, she is simply an object exchanged by men. It's in this way that 'patriarchal ideology' makes women both marginal and central, mere chattels and the repositories of ultimate value. Assumptions, prejudices, stereotypes: as a child reading *King Arthur*, I drank them in. I thought that all women should be like Guenever – beautiful but cold, desirable but cruel.[64]

Briggs does little to question traditional gender roles. But in the case of Guenever, there is an undercurrent which, I suspect, had a more damaging impact on my 8-year-old self. Briggs cut the passage in which Merlin tells Arthur that Guenever is "not wholesome for him to take to wife". But in the *Morte* and, in a more diluted way, in *King Arthur*, the feeling that there is something wrong with Guenever surfaces time and again. And Malory seems, far more than Briggs, to present the Queen as a type of 'woman' in general. Launcelot and Arthur, Gawaine and Mordred: they each play their part in the collapse of the Round Table. Yet the growing pile of corpses is partly Guenever's fault. In an unusually direct passage at the end of Book XVIII, Malory tells us that the rules of love are not what they were. Men and women once loved each other better than themselves: this was "virtuous love". But "nowadays":

> men cannot love seven night but they must have all their desires: that love may not endure by reason; for where they be so soon accorded, and hasty heat, soon it cooleth. Right so fareth love nowadays, soon hot soon cold: this is no stability.[65]

The phrasing here is less familiar than the sentiment, which to members of my parents' generation tended to come through in response to cases of divorce among younger couples who *couldn't make a go of it* and failed to realize that marriage was *hard work*. Easy come, easy go: this was love 'nowadays'. And so too for Malory: "soon hot soon cold"; love is mutability; without measure, we wander on shifting sands. But how should we see the love of Launcelot and Guenever? Malory wants to present it as an instance of "old love" – a passion which endures. This, perhaps, is why he doesn't mention any "disports" in Book XX. In Book XIX, however, the bleeding Launcelot takes "his pleasance and his liking until it was in the dawning of the day". Archibald rightly observes that there is "no reference to Guenevere's pleasure" at this point. But I don't think Malory failed to include references to the Queen's feelings merely because he was a man. He wanted to preserve the possibility of "virtuous love", even if it required an act of trickery. When Launcelot describes Guenever as a "true lady", it is a noble lie. We know the truth, even if we can't admit it: this is "lycours lust", and the relationship between Launcelot and Guenever is characterized by precisely the instability which defines love "nowadays". We may blame Launcelot for this, and it's true that during the quest a hermit speaks of his "unstableness". Yet it is surely Guenever rather than Launcelot who incarnates instability. The Queen is nothing if not "soon hot soon cold": she is mutability itself, now fire and now ice. Guenever waxes and wanes, bringing change to the fortunes of men, casting some down and raising others up, impersonally, implacably.

"Not wholesome": Merlin's remark makes Arthur's future wife sound like fast food. But there is in the *Morte* a sense, not only that Guenever's love is innutritive and even toxic, but also that she destabilizes the 'whole'. Guenever splits her subjects more effectively than a sword through the skull.[66]

5

The Great Default

To read *King Arthur* at the age of 8 was to be confronted with a story of desperate desire, transcendent but hopeless love, sin and sorrow, devastation and death. I'm surprised that I was allowed to read the book in the first place. Was it possible that depictions of smitings and cleavings were considered suitable material for children at this period? Possibly so; yet I can't imagine that adultery would have been seen as an acceptable topic in literature for the under tens. I don't think I knew the word 'adultery', so I wasn't in a position to make the inference that it was something grownups did. But it was there, nonetheless: Briggs couldn't do anything about that. *King Arthur* gave me a glimpse of another world. It led me and misled me, but it also helped me to understand that I didn't understand.

I'm not sure I understand now, if I'm honest. But it isn't as if the *Morte* is a locked room; Malory's preoccupations are often evident in a phrase. In Book XIII, Launcelot admits that his love for Guenever is "out of measure". The condition is contagious. Launcelot says that Elaine of Astolat loved him "out of measure". She agrees: she has loved Sir Launcelot "out of measure". Just like Elaine of Corbin. "For wit you well", as Malory tells us, "out of measure she loved him". The loss of measure has its origin in matters of the heart. But it doesn't end there: when Launcelot breaks into Meliagrance's castle, he is "wroth out of measure". On the battlefield near Salisbury, the King is likewise "wroth out of measure" when he sees "his people so slain from him". Then he finds Mordred leaning upon his sword near "a great heap of dead men". Arthur runs his spear "more than a fathom" through the body of his son. And in his dying act – Malory seems to have invented this detail – Mordred thrusts himself along the spear and cleaves the "helmet and the brain pan" of his father. We've seen such wounds before. But by this stage Arthur's victory over Lucius is an age ago, in England's springtime. It's longer still since the commons cried: "We will have Arthur unto our king". It's a cold world: the nights are closing in; the state is out of measure; anger begets anger and violence, violence. In the moonlight, on the battlefield, robbers are killing the wounded "for their harness and their riches". Malory points the moral for those whose "common voice" led them to side with Mordred rather than with "he that was the most king and knight of the world". The fact that "there may no thing please us" is "a great default of us Englishmen". England itself lacks "measure" for we, as Malory puts it, are "new fangle".[67]

And by this stage, in a different sense, the reader might well conclude that England – Englishness – is terribly hard to measure. We've seen that Malory's geography is vague indeed (the final battle of the *Morte* takes place near Salisbury but also "by the seaside").[68] Space is nevertheless defined more clearly once Arthur becomes King. He brings the nation into being, shaping its extent and limits. Arthur invents England – re-invents it, perhaps, for if the King wants "to get all England into his hands" he must have a prior idea of what 'England' is. Yet boundary lines remain unclear when Malory sets out the state of play at the start of Book VIII:

> At that time King Arthur reigned, and he was whole king of England, Wales, and Scotland, and of many other realms . . . in Wales were two kings, and in the north were many kings; and in Cornwall and the west were two kings; also in Ireland were two or three kings, and all were under the obeisance of King Arthur. So was the King of France, and the King of Brittany.

In Geoffrey of Monmouth, Arthur is King of Britain and the conqueror of other realms. In Malory, Arthur is King of England and other kingdoms recognize his authority. The internal consolidation of England and the defence of the new nation from external threat in Books I–IV of the *Morte* is a relatively straightforward tale, though it looks less familiar in Caxton, where Arthur wants "to gete al Englond in to his hand" and to be "hoole kynge of Englond". As a geographical entity, however, 'Logris' is more mysterious.[69]

When Tristram decapitates Sir Nabon le Noire in Book VIII of the *Morte*, he defeats a knight of "North Wales" and wins a victory for "the realm of Logris". But where is Logris? In Book IX, King Mark asks for tidings from "the realm of Logris" and the main item of news – Tristram's performance at a tournament – relates exclusively to England. Malory subsequently underlines this identification. In Book X, Tristram offers to take Isoud to "the realm of Logris" – a place which, as Malory immediately adds, "is this land". In Book XII, still more unambiguously, Launcelot is banished "out of the country of Logris . . . that is for to say the country of England". But why have two words for the same place? Malory is employing terms from different languages. 'England', 'English': the land and its language are named for the Angles. In sixth-century Welsh, however, as N. J. Higham notes, the word *lloegr*, which "can mean any neighbouring people", would usually have referred to the English. Malory's Arthur is King of England, and the *Morte* represents this country as a territory achieved through battle: England expands by conquering other lands which it has previously categorized as English. But this sense of possession achieved, of some entity brought into existence by an act of political will, is undermined by the references to Logris. We may pretend to know who we are, but because it names us in the language of others, 'Logris' makes us foreign to ourselves. The effect is unnerving but also exhilarating, for Logris is much more exciting than dull old England.[70]

I hadn't heard of Logris when I read *King Arthur*. My reflections on 'England' related less to history than to the "new fangle" world of the 1960s. I've mentioned that the Arthur stories encouraged me to think of England as the mixture for a Christmas cake. The Union Jack resembled a pie cut into slices, or a more complicated version of Battenberg cake. But when I began to think about the names of the things we ate at home I became increasingly bemused. Beef was British, but our lamb came from New Zealand and our bacon from Denmark. I remember the first time my mother prepared a Danish open sandwich, and it was well worth sacrificing a second slice of bread in order to have more ingredients on the first, though it was hard to see what was 'Danish' about that. Moreover, the ingredient which preceded the ham, tomato and lettuce was (at least in my mother's version of this dish) a layer of something called 'Philadelphia' – a cream cheese named, I was told, after a city in the United States. I wasn't aware that my breakfast favourites – Kellogg's Special K and Frosties – were American. I thought Spam was as English as Shippam's potted meat or Wall's sausages. Not knowing the origins of companies such as Green Giant and Heinz, sweet corn and baked beans seemed thoroughly native to me. Foreign foods were reaching the table in disguise: I remember being astonished to discover that Golden Delicious apples came from France.

At breakfast, lunch and tea a multitude of words posed their problems before being consigned to an increasingly distended mental file labelled 'England'. To turn to *King Arthur* was to become still less sure about the nature of the nation. Briggs referred to Arthur as the ruler of "all the North and Scotland and Wales and all the fair rolling lands of England". But didn't the "North" form part of England? Didn't Scotland and Wales have their own kings? The issue of nationhood is still more vexed in the *Morte*. As I've already suggested, the May Day tournament at Lonazep can be seen as the apogee of Arthur's reign. The idea is that:

> all the knights of this land, and of Cornwall, and of North Wales, should joust against all these countries, Ireland, Scotland, and the remnant of Wales, and the country of Gore, and Surluse, and of Listinoise, and they of Northumberland, and all they that held lands of Arthur on this half the sea.

It's a lovely list, but a baffling one. Why aren't Cornwall and Northumberland part of England? Why pit "North Wales" against its "remnant"? Where are "Surluse" and "Listinoise"? And what does Malory mean when he talks about lands on "this half" of the sea? Where is the other half? Is there another England somewhere else?[71]

The question of nationhood isn't simply a matter of borders, however: affiliation is as important as location. And the more I read *King Arthur*, the more I began to ponder the nature of Launcelot's citizenship. On the face of it, everything was straightforward: Arthur was King of England; Launcelot was his best knight. Launcelot, therefore, was English – wasn't he? I assumed that Joyous Gard, Launcelot's castle, was in England, and Malory confirms that it is to be found either at Alnwick or, as "some men say", Bamborough. Yet this isn't Launcelot's only or his earliest home. When Merlin meets the young Launcelot in Book IV, he travels "over the sea unto the land of Benwick". This is not simply a trip along the English coast, for in Book XX it emerges that Launcelot comes from Bayonne or, as "some men call it", Beaune. Briggs made no mention of Launcelot's origins when he first appeared at Camelot. But in the concluding chapter Gawaine commands him, in the name of the King, to "go back to your own realms in France". As a child, I realized with sudden perturbation that Launcelot was as French as a Golden Delicious apple.[72]

At the end of the *Morte*, the constituents which Arthur mixed together separate out again. The King is not a multinational food company, but he pursues a policy of mergers as single-mindedly as Kraft or Nestlé. Camelot is the headquarters of England plc (www.knightsoftheroundtable.co.eng) and the Round Table is the nation's most trusted brand. Even so, as it eventually proves, England is more like oil and vinegar than Christmas cake. The kingdom's division – its fissiparous nature – means that all the time, beneath the repeated festivals of Englishness, the various parts of the nation have retained a sense of their separate identity. Yet the *Morte* highlights a still deeper problem with the notion of nation. The issue is not that Launcelot isn't English. It's that England itself – deep down – is un-English: there has been something foreign about us from the start. At the beginning of Book V, Arthur argues that he owes "no tribute to Rome" and asserts the right "to claim the title of the empire". On what basis? The King is clear: it is because "we" are "descended of them". It's incredible: the English monarch is a Roman.[73]

When the King puts the case for continental war, Malory is nodding in the direction of Geoffrey of Monmouth, who claimed that Brutus, the great-grandson of Aeneas, was the "first king of the Britons", attributing to Arthur, in N. J. Higham's words, a "lineage equal, or even superior . . . to the Romans". Unlike his predecessor, Malory refers to Arthur as the King, not of 'Britain', but of 'England'. It's a crucial shift of emphasis, although Malory is as interested as Geoffrey in giving his imagined community a pedigree. The national mixture isn't simply created by Arthur's ability to draw the different elements of his realm into a unified order in the present. Malory also wants to show that Englishness extends backwards in time: at root, we always were what we would become. Yet this concern with origins unsettles the concept of national identity as much as it extends it. Almost accidentally (or driven, perhaps, by a deeper insight into the nation's nature) Malory begins to unpick the fabric he has woven. Whether the English go back, via Brutus, to Aeneas and Troy or, via the Caesars, to Rome, the English come second. Having no foundations to call our own, no clear beginning, we can neither tell how 'we' are different to 'them' nor recognize the deep connection between them and us.[74]

Ing-lund. I knew this was what *King Arthur* was about. I knew the concept was unstable and suspect I was dimly aware that Arthur's knights would not have extended the category of Englishness to me. I certainly remember feeling that the nature of nationhood was again at issue when the quest began. A number of knights went overseas in pursuit of the Grail. The presence of English knights in the Holy Land wasn't entirely unfamiliar to me: one of my Ladybird books contained a picture of Saladin slicing through a silken cloth with his scimitar whilst Richard the Lion Heart shattered an iron bar with his sword. Saladin . . . silk . . . scimitar: it was all very sibilant, subtle, and sinister, but it was strange that Richard's foremost quality was brute force. I wondered at the time whether breaking things with broadswords was the best that England could do. In the Ladybird illustrations, flags flew from the towers of Acre; English chain mail glinted in the sun. My ready-made iconography for the encounter between East and West had a second source: Christmas cards showed conifers and camels, sand and snow – sometimes simultaneously.[75]

When Canterbury came into contact with Jerusalem, prefabricated pictures thronged into my mind: there were swords and armour, but also robes of biblical blue and gold like those I drew in Mrs Bullough's class one summer's day in 1970. Medieval . . . Mediterranean . . . it was mixed up in the middle of my head. Though his geography is idiosyncratic, Malory sees more clearly. The East isn't just a distant land to fight and die in. Unlike the meeting between Richard and Saladin, in which cultures uncomprehendingly collide, each appearance of the Grail – that ancient and holy vessel – represents a projection of the past into the present, and this adds significantly to the frisson created by the meeting of orient and occident. In the penultimate part of the *Morte*, the quest makes the Mediterranean world a felt presence. But Biblical echoes can be heard at earlier points in the story, for in England itself, the East occasionally comes to the West, the past to the present.

But is it England? In Malory's hands the nation repeatedly seems more foreign than familiar. We first encounter the Grail in Book XI, when Launcelot releases the needle-naked woman from the stew-hot room. After slaying a "fiendly" dragon, Launcelot meets King Pelles, the guardian of the Grail. His daughter, the "fair Elaine", will shortly become pregnant with Galahad. Launcelot clearly makes a big impression in a short space of time, but the location of Pelles's castle – "over the pounte of Corbin" – is not nearly so obvious. We are presumably still on "this half" of the sea: Launcelot starts his adventures at Arthur's court and no voyages are mentioned. But when Pelles introduces himself as "king of the foreign country" we seem to be in another place altogether. And any sense of ambient Englishness becomes still more attenuated when Pelles details his lineage: he is "cousin nigh" to Joseph of "Armathie".[76]

The references to the Grail make England into a "foreign country". And Malory now provides a good deal of information. Percivale discovers that Joseph of "Aramathie" brought the Grail "into this land" when he was sent by Christ "for to . . . preach the holy Christian faith". Joseph came with King Evelake, who was struck "almost blind" centuries ago. Like Launcelot, Evelake is a moth to the Grail's flame: he was always "busy to be thereas the Sangreal was" and seems one day to have got too close. Evelake prays to live until a descendant "of the ninth degree" is able to "achieve the Sangreal". We know that Launcelot is "of the eighth degree" and Galahad "of the ninth degree". But it is not entirely clear whether the Du Lacs are descended from Evelake, from Joseph of Arimathea or from "our Lord Jesu Christ". The third option seems the least likely, but it is the one favoured by Guenever: according to her, Launcelot is "of the eighth degree from our Lord Jesu Christ" and Galahad "is of the ninth degree".[77]

When Percivale, Bors and Galahad reach Castle Carbonek in Book XVII it is time for the quest to be "fulfilled". The holy vessel is accompanied by four angels who carry in a chair an elderly man with letters on his forehead: "See ye here Joseph, the first bishop of Christendom". Once again the story reaches back to the Holy Land, to the rich man who begs Jesus' body from Pilate and lays it in a tomb, rolling a "great stone to the door". But this isn't simply another instance of a national narrative mingling with other, older tales. The encounter with Joseph of Arimathea carries a message still starker than Malory's remarks on the "great default" of the English. We see a figure with the "signs of the passion" who tells the three knights that they must remove the Grail from "the realm of Logris". As we come to terms with the fact that the king of the "foreign country" is resident in these lands, Pelles explains why the Grail has to be returned to the place from which it came:

"wotest thou wherefore? For he is not served nor worshipped to his right by them of this land, for they be turned to evil living; therefore I shall disinherit them of the honour which I have done them".

Briggs doesn't reproduce the line about "evil living". She is nevertheless clear that the Grail must be taken to Sarras because "the people of this land" – having "turned aside after riches and vain things" – are "no more worthy that it should be among them".[78]

Adam and Eve were expelled from Eden to wander far from grace. But in the *Morte* we see the fall of "this land", a whole nation. Malory calls it 'Logris', but the word merely softens the blow: we know it is England. And now we may remember a tale of long ago. In a time of war, famine and pestilence, two kings met in battle. One cleft the other with the "first stroke of his sword'. Afterwards, the "realm of Logris" acquired another name: it was England, and also the "waste land".[79]

CHAPTER
6
Being Launcelot

Towards the end of the summer term, a tournament known as 'Sports Day' was held at school. Divided into our houses (Normans, Tudors, Stuarts and Hanoverians) and watched by parents, we sat in lines on a bank overlooking the running track. The tarpaulin felt rough against our crossed legs; a sweet smell went up from the crushed grass. *Don't fidget!* The hissed instruction of a teacher was hard to obey when one had been immobile for what seemed like hours. *Do your best – but don't show off!* This advice was at least more knightly. In the egg and spoon race I usually came last, feeling clumsy and flustered. But one year I won the sack race. I can still feel and smell the hessian sack as I wait for the whistle to blow. I concentrated so much on jumping that I didn't even realize I was in the lead.

The Arthur stories were filled with what a film classification board might describe as 'adult themes', but one of their fascinations was that childhood was built into their structure. Briggs revealed a world that was new to me, although one of the oddest things about adults was that they often resembled children. When Arthur returns from Rome, his knights "made jousts and tournaments". It was as if, having done their work, they could go out to play. If it wasn't for Mordred, I thought, life at Camelot could have been an endless holiday. Had I been reading the *Morte* rather than my Dean & Son abridgement, I might have been surprised to notice that Arthur's knights taunt each other like children in the playground. Tristram suspects Palomides will not keep their appointment to do battle for, as he boastfully points out, "I am much bigger than ye". A knight is killed for having the temerity to suggest that Launcelot is a "better knight than Sir Gawaine". *Nuh nuh ni-nuh nuh!*[80]

C. S. Lewis remarks on the scenes of penitence with which medieval romances conclude. "We hear the bell ring", he writes, "and the children, suddenly hushed and grave . . . troop back to their master". Lewis's point is that obedience infantilises. But one doesn't need to see it this way, for renunciation – the repression of desire – is a manifestation of the 'reality principle' which Freud associated with adulthood. In the end, the division is not so much between the child and the adult as between the wild and the tame. And despite his pleas for restraint in matters erotic and political, in spite of his emphasis on order, Malory knows that it's wildness which makes and unmakes relations between men and women, doing and undoing narratives and nations. In spite of himself, he sometimes forgets about 'measure' and seems instead to be saying that smiting and kissing, clipping and cleaving are the only things worth doing. We can't help it; we're errant.[81]

Even as a child I found myself enlisted on the side of wildness. The King gained a kingdom and held it to his last breath. But Launcelot threw everything away – for love. Tennyson brings this out rather beautifully at the end of "Sir Launcelot and Queen Guinevere":

> A man had given all other bliss,
> And all his worldly worth for this,
> To waste his whole heart in one kiss
> Upon her perfect lips.

As a child, I would have recognized this emotional extravagance instantly. I didn't realize at the time, but Brigss was almost as indebted to "Idylls of the King" as she was to the *Morte*. Take her description of Launcelot:

> He had a fine figure and was darkly handsome . . . high and fierce was the glance of his dark eyes; his slightly waving hair hung to his shoulders and was also softly dark so that the gold circlet upon his brows shone by contrast. Strong were his muscles, so that men could mark the swell and curve of them beneath his purple silk robe.

Malory could never have written anything like that (he didn't even use the word 'purple' in the *Morte*). Briggs is embroidering upon Tennyson, who writes in "The Lady of Shalott" of Launcelot's "broad clear brow" and "coal-black curls".[82]

At the age of 8, I might have been surprised to discover that my image of Launcelot – of Camelot itself – was rooted as much in the Victorian period as in the Middle Ages. At the time, however, my interest in the Arthur story had nothing to do with the *Morte*'s adaptations: it was more urgent and more personal. My contemporaries thought of Mick Jagger and Bryan Ferry, but for me – silly me – Launcelot was the embodiment of 'style', an elusive quality involving wildness, waste and sacrifice. Style was about throwing things away and

not caring. I sensed it in Briggs – that primal impulse couldn't be beaten
out of the narrative. Yet wildness would have been more evident if I
had read the *Morte*. When he sleeps with Guenever, Launcelot sacri-
fices perfection itself. Caught naked in the Queen's bedroom, he would
rather have a suit of armour on him than be "lord of all Christendom".
In his own words, Launcelot is the "unhappiest man that liveth". But
isn't the price worth paying? Arthur is put into a barge and Sir Bedivere
weeps in the forest. But when Bors finds Launcelot "stark dead" in his
room, there is more general sorrow for this marred and melancholy
man. In the lament of Launcelot's brother Ector, the dead man is the
"courteoust knight" and "the truest lover". He is "kindest" and "goodliest", "meekest" and "gentlest". In the choir at Joyous Gard there is
"dolour out of measure". When *The Tale of Peter Rabbit* was read to me
as a very young child, I entertained an image of myself as Peter Rabbit.
As my hero and model, Sir Launcelot was infinitely more compelling.
If one wanted a reason to break the rules, ladies came well ahead of
lettuce.[83]

Peter Rabbit enjoyed French beans and radishes as well as lettuce.
And so, in English children's writing – and in my reading – it went on.
The Wind in the Willows has hardly started before Mole and Rat break
for "coldtonguecoldhamcoldbeefpickledgherkinssaladfrenchrollscresssand-
widgespottedmeatgingerbeerlemonadesodawater". On their first trip to the
island in *Swallows and Amazons*, Ransome's children take "bread, tea,
sugar, salt, biscuits, tins of corned beef, tins of sardines, a lot of eggs
. . . and a big seed cake". But these are just the daily provisions. After
the battle in Houseboat Bay, Captain Flint serves "ices, strawberry ones
. . . parkins and bath buns and rock cakes and ginger-nuts and choco-
late biscuits", "mountains of sandwiches", and a cake with "a picture of
two little ships done in pink and white icing". Yet the convention of the
ritual meal flourished long before this. Chrétien de Troyes's Erec and
Enide enjoy "pike and perch, salmon and trout . . . raw and cooked
pears". In the *Morte*, by contrast, the plates seem empty: we know only
that there is meat and fish. It's not surprising that Briggs elaborates. At
Arthur's wedding, the guests tuck into "boars' heads . . . pasties and rich
meats". Tor and his squire feast on "capons and pasties". Re-reading
King Arthur as an adult, I found the popularity of "pasties" in Briggs's
Camelot rather surprising, and wondered frivolously whether Sir
Ginster produced them in the castle kitchens. According to Chrétien's
translator, however, Eric consumes "cold meat pies". In another tale
there are "venison meat pies" which are "not displeasing".[84]

Questions about the authenticity of Briggs's version of the *Morte*
wouldn't have been on my mind as a child. I was 8 years old. I wanted

to be Sir Launcelot, and I was prepared to experiment. On Sundays, we sometimes drove to Smithills, a former coaching house which had become a carvery with a Dickens theme. The restaurant was all Dick Swiveller and Mr Micawber, booze and bonhomie. Pictures of Mr Pickwick's roseate face, pot belly and surprisingly slender shanks appeared above the door to the restaurant and on the cover of the menus. At the time, none of this seemed tacky: I liked the fact that we ate our lunch in the 'buttery': it sounded, well, *buttery* . . . softly salty and deliciously unctuous, just like the black puddings which I consumed at every opportunity. I see them still: the blood-darkened matrix, the flecks of fat. They called it 'Joe the Fat Boy's Snack' and nobody knew why I was besotted with it, including myself. It's only now, reading Briggs, in which Launcelot is at one point served a "black pudding", that I see the truth. I was trying to become Sir Lancelot by consuming what he ate. It was an act of sympathetic magic.[85]

Needless to say, the consumption of black pudding didn't make me darkly handsome, and in my more realistic fantasies I contented myself with being one of Launcelot's young friends – Gareth, perhaps, or Lavaine. And yet, just once, I cut almost as fine a figure as Sir Launcelot. One winter's day at school, we were allowed to play in the snow. Children circled like horsemen; snowballs flew through the air. The tallest boy in the class began to pelt an undefended girl. I hardly ever talked to her: she was far too beautiful. Dark hair, pale face, black eyes: she was a maiden straight from the pages of *King Arthur*. To defend her honour – to offer succour – I threw my snowball and saw it hit. And for that brief moment I was my hero. Then the boy-giant roared with pain, the fair damosel cast me a grateful look, and I ran away as fast as I could.

When I was young, relations in space were the first to be apprehended: dampness and shade in the back garden, brightness on the other side of the house; the world at the back and the one at the front. Time took longer: I awoke and went to sleep, but there was no particular sequence, to the hours and days. Perhaps this was why I found it easy to accept the sudden lurches in the time-scheme of *King Arthur*. As a child, time happened as quickly as a fall or a cut, but it also congealed. Christmas noticeably dammed the stream: in November, the coming event flowed sluggishly towards me. But then the trickle stopped: my advent calendar – one tiny window after another – converted days into weeks.

Christmas was the end of the year and a week later another one began. Yet time was divided in other ways. The school year ended in July and began again in September. In the middle came my birthday, which was the end of one year and the beginning of another. The years turned also to the rhythms of my illnesses: bronchitis in October, hay fever in June. This isn't to say that I didn't notice changes. In May, I looked for caterpillars on the underside of hazel leaves. I remember the bare branches of the trees in January, the rustling leaves I kicked up on the way home from school in November, the deep-dark foliage of July. But none of this happened in any particular sequence. It wouldn't have disturbed me if winter had followed spring or summer autumn.

As a child I read *King Arthur* with less sense of temporal disorientation than I experience now. It's only as adults that we learn linear time, realist time: as children we're modernists – or medievalists – untroubled at any rate by chronological contortion. "Now turn we": Malory's formula isn't a sign of disorganization but a way of putting into sequential form a series of episodes whose meanings revolve in vast orbits. This is why Arthur's reign seems to have the rhythm of a single year. It begins in spring; a gloriously extended summer follows. After the quest, the narrative descends into autumn before dwindling finally into the depths of winter, when a hand grasps Excalibur and draws it back into the depths. The story of King Arthur made shapes with time, converting sequences into resonant circuits of significance.

7

Pentecost

C. S. Lewis draws attention to the "constant connexion" in medieval romance "between the god of Love and the month of May". Lewis outlines the scenario of the *Romance of the Rose*:

> The poet, "Wisshinge and wepinge al min one", and wandering in the usual May morning, meets Venus and is handed over by her to the priest Genius, to confess himself as regards the code of love.

"The usual May morning": Lewis identifies the convention almost wearily. He doesn't comment on the more significant fact that May is a time of "wepinge" as well as "wisshinge".[86]

Time made shapes in *King Arthur*, and the main parts of the story had their seasons. In the *Morte*, however, Malory's temporal rhythms are more complicated and also less reassuring. There's the linear historical plot, which covers several decades: Arthur is born; he becomes King; he marries Guenever. There are battles and tournaments; the knights swear an oath; the fellowship of the Round Table waxes and begins to wane. And finally, the King dies. But the narrative also turns upon itself. On May Day, at the height of his power, the King declares "a jousts before the castle of Lonazep". To celebrate the arrival of Tristram and Isoud, he will bring together knights from Cornwall and Wales, from Gore, Surluse, Listinoise, and "all they that held lands of Arthur on this half the sea". But if May marks the point at which Arthurian England reaches its zenith, this month also heralds the kingdom's demise.[87]

At the end of Book XVIII, Malory pauses to celebrate the "lusty month of May". When things begin to "fruit and flourish", he suggests, lovers should "call again to their mind . . . many kind deeds that were forgotten". May is the point in the calendar when 'measure' is restored. It's the time to balance the books, emotionally speaking, to make repayment for kindness past. May renews mind and body, the inner self as well as the outer world. And it's perhaps because this month is a junction between the old and the new that Malory associates it with stability and balance: in climatic terms, May is neither too cold nor too hot, not too bright nor yet too dark.[88]

The ameliorating influences associated with the month of May have implications in the political as well as the erotic sphere. Gawaine refuses to join the conspiracy led by his brothers because Launcelot's "kind deeds . . . should be remembered". This comes at the start of Book XX and recalls Malory's remarks on May as the month to remember "kind deeds" two books earlier. Gawaine's refusal to share the "privy hate" of Agravaine and Mordred is significant, for he has previously been presented as a hothead. Once again, Malory is hinting at a seasonal connection. May is the "lusty month", and there is no lustier knight than Gawaine. Back in his own and the kingdom's salad days, Gawaine spent two days and nights in Lady Ettard's pavilion, and it's not surprising that this affair took place in "the month of May". So Malory associates Gawaine with May's surging germinations and ejaculations, though also and additionally with its countervailing values: temperance, gentleness and restraint. The year's green hinge can turn either way, producing beginnings as well as endings, death in addition to life.[89]

"Wepinge" as well as "wisshinge": spring's obvious association with rebirth is for Malory only part of the story. By the time of the tournament at Lonazep, there is, as Launcelot informs Arthur, "great jeopardy". The King is "passing glad" to see Tristram and Isoud, but their elopement has stirred slumbering enmities. And if Arthur wants to "get all England into his hand", he has a funny way of doing things. The King would have "this land" – England – "joust against" Ireland, Scotland and Wales, against Gore and Surluse and Listinoise. In former days, the institution of the Round Table was a way of ensuring that rival groups recognized a single sovereign. Once upon a time, each of Arthur's knights occupied a separate arc within a single circle of glory and of power. As late as Book VIII Malory suggests that kings in Scotland, Wales, Cornwall and Ireland, as well as in France and Brittany, are "under the obeisance of King Arthur". He is "whole king". At Lonazep, however, Arthur seems to divide up his subject realms for sport.[90]

Elizabeth Pochoda suggests that the Round Table might be a victim of its own success: if Arthur's knights won all their battles, they would eventually "run out of enemies". The logic here is linear: the quantity of enemies is fixed and therefore exhaustible. But May's logic is one of circularity and renewability: it is the month when old friends become enemies. And although tournaments are play-fights, Arthur draws the battle lines at Lonazep so aggressively that he alienates his own subjects. The idea of the whole seems to have been forgotten. An emphasis on singularity – purity, even – displaces the earlier sense of Englishness as mixture. According to the original recipe, the English are this and that, one thing and another. We're different – diametrically opposed to each other, perhaps – but part of a single circuit (except for cowherds, of course). Once upon a time, the Round Table was a hub with radial spokes. But now a thick-edged line surrounds us all, restraining centrifugal impulses. It's insiders against outsiders, 'us' *versus* 'them'. And if 'we' are also 'them' – if we have loyalties on each side of the line – then we're no longer really English. May is the time when things come together, and also when they fall apart. The month brings new life to ancient forms, but might also make youth itself decrepit. In May we repair "winter rasure"; without care, however, we also "deface green summer". And when May is out of measure, the regular return of the seasons gives way to another order altogether.[91]

When Guenever goes "Maying into woods and fields beside Westminster", time's path is already a descending one. It is, in Lewis's phrase, the "usual May morning", and what usually happens in May is something entirely unexpected. Unknown to Guenever, Sir Meliagrance has been watching his chance. He has loved the queen "passing well" for years and knows this is "best season to take the queen". Guenever is apprehended, along with the ten knights in her company, several of whom are "dolefully wounded". But the Queen manages to send out a '*m'aidez*' – her ring, carried on the swiftest horse by "a child of her chamber". Launcelot responds instantly. He crosses the Thames at Lambeth and, when his horse is shot from under him by Meliagrance's archers, presses on through "ditches and hedges". Moving at ground level quickens Launcelot's perceptions, though not his sympathies. He catches glimpses of the common folk at their work, but for him this England is merely a space to be traversed. He commandeers a wood-cart. The carters do not protest, but Launcelot strikes one of them a fatal "buffet"; the other prudently drives him to Castle Meliagrance, where Launcelot breaks a porter's neck "in sunder".[92]

It's not surprising that Briggs's Launcelot refrains from casual murder. For her, the Maying episode is an opportunity to achieve vividness – a last spot of colour before gloom descends.

Queen Guinevere and her knights gathered daisies with the dew still on them, and made chains and crowns very fair to see. They cut branches of green tasselled birch and bunches of forget-me-not, primroses, celandines and sweet-smelling herbs, so that they were all decked with Nature's jewels and blazons.

In the equivalent passage in the *Morte*, the Queen simply gathers "herbs, mosses and flowers". Still, it's surprising that Briggs is at least as graphic as Malory when it comes to the cleaving of Meliagrance – in general, violence in *King Arthur* is toned down. In the *Morte*, the Queen's captor receives a stroke which "carved the head in two parts". In *King Arthur*, Briggs has Launcelot's blow cleaving "steel and bone and brain". For Briggs, it would seem, adultery is one thing and treachery quite another. But she misses the point about May. Meliagrance's abduction of the Queen intrudes into the natural order: there is no sense, as there is in Malory, that the garden of May contains the opposite of everything one wants.[93]

The terms of retribution in Book XX are familiar enough; so is Launcelot's contempt for ordinary people. But time is out of measure; adultery, like blood, will out. Malory drives the point home at the beginning of Book XX. May is when lusty hearts "flourisheth and burgeoneth", but also the time when "a great anger and unhap" begins to destroy "the flower of chivalry of all the world". Gawaine initially heeds May's message but then falls victim to this anger – and is that anger's victim, dying at Dover of an old wound. Malory has waited a long time for this moment, for as early as Book III Gaheris reproaches Gawaine for beheading a woman. Gaheris himself goes on to behead his mother and to have his head cloven by Launcelot. Gawaine dies of a reopened head wound originally inflicted by Launcelot. The smiter smitten: it's poetic justice. But here as elsewhere, Malory's seasonal irony is acute: Gawaine dies on "the tenth day of May".[94]

Like many of the more important events in the *Morte d'Arthur*, the quest for the Grail begins at Pentecost. It's at this point in the year that Arthur is acclaimed king. It's at Pentecost that the knights of the Round Table swear to "succour" ladies. This is a time of wonders and portents, of damosels and doves. It's at this time that Galahad takes his place in the Siege Perilous; at Pentecost, too, that the quest for the Sangreal begins. As a child, I didn't know when Pentecost took place any more than I knew what samite was: I just liked the sound of the word. In the Christian tradition, however, Pentecost falls on the seventh Sunday after Easter, on Whit Sunday. Visited at Pentecost by a light which shines more brightly than the sun, Arthur's knights are the modern counterparts of Christ's disciples. After Easter - the crucifixion, the resurrection – after long weeks of prayer, the disciples discover that Jesus' spirit has been born again in them. They hear a "rushing mighty wind" and see "tongues . . . of fire". Previously, these men merely followed Christ; at Pentecost, they become Christians. And they are given the ability to speak with men "of every nation":

> Parthians, and Medes, and Elamites, and the dwellers in Mesopotamia, and in Judaea, and Cappadocia, in Pontus, and Asia.
> Phrygia, and Pamphylia, in Egypt, and in the parts of Libya about Cyrene, and strangers of Rome, Jews and proselytes,
> Cretes and Arabians . . .

In the *Morte*, the power of the Roman Emperor is a power over places: the imperial centre can call upon resources from Alexandria to Damascus, Damietta to Tarsus. But the power of Christianity is a power over peoples and tongues, a power embodied in the word. Lucius and his agents reach out and grab you; Christians whisper in your ear. In either case, however – whether authority is achieved through external or internal means, whether it's the body or the soul which is made captive, whether empire is worldly or otherworldly – the subject remains what he always was: Syrian, Turkish or Cretan. Camelot is different in this respect, for Arthur represents a new form of power. It is not Roman or Christian: it is English.[95]

In some ways, it looks as if the King's authority is weaker than that of Jerusalem or Rome. Religious or secular, the old empires were nothing if not outward-looking: they grew by voracious accumulation. But Arthur's power is defensive, even introspective: it depends on subtraction and exclusion. The Round Table joins Arthur's knights in "one accord", like the disciples. It offers membership of a social structure which is the focus of the knights' existence and to which, far as they travel, they must return. For the disciples, however, Pentecost is the beginning of a journey outwards to others; the order they glimpse exists not here and now but in a future communion. Arthurian Englishness nevertheless involves a more fundamental adjustment to one's sense of what one is than either Jerusalem or Rome would ever have demanded. One can be a Christian or a subject of the Empire and remain a citizen of wherever one happened to be born. But to be part of Arthur's world one has to become English, committing oneself to life inside a verbal entity. The walls of Rome and Jerusalem stand firm but will never contain their inhabitants' lives. 'England' is only a word, but one which holds its subjects more firmly than stone.

The biblical Pentecost marks the end of the beginning. It's a point of congregation and foundation: the disciples are visited with tongues of fire in a closed and private space, where the expansive force of organized faith is building up. In the *Morte*, by contrast, Pentecost is more a matter of light than heat. And the force here is ultimately centripetal: after it has been stretched to breaking point, the system falls in upon itself. Pentecost marks the beginning of Arthurian civilization, but also the end. For it is May – or early June at the latest – when Arthur realizes that he will never see his knights "again whole together". It feels like the final battle, when Arthur's knights fall to the "cold earth", takes place in winter, and Tennyson explicitly sets the closing books of the "Idylls of the King" at the end of the year. In the *Morte*, however, the last battle takes place soon after Trinity Sunday, eight weeks after Easter and a week after Pentecost. The *Morte* ends in May, and in concluding comes full circle, for Mordred, as we only now recall, was "born on May-day".[96]

The *Morte* is such a ghostly text. This isn't because Percivale comes back from the dead or because Galahad is more spirit than flesh. It has to do with space – and time. In its circles and still more in its broken circles, the text remembers itself – the last May recalls the first – and also anticipates: each subsequent May is present from the beginning. The text almost thinks: it watches you, even if you aren't aware of it. I wasn't aware of it when I read *King Arthur* on summer's evenings in 1970. I had no idea when I bought my copy of the Everyman *Morte* that autumn day in 1981. I didn't realize it one night in October 1987 when I walked back to my lodgings in Cambridge after a party in the rooms of a Trinity don – a party during which a violent storm rattled the ancient windows in their frames. If on the following day I had read the newspapers, I would have concentrated on reports of the 'Great Storm'. I wouldn't have turned to the obituaries and thought about the man who, fifty years earlier, discovered a manuscript of the *Morte d'Arthur* and in that moment did as much to help this work survive as anybody in five hundred years.

Part II

The Life

CHAPTER
8

The Fat Book

There was once a librarian, a man who loved old books and was familiar with the "fine brown powder" which drifted through the air when readers disturbed their repose. He was also a teacher, and wanted to "thrill" his pupils by using Mercator's atlas of 1570 to investigate the history of "exploration and empire". He worked in a public school with a large collection of old books and manuscripts. He believed, perhaps, that there were unknown worlds within their pages – islands to map on some Mercator of the mind. New discoveries could still be made: it hadn't been long since a "bedside mat" in one of the rooms at school had been identified as a tapestry "probably woven for the occasion of the christening of Prince Arthur, Henry VIII's oldest son". But what he found that day didn't at first seem of much interest. It was a manuscript, but the binding was relatively modern, and the work was written on paper – 473 leaves of it – rather than vellum. For him – at first – it was just a "fat" book.[97]

The man was Walter Oakeshott. The school was Winchester College. The bedroom was that of the Warden; it contained a safe which housed various ancient documents. And the fat book turned out to be a manuscript of the *Morte d'Arthur* – the only one in existence. It was 1934, and Oakeshott had just made one of the greatest literary discoveries of the twentieth century. At first, however, he had no idea what he'd found. Nor did those who had been there before him: the college had catalogued the volume in the nineteenth century; M. R. James had examined it "more than once". It wasn't as if the manuscript was unknown. And its subject matter was also familiar: as a young man in the 1920s, Oakeshott had taught both Malory and Tennyson at Merchant Taylor's school. By this stage of his career, however, he was more interested in twelfth-century illuminations. It wasn't until the Easter of 1934, while preparing an exhibition in the new library, that Oakeshott came upon a reference to Malory in the *Cambridge History of English Literature*. "No manuscript of the work is known": the line made his heart miss a beat. Oakeshott bought a copy of the Everyman *Morte* at Wells's bookshop in College Street. Comparing the two texts, he realized that the manuscript he had found was quite unlike Caxton's text. Oakeshott placed the newly discovered work in his exhibition, where it was seen by H. D. Ziman, literary editor of the *Daily Telegraph.* Ziman printed a report of the "remarkable discovery" on Monday 25th June. *The Times* picked up the story the next day.[98]

The following Saturday, Oakeshott was due to host a lunch on the first day of the cricket match between Winchester and Eton. One imagines him setting out the napkins and arranging the cutlery whilst his children – Helena, a girl of three; Evelyn and Robert, twins of just eleven months – were having their hair brushed by Noel, Oakeshott's wife. The guests had already assembled when the doorbell rang, at which point, as his biographer John Dancy records, Oakeshott left the "salmon and . . . strawberries" and opened the door to a man he had never met before – a man who had travelled hotfoot from Manchester on hearing reports of the "remarkable discovery" and introduced himself as Eugène Vinaver. It was a somewhat chilly meeting: Oakeshott showed Vinaver the manuscript in its showcase but refused to allow his guest to touch so much as a page of it.[99]

Oakeshott initially considered editing and publishing the 'Winchester manuscript' (as it had now become) on his own account. But he shortly ceded this task to Vinaver, though by his own admission he "skimmed the cream quite unscrupulously" in articles published in *The Times* and *The Times Literary Supplement.* As a scholar of medieval romance, Vinaver was more qualified to undertake an edition of the *Morte*; one suspects that he was also very persuasive. Yet Vinaver's feelings must have been mixed: he had spent the previous three years collating all known sources of the *Morte.* The discovery of a manuscript of this work drew attention away from the question of influences and back to the text. But it was too good an opportunity to miss. Vinaver had the manuscript sent up to the John Rylands Library in Manchester. It was here, in Deansgate, that he produced his edition – the one now generally used by Malory scholars. It took thirteen years, but Vinaver had decided what he had on his hands almost immediately: a manuscript which was "more complete and authentic" than the Caxton text; a version of the *Morte* which brought us "nearer to what Malory really wrote".[100]

It's rather a lovely story: it makes me think of C. S. Lewis and J. R. R. Tolkien tucked up in the Eagle and Child with beer and tobacco to hand: the little world left outside and only the vastness of literature within. Yet the discovery of the Winchester manuscript was announced a few days before the Night of the Long Knives; by the time Oakeshott published his article in *The Times* Hitler was Führer. As the catastrophe in Europe unfolded, people packed their bags and went off to work, unwrapped their lunchtime sandwiches, gazed through the windows of train carriages as the sun set behind suburban roofs. Newspapers were read and books written. Scholarly reputations were made, and the name of Vinaver became permanently associated with the *Morte d'Arthur*.

It's odd to think of Vinaver toiling in a library between 1934 and 1947 – odder still to contemplate what residents of Guernica, Dresden, Auschwitz or Nagasaki might have thought of his endeavours. Both Vinaver and Oakeshott were scholars; both were vulnerable to the charge of living in ivory towers. But Oakeshott was by no means a disengaged intellectual. *Commerce and Society* (1936) was, in Dancy's words, a "lively history of trade, empire and seamanship". It also contained a distinctly leftist explanation of the Depression. And although Oakeshott's enthusiasm for Drake, Hawkins and Raleigh resurfaced in *Founded Upon the Seas* (1942), this later book was not so much a defence of imperialism as a contribution to the war against Fascism. As a school debater, Oakeshott had in 1933 argued the case for dictatorship. But this was a rhetorical exercise. Oakeshott lectured in Working Men's Colleges during the 1920s. He supported the Republican cause in Spain and contributed to *Men without Work* (1938), a report which influenced the social programme set out by William Beveridge in 1942.[101]

The "fat" book turned Vinaver into one of the great Malory scholars but it also affected Oakeshott's career. On one occasion, he took his pupils to the Minster – the very building in which, according to Malory, Arthur's knights attended Whitsun service before jousting in a nearby meadow. It was easy, Oakeshott felt, to "people that piece of land with those knightly figures – though", as he immediately added, "they had never existed". Perhaps they never had. But think of that summer's day in 1934. The meal on the table; cricketers resting on their bats; a stranger at the door: the meeting between Oakeshott and Vinaver has something legendary about it. And also something miraculous, as if charged particles continued to emanate from the *Morte* well into the twentieth century.[102]

Oakeshott was not to edit Malory, but he didn't do a bad job of "skimming the cream". His *TLS* article argued that the Winchester manuscript was an intermediate copy and not a Malory holograph (Vinaver later argued in more detail that the Winchester text and the copy used by Caxton were derived from two manuscripts which were themselves copied from a single text and that this manuscript was itself a copy of what Malory originally wrote). This would have fascinated Malory scholars. Yet Oakeshott's article in *The Times* might have attracted the attention of a wider audience. The American scholar G. L. Kittredge had proposed that the author of the *Morte* was Sir Thomas Malory of Newbold Revel in Warwickshire as early as 1894. Oakeshott argued that the Winchester manuscript increased the likelihood that Kittredge's hypothesis was correct. Caxton had carved up his version of the *Morte* into twenty-one books and at the end of Book IV, after Malory's account of Uwaine's adventures, printed the legend "*Explicit liber quartus*" – "Here ends Book Four". In the Winchester text, however, there was at this point (see the front cover of the present volume) a passage unknown to previous readers of the *Morte*:

> Thys was
> drawyn by a knight prefoner Sir Thomas Malleore
> that god fende hym good recouer amen

Oakeshott had the lines photographed and sent them off to the States. Replying to Oakeshott in September 1934, Kittredge wrote that he had been profoundly "stirred": the lines in the Winchester manuscript were "a voice from the great deeps".[103]

The *Morte* is such a vast and intricate work: C. S. Lewis described it as a "cathedral of words". And in many respects, Malory's life – like those of the cathedral-builders – remains a mystery. P. J. C. Field suggests that the *Morte* displays a high degree of "self-effacement". Action precedes thought; incident precludes reflection. The author of the *Morte* is intent on describing the world he sees in his mind's eye: he isn't interested in himself. So it's natural to wonder what kind of man Malory was. A bookworm who inhaled the fine brown powder which fell from the volumes on his shelf as if it was the scent of lilacs in spring? An English Quixote who thought the age of chivalry had not passed? Or some Home Counties colonel, regaling guests with interminable tales of lopping and chopping?[104]

When Malory has recounted the deaths of Arthur, of Lancelot and Guenever, his tale is almost done. Constantine becomes "chosen king of England" and Bors goes to the Holy Land to fight "the miscreants or Turks", there to die "upon a Good Friday". Death is everywhere – as is resurrection. Then, in the last lines of the *Morte*, we catch a glimpse of the author – the builder whose plan is surpassed by the structure which now stands before him. In Caxton's text (see fig. 7), Malory asks his readers to "praye for me whyle I am on lyue that god fende me good delyueraunce / & whan I am deed I praye you all praye for my foule".

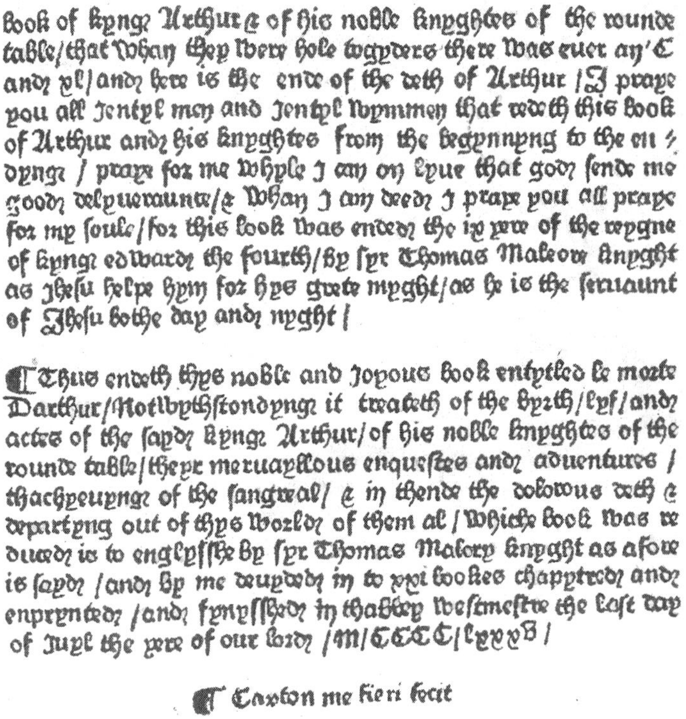

Booß of ßyng? Arthur & of ßis nobße ßnygßtes of tße rounde
tabße/tßat wßan tßey wer ßoße togyders tßere was euer an' C
and xl/and ßere is tße ende of tße deth of Arthur /J praye
you aß Jentyl men and Jentyl wymmen tßat redtß tßis booß
of Arthur and ßis ßnygßtes from tße begynnyng to tße en ꝛ
dyng / praye for me wßyße J am on lyue tßat god sende me
good delyueraunce/& wßan J am deed J praye you aß praye
for my souße/for tßis booß was ended tße ix yere of tße reygne
of ßyng? edwarde tße fourtß/By syr Thomas Maßeor ßnygßt
as Jßesu ßelpe ßym for ßys grete mygßt/as ße is tße seruaunt
of Jßesu botße day and nygßt /

☞ Thus endetß tßys nobße and Joyous booß entytßed ße morte
Dartßur/Notwytßstondyng it treatetß of tße byrtß/lyf/and?
actes of tße sayd ßyng? Arthur/of ßis nobße ßnygßtes of tße
rounde tabße/tßeyr meruaylßous enquestes and? aduentures /
tßachyeuyng? of tße sangreal/& in tßende tße doßorous detß &
departyng out of tßys worßdꝛ of tßem aß/Wßicße booß was re
ducedꝛ in to engßysße By syr Thomas Maßory ßnygßt as afore
is sayd?/and By me deuydedꝛ in to xxi booßes cßappytred? and?
enprynted?/and? fynysßedꝛ in tßabbey wesmestre tße ßast day
of Juyß tße yere of our ßordꝛ /M/CCCC/lxxxv /

☞ Caxton me fieri fecit

FIGURE 7 The last page of Caxton's *Morte*. Reproduced by courtesy of the
University Librarian and Director, The John Rylands Library, The University of
Manchester (Incunable Collection 18930, folio ee62).

Again there is the prospect of death, final and ineluctable – and again,
hope of "delyueraunce". Then we are suddenly confronted with
concrete facts: the author tells us that his book "was ended the ix yere
of the reygne of kyng edward the fourth" and was written by "fyr
Thomas Maleore knyght . . . the feruaunt of Ihefu bothe day and
nyght".[105]

So we know the *Morte* was completed sometime between 4 March
1469 and 3 March 1470 – the "ix yere" of Edward IV's reign. But
'Maleore'? Medieval spelling, as William Matthews points out, "was
always flexible". Even so, modern readers might well feel confused. In
his preface, Caxton talks not of 'Maleore' but of 'Malorye'. And in the
Winchester manuscript, the name is 'Malleorre'. In spite of its
geographical and anatomical mistiness, the *Morte* is nothing if not
substantial. But the name of its author is strangely impalpable and this
is still more true of the man himself: so eminent a scholar as P. J. C.

Field is prepared only to say that Thomas Malory, Knight, of Newbold Revel in Warwickshire, is the "most likely" author of the *Morte*. It remains possible, if unlikely, that the work was written by Thomas Malory of Holcot in Northamptonshire or Thomas Malory of Papworth St Agnes in Cambridgeshire. It might have been penned by Thomas Malory of Tachbrook Mallory in Warwickshire or Thomas Malory of Long Whatton in Leicestershire. It might even have been composed by Thomas Malory of Hutton Congers in Yorkshire.[106]

This parade of Malories passes before us: one dandling a child on his knee; another in embroidered robes; still a third, bright-eyed but hollow-cheeked, his hand resting on a book which might be a Bible or a ledger. Different faces but the same name – and only one of them is the man who wrote the *Morte*. And the mystery deepens: the *Morte*, as Elizabeth Archibald and A. S. G. Edwards observe, is the "first major work of secular prose fiction in English". But its author – if he was indeed Sir Thomas of Newbold Revel – had been prosecuted as a "thief, rapist [and] would-be murderer" and was also an "oft-imprisoned felon".[107]

The Newbold Revel Malory first pops up on the grid in 1443, accused of having wounded Thomas Smythe of Spratton in Northamptonshire and stolen £40-worth of goods. For a time, the Smythe incident looks like a one-off. We know nothing of Malory for the next seven years. Nothing to his discredit, at any rate: Malory probably serves as Member of Parliament for Warwickshire in 1445; in 1449 he becomes MP for Bedwin in Wiltshire. At this point, Malory's life takes a different turn. Parliament is prorogued on 17 December 1449. Sometime during the next two weeks, Malory and twenty-six armed men seem to have attempted an ambush in the abbot's woods at Combe. Their target is Humphrey Stafford, Duke of Buckingham. And now the criminal spree begins in earnest: in May 1450, Malory's behaviour becomes erratic – crazy, even. He is first accused of having raped Joan Smith at Monks Kirby. A week later, it is alleged, he extorts 100 shillings from Margaret King and William Hale, also of Monks Kirby. Three months after that, in August – one notices an emerging pattern – it would appear that Malory rapes Joan Smith again. This incident takes place in Coventry and, as in the case of the Spratton Smythe, Malory appears to have compounded his crime by stealing goods to the value of £40. Towards the end of the month there is another allegation of extortion, the victim on this occasion being John Milner of Monks Kirby.

Everything goes quiet for a while. But then, in June 1451, at Cosford in Warwickshire, Malory and five other men allegedly steal seven cows,

FIGURE 8 Malory's Warwickshire. A detail from William Dugdale's map of the Knightlow Hundred in the 1656 edition of *The Antiquities of Warwickshire* (between pp. 2 and 3). Caludon is to the east of Coventry; Combe Abbey is to the south-east of Caludon. In the triangle formed by the intersection of the Fosse Way, Watling Street and the River Avon, Monks Kirby, Cosford and Newbold Revel can be seen. As the crow flies, it is 9 miles from the centre of Coventry to Monks Kirby. For more information on early maps of Warwickshire, see n. 109, this volume. Reproduced by kind permission of Maurice Tennant.

two calves, 335 sheep and a cart worth £22 belonging to William Rowe and William Dowde of Shawell. In the following month, in a case reported to Henry VI himself, Malory seems to have broken into the Duke of Buckingham's deer-park at Caludon, stealing six does and causing £500-worth of damage. He is arrested and held at the manor-house of Sir William Mountford in Coleshill; he escapes that same day by swimming the moat. The following night, with ten other men, Malory apparently gains access to Combe Abbey using battering rams. He steals ornaments and money to the value of £86 from two of the abbot's chests. A couple of days later – the sums have changed but the pattern of repetition remains evident – Malory again breaks into Combe Abbey. On this occasion, he is supposedly accompanied by more than a hundred men, among them eleven yeomen, three husbandmen, two labourers, a gentleman, a groom, an armiger and a smith, together with a cook whose name was Cook and a harper called Harper. Malory and his cronies proceed to break down eighteen doors, force open three iron chests, insult the Cistercian abbot and, along with £40 in cash (£40 again!), make off with "five rings, a small psalter, two silver belts, three rosaries (of coral, amber and jet), two bows and three sheaves of arrows".[108]

The authorities now respond in a more concerted way. In August 1451, charges of "divers felonies" are laid at Nuneaton. Malory is apprehended and, in January 1452, produced at the King's Bench Court. He pleads not guilty and is committed to Ludgate prison. But Malory's criminal career isn't over yet. Early in 1453, he appears to have broken the terms of his bail. It's likely to have been during the spring or early summer of this year that (as is again alleged) he steals four oxen from Sir William Peyto's estate at Sibbertoft and threatens a bailiff before attempting to drive the oxen to Fenny Newbold. During a further period of bail in 1454, Malory seems to change the field and mode of his operations. His servant John Aleyn is engaged in some horse-rustling around Great Easton in Essex and, early in July, Malory accompanies Aleyn to Braintree. They break into the house of John Green at Gosfield and then – that pattern again – try the same trick a few days later. On this occasion, Malory ends up in Colchester prison. Undaunted, he makes use of "swords, daggers, and langue-de-boeufs" in a second breakout. He doesn't appear at the King's Bench when his bail expires in October 1454. In November, however, this double-dappled man is again apprehended by the authorities and committed to the King's Bench Prison, where – with spells in a number of other London gaols – he remains until 1460.[109]

CHAPTER

9

Bricks without Straw

According to William Matthews, "we now know more about Sir Thomas Malory of Newbold Revel than about any other Warwickshireman of his time". This knowledge has been established by more than a century of scholarly endeavour. And yet – in the end – we know so little. Discussions of the Newbold Revel Malory remain, for Christine Carpenter at least, "strangely unilluminating". Writing a biography of Malory is, as P. J. C. Field puts it, "like making bricks without straw". We don't even know when the Newbold Revel Malory was born, though Field thinks it "must have been between 25 April 1415 and 22 May 1418". Parts of Malory's life during the late 1450s and early 1460s are a "complete blank". We don't have a contemporary account of Malory – there's no Aubrey or Boswell. There is not a word – even of reproach – from Elizabeth his wife.[110]

We're not completely at sea, however. We're almost certain that Malory died in 1471 (if Field is right, Malory would then have been in his mid-fifties). We know, too, that in his *Antiquities of Warwickshire* (1656) William Dugdale reported that Malory was "buryed under a marble in the Chappell of St Francis at the Grey-Friers, near Newgate". His gravestone apparently carried the following inscription –

HIC IACET DOMINUS THOMAS MALLERE
VALENS MILES
OB 14 MARCH 1470
DE PAROCHIA DE MONKENKIRBY IN
COM WARWICI

– which seems reassuringly definite, though it adds a fourth spelling of the name (Maleore, Malorye, Malleore and now Mallere) and the year should be 1471 rather than 1470. But the greater mystery is how Malory's mortal remains ended up in Greyfriars. It was close to the prison in which he was held during parts of his second term between 1468 and 1470. Since Malory seems to have died not long after his

67

release, Greyfriars may well have been the nearest and most convenient place of interment. Yet even allowing for the fact that Malory (as Field points out) "was never tried" – far less convicted – "on any of the charges brought against him", it's hard to see why a provincial gentleman with so chequered a history should be left to await Judgment Day in what Matthews describes as the most "ornate and fashionable" London cemetery – a place of burial which contained the residuum of "two queens and a king, nobles, goldsmiths, scholars, monks, physicians, judges, and rich merchants from Florence, Genoa, Gascony, Sicily and Spain".[111]

Malory's criminal career does indeed seem to have been remarkable: in the 1930s, A. C. Baugh wrote disapprovingly of an "orgy of lawlessness"; in the 1950s, Muriel Bradbrook felt that the idea of Malory as a "gangster" was "depressing". For C. S. Lewis, the lack of connection between the *Morte* and what we know of its author is the first of five paradoxes which together form the "single grand Paradox" of Malory. Matthews agrees: as a man and a writer, Malory presents us with a "moral paradox". We needn't expect artists to lead lives of exemplary virtue but – for Matthews at least – the paradox of Malory remains "too absolute". The man and the work seem to come from different worlds. The *Morte* is as solid as a cathedral; the man is a will-o'-the-wisp. Malory may have been a prisoner in life, but he escaped from the gaol of posterity.[112]

Bricks without straw: we know the charges, but there are more questions than answers. Who was Smythe? How serious was the assault? What was stolen? We might picture Malory as a boozer and brawler, vomiting in gutters, getting into late-night scuffles, ending up in a police cell, and then being hauled up before the beak. But Malory was (by Field's reckoning) at least 31 when the crime spree of 1450–4 began – hardly a juvenile delinquent. Still, it's worth considering Malory's family situation during these years. He had lost his father by 1434; an uncle died in 1440 and another uncle in 1443. His mother was dead by 1445. When Malory took charge of his estate, he may well have been the oldest surviving member of his family – alone in the world, without more senior sources of advice. This would have been common in medieval England. But that's not to say that an absence of family support didn't play a role. Perhaps a sense of isolation and disorientation was widespread. Perhaps, as a result, the English social system was more affected by unguided young men than it might otherwise have been. As Field points out, the Smythe allegation is "not unusual": the Warwickshire gentry "accused one another of scores of comparable crimes during the fifteenth century".[113]

But what about the rape? Elizabeth Malory must surely have asked the question, and one is at a loss to imagine her partner's answer. Another question: did 'rape' mean the same thing in 1450 as it does today? Several critics have their doubts. Kittredge felt that the charge against Malory was "absurd – a mere legal formula". Edward Hicks agreed: the rape charge was a "legal fiction". In an even more charitable spirit, C. S. Lewis suggested that Malory took Joan Smith away from her "knave of a husband" in order to prevent her receiving a pair of "black eyes". This is hardly Launcelot rescuing Guenever from Meliagrance but it's not rape as we know it. Some years after Lewis, Edmund Reiss hastened again to Malory's defence: the charge was at best "ambiguous". William Matthews also considered the possibility that the offence against Joan Smith was "less offensive than it now seems": perhaps she had merely been "abducted". For Matthews, however, the specific charge – *"felonice rapuit et cum ea carnaliter concubit"* – makes it clear that Malory was accused not of mere abduction but of behaving *carnaliter*–"carnally". Field concurs: the charge of *raptus* could indeed refer to abduction, "but in this case . . . did not: the charge was sexual assault". This, then, was rape in the "modern sense".[114]

Yet one doesn't need to be an apologist for Malory to recognize that the nature of his act is unclear. Field acknowledges that the charge against Malory was pressed by Joan Smith's husband under a statute whose purpose was "to make elopement into rape despite the woman's consent". Malory was accused of a sexual crime and not of abducting or eloping with Joan Smith, but it's possible that the charge against him was brought maliciously. Perhaps Mr Smith needed to see his wife's infidelity as rape. Perhaps Malory's crime was to have transgressed the sexual conventions of his time. Perhaps his was a case, not of wickedness, but of wildness.[115]

The idea of Malory as a "modern" sex criminal may or may not deepen Matthews's "moral paradox". For Catherine Batt, however, this paradox – Malory the writer *versus* Malory the rapist – involves a "false dichotomy". Batt argues that critics from Kittredge to Field have considered the rape from a male perspective. But the question for her is not whether rape (according to Malory's definition or Mr Smith's or that of a fifteenth-century judge or a twentieth-century critic) took place or not. All these approaches reveal the way in which men have used rape to define women. Whether Malory is retrospectively exonerated or convicted, we are looking in a mirror. So perhaps my suggestion that Malory was wild is just another occlusion. He was clearly a resourceful man and not just crazy. He could raise support at short notice; he could

improvise. What is wildness, anyway? A name for something unmea-
surable – and wholly personal. There's nothing wrong with
explanation on the basis of individual character, of course: Malory's
motives may be unclear, but his life is stamped with a unique, even
perverse waywardness. Yet we shouldn't forget that the author of the
Morte was writing during a period of instability "unparalleled", in the
words of Bruce Webster, "since the Norman Conquest". It's not easy
to see how a rape could be explained in terms of the Wars of the Roses.
But an assault on an abbey must surely have had a political dimension.
And then there is Malory's attempt to assassinate the Duke of
Buckingham.[116]

In 1950 Richard Altick suggested that Malory's actions at Combe
Abbey expressed popular feeling against the "bloodsucking privileges
of the religious houses". Edward Hicks notes that complaints against
the Abbot of Combe had been made, going on to argue more specu-
latively that although Malory may not have been a dissenter,
"discontent with the monastic system was not confined to Lollardy".
For Hicks, Malory was a "political" rather than a "doctrinal" Lollard.
But the manor at Newbold Revel was only six miles from Lutterworth,
the "fountain-head of Lollardy", and scarcely further from Coventry,
"one of the hot-beds of . . . militant Lollardy". And Humphrey Stafford,
the Duke of Buckingham, was a staunch anti-Lollard.[117]

Was Malory's attempt on the Duke's life the result of a "personal
quarrel" or an expression of "dissent"? Field concludes that Malory's
motives were "private" and that "much of the picture remains obscure".
A personal difference or a point of principle? At the distance of half a
millennium it's not always easy to say which is which: they might sometimes have been one and the same. We need to know what Malory felt
and what he thought. What was going through his mind in 1450, in
1460, in 1470? Yet this question may not only be unanswerable but also
misplaced, particularly if we regard the Wars of the Roses as a dynastic
conflict. If we do, the story runs as follows: the Lancastrian Henry VI
held the throne when Malory began his career in crime; Henry VI was
the son of Henry V; Henry V was the son of Henry IV, and Henry IV
was the son of John of Gaunt, 1st Duke of Lancaster, the fourth son of
Edward III. Back in 1399, Henry IV (Henry Bolingbroke as was) took
the throne from Richard II, the son of Edward the Black Prince,
Edward III's first son. In 1461, Edward IV (formerly the Earl of March)
deposed Henry VI and ruled until 1483 (with an interval between 1470
and 1471, when Henry was restored to the throne). Edward, the Yorkist
king, was the son of Richard, Duke of York; Richard was the son of
Richard, Earl of Cambridge; the Earl of Cambridge was the son of

Edmund Langley, 1ˢᵗ Duke of York. And Edmund was the fifth son of Edward III. Edward IV's title to the throne, however, was strengthened by descent through the female line: the Earl of Cambridge's wife was Anne, and she was the daughter of Lionel of Antwerp, 1ˢᵗ Duke of Clarence, the third son of Edward III (the second son died in infancy).

Set out in this intricate but arid way (Mortimer's speech in *1 Henry VI* provides a more vivid but also still more confusing backstory) the Wars of the Roses are a genealogical not an ideological conflict. There was no argument about whether we should have a monarchy: the Wars of the Roses were not the English Civil War. Our own political paradigms – left, right; liberal, conservative – don't wholly explain the 1640s and are still less useful when it comes to the 1450s. Yorkists and Lancastrians argued about the king's finances and the war in France, but neither side possessed what we would recognize as a set of policies. Nor can the conflict satisfactorily be seen as regional: Yorkists didn't necessarily come from Yorkshire or Lancastrians from Lancashire. The Wars of the Roses were not a county cricket match.[118]

The lack of debate about political principles in the 1450s (what we would recognize as political principles, I mean) makes it easy to conclude that the English élite were unprincipled power-grabbers. Christine Carpenter highlights "collective political action" rather than "rampant individualism" during this period. But the key concern – "where power lay" – seems to have been uncluttered by arguments between radicals and reactionaries, centralizers and devolvers. It's true that the Duke of York (as Carpenter notes) "took his political stand in the 1450s upon the common weal". It's also the case that York presented himself as a representative of the "ancient nobility" and cast his rival, William de la Pole, 1ˢᵗ Duke of Suffolk, as a bungling upstart. The idea that Suffolk was responsible for the loss of England's territories in France certainly gained ground in parliament and the "popular consciousness". But it was, Carpenter is clear, a "myth". Somerset, Suffolk's successor at court, might equally have been seen to stand for the "ancient and conventional virtue of obedience to the ruler" with York representing "the non-household nobility and . . . the lesser ranks of political society". But these contrasts were artificial ones: the parties to the Wars didn't neatly separate into traditionalists and innovators, the old guard and the young Turks. There was no fixed division between "ins and outs" and York's allusions to the failure in France (in 1452 he referred to the "derogation, lession of honour and villainy reported generally unto the English nation") were, as Carpenter argues, "self-justifying".[119]

The most obvious aspects of any historical period are often the most misleading ones. Perhaps, then, the real mystery is not Malory the man but the age he lived in. For Carpenter at least, this "very difficult period" cannot wholly be understood in terms of the conflict between Yorkists and Lancastrians, the white rose and the red. It's not entirely clear that it is right to call the Wars of the Roses 'wars'. There was widespread disorder and, at certain points, high levels of violence: thousands lost their lives at the Battle of Towton in 1461. But Carpenter describes the first Battle of St Albans as "an affray" and reminds us that, throughout the Wars of the Roses, "armies were mostly not large and campaigns were short".[120]

It's not even clear when the Wars started. As far back as 1399, when Richard II was deposed and the House of Lancaster sowed the wind? Or only when England reaped the whirlwind? At the first Battle of St Albans in 1455? Or not until the Battle of Blore Heath in 1459, as Carpenter suggests? When did the Wars end? One would usually say that it was at the Battle of Bosworth in 1485, with Richard III dead and Henry VII set to unite the houses of York and Lancaster by his marriage to Elizabeth, the daughter of Edward IV. But the Yorkist forces – admittedly under the pretender Lambert Simnel – weren't finally defeated until the Battle of Stoke Field in 1487. And some historians would argue for a much earlier conclusion: Bruce Webster claims that the troubles were not "essentially dynastic" after Edward was crowned in 1461. Depending on the dates one chooses, the Wars of the Roses lasted for almost a century (1399–1487) or a couple of years (1459–61). This is perturbing enough. But it has been further argued that the Wars of the Roses didn't actually happen. In *1 Henry VI*, Somerset plucks the red rose of Lancaster and Warwick the white rose of York. The King later pronounces the wearing of these emblems "madness" – before himself putting on a red one. It is a characteristically crazy act. But Yorkists and Lancastrians may not actually have used the rose as a badge. In the final scene of *Richard III*, Henry Tudor vows to "unite the white rose and the red"; Henry VII certainly used the Tudor Rose as an emblem. But nobody at the time spoke of the 'Wars of the Roses'. Even now, for Webster at least, the term is an "inadequate label". One might think that the title of Carpenter's book – *The Wars of the Roses* – is self-explanatory, but the first line reveals our mistake: "This is not, strictly speaking, a book about the Wars of the Roses". As Carpenter's subtitle makes clear, her subject is "politics and the constitution" rather than the familiar field of dynastic and military conflict. A "difficult period" indeed.[121]

CHAPTER

10

The Coal-Face

In the traditional account, the Wars of the Roses were the product of dynastic conflict and aristocratic unruliness. But for Carpenter, the constitution of late-medieval England was "perfectly workable". The loss of French territories, the crown's financial weakness, declining trade revenues, the instability brought about by the Black Death – these explanations are necessary but insufficient. For Carpenter, the crisis wasn't caused by the 'over-mighty' barons of historical cliché: it began at the top, in the person of Henry VI. Three depositions, two protectorates, a dozen battles between 1454 and 1471: for Carpenter all this was "rooted in the king's personal incapacity".[122]

Carpenter may be right to reject the idea that regional power struggles undermined the monarchy. Still, the conflicts unquestionably existed: as early as the 1440s, Carpenter finds a widespread "lack of local stability". In Warwickshire, a "power vacuum" produced "attendant disorder among the gentry" and by the early 1450s there was "growing division and disorder" (some of it emanating from Newbold Revel, as we've seen). So it may be in the county context that Malory's actions begin to make sense. Carpenter argues that, like other areas of the country, fifteenth-century Warwickshire operated under a system of 'affinities'. "By the affinity", she writes, "we mean all those lesser landowners connected to [the lord] by anything, from indenture and contract to nothing more tangible than a sense of loyalty or obligation". The major aristocratic influences in Warwickshire during the 1450s were Humphrey Stafford, since 1444 the 1st Duke of Buckingham, and Richard Neville, created 16th Earl of Warwick in 1449 – Shakespeare's "setter up and plucker down of kings". Yet, as Carpenter points out, county networks were "immensely complex and often included . . . intertwined affinities".[123]

In an earlier study of Warwickshire landed society, Carpenter acknowledges that her decision to discuss the county as if it were a single entity is a matter of "convenience": most counties had "little existence as political and social units until the later sixteenth century" and Warwickshire was in any case "particularly fragmented". Still, the fact that the system of affinities extended beyond the county boundary doesn't mean that it didn't exist, and it remains possible that Malory's actions can be explained with reference to this system. For Kittredge and Oakeshott, the passage in the Winchester manuscript about the "knyght presoner" lent support to the idea that it was the Newbold Revel Malory who wrote the *Morte*. Yet the most significant word here might be 'knyght' rather than 'presoner'. Documents cited by Field describe Malory as an "esquire" in 1439 and a "knight" in 1441, when he would have been one of perhaps 2,000 armigerous gentry. In the seventeenth century, William Dugdale reported that Malory had been knighted in "23. *H.* 6." – that's to say in 1445. Field thinks Malory "may well" have been knighted by Henry VI, although this event occurred "by 8 October 1441". Either way, Malory belonged to the upper ranks of the gentry: he wasn't just a 'gentleman'. Later on, as a 'knight of the shire', Malory would have been one among 74, since two such knights were appointed for each of England's 37 counties. Malory wasn't quite at the top of political society but, as a member of the class which exercised rule in the shires, at what Carpenter describes as the "coal-face of government", he was at the bottom of the top. Yet this position may have been precarious: if Malory was indeed knighted for military service, then his status, according to Carpenter, was "something to be valued". In comparison with the fourteenth century, however, this class of knights was declining if not yet threatened: military service was becoming a "specialist activity". But Malory's problems may have been less to do with his title than with his finances: Field thinks his income was "less than half . . . the average" for a knight. Despite his lavish burial, Malory's spell in the King's Bench Prison seems at points to have been an impecunious one. And it's possible that the two occasions on which Malory was alleged to have taken goods to the value of £40 and the further occasion on which he was accused of stealing £40 in cash would have had particular significance. An act of 1445 stipulated an annual figure of £40 for knights sitting in Parliament. For Malory, these thefts would have bought a respectable career.[124]

Thomas Malory wasn't by any means a nobody. According to Carpenter, his "property and geographical placing" made him a man whose support was "worth cultivating". As a "poor knight", however, it's possible that Malory was punching above his weight. Malory would have had obligations to those above him. But those below – the dozens of men involved in his escapades – were also part of the affinity system, and would in return for their assistance have demanded recompense. Perhaps Malory was too small a fish to swim in his chosen pond. But this doesn't explain the split with Buckingham. And a split it must have been, for Malory had once enjoyed close relations with Humphrey Stafford. Hicks thinks it "highly probable" that, in 1431, Malory saw Joan of Arc burned at the stake in Rouen – an event at which Stafford was present. Carpenter believes that Malory was a member of Buckingham's entourage "from 1439". Field suggests that Malory "may" have served under Philip Chetwynd in Gascony around 1442: Chetwynd was related to Malory's mother and belonged to Stafford's affinity. The connection between Malory and Buckingham seems to have deepened: in Field's view, Malory's position as MP for Warwickshire during the 1445–6 parliament identifies him as one of Buckingham's "associates". In the 1449–50 parliament, Malory was returned for Bedwin in Wiltshire: for Field this represents another "provable connection" between Malory and Buckingham because the Staffords had been "lords of Bedwin for three quarters of a century". Field therefore finds it "easy to believe" that the Duke, having found Malory "useful" four years earlier, "used his influence" to get Malory his Wiltshire seat. Such links were soon broken, however: parliament was prorogued in December 1449 and, early in 1450, Malory set out to kill his former patron, the King's "most wealthy subject", holder of land in twenty-two counties and the leader of an affinity consisting of some ten knights and twenty-six esquires.[125]

At this point our subject's life becomes complicated to the point of incoherence. After the attempt on Buckingham's life, Malory – still serving as MP for Bedwin – might have returned to Westminster in order to attend the second session of parliament in late January 1450. He might then have followed parliament to Leicester in April. By this stage, however, the honourable and gallant member would have had other things on his mind: in May he allegedly raped Joan Smith; by the time parliament reconvened in November, he is supposed to have raped her once again. Like any modern-day politician in a tight spot, Malory needed career-management skills. And by the time the new parliament met in November 1450, Malory had managed to become MP for Wareham in Dorset. It was a seat which, as Field points out, "belonged to the Duke of York". The implication is clear: Malory too "belonged to York".[126]

The problem, however, is that we don't know how national and local politics meshed in Malory's case. In the 1449–50 parliament, Suffolk was blamed by Yorkists for the English failure in France (the Commons brought eight charges of treason against him in February 1450 and there were calls for his execution in April). It's true that English foreign policy had been a disaster: Maine had been lost in 1448; Normandy was overrun early in 1450; Cherbourg, the last English bastion, fell in August. It's likely that Malory "belonged" to York by November 1450, but whether or not he was part of the campaign against Suffolk at the start of that year remains unclear. Even if he was, a break with Buckingham wouldn't necessarily have followed: the Duke was no Yorkist but nor was he closely associated with Suffolk. Indeed, he was thought in some quarters – probably incorrectly – to have been unfairly excluded from power by Suffolk. Feelings against Suffolk were certainly running high: in May 1450, the ship taking him into exile was intercepted by a privateer, the *Nicholas of the Tower*. According to Carpenter, Suffolk was put through a mock trial and then, in the name of the "community of the realm", expeditiously "beheaded with a rusty sword" on the gunwale of a boat (his "headless body", as John Wolffe reports, was later "found on Dover sands"). Suffolk's execution was, as John Watts puts it, the "first act in a summer of mayhem that was to change the face of English politics forever". But this hardly explains why Malory staged his own "summer of mayhem" or why he wanted Buckingham dead.[127]

It's by no means clear that Malory's attack on Buckingham was motivated by hostility to the Lancastrians. Buckingham was admittedly killed fighting for the Lancastrian army in 1460. He also led Henry's forces at the first Battle of St Albans in 1455 and was injured as a result (in *3 Henry VI*, York's son, the future Edward IV, boasts that "I cleft his beaver with a downright blow"). In general, however, the Duke tried to remain impartial. When the young Buckingham was a leading figure in the King's household in the 1420s, he attempted, according to Carole Rawcliffe, "to moderate between the warring factions". Although he negotiated on behalf of the king in 1455, Buckingham was by no means committed to Somerset in the days before St Albans. Rawcliffe speaks of the Duke's "ungovernable temper", and it's true that he once physically threatened Joan of Arc. It's also true that Buckingham didn't walk away from a feud. In May 1448, the Duke's son, Richard Stafford, was killed by Robert Harcourt in an affray which Carpenter describes as the "single most shocking outbreak of violence in Warwickshire in the 1440s" (according to one of the Paston letters, Harcourt smote the young man a "grette stroke on the hed with hys sword"). Buckingham responded by leading a "small army" to Stanton Harcourt in Oxfordshire. The church into which Harcourt and his men had retreated was torched, arrows were fired into the tower, and Buckingham's forces left a "trail of devastation" behind them. When it came to national politics, however, the Duke was by instinct a peacemaker. Although he was later drawn into "confrontational positions",

Buckingham escaped penalties under York's second protectorate and in 1456 demonstrated his open-mindedness by objecting to Queen Margaret's dismissal of York's men. It was only in 1457 or 1458 that the Duke became identified with the Queen's group – and this at a time when Margaret had adopted "bi-partisan politics". Perhaps, then, the ambush in Warwickshire was motivated by local factors and Malory's support for the Yorkists was a separate matter.[128]

It's not the least of the mysteries of these years that Buckingham did not react more quickly to Malory's attempt on his life. The ambush was an organized insurgency, and one would have thought that it merited a prompt and forceful response. Yet Buckingham took no action against Malory for eighteen months, waiting until after the attack on the deer-park at Caludon before laying charges in August 1451. When the Duke at length made up his mind, however, he exercised all the influence which he possessed. Stafford was one of the presiding judges when the charges against Malory were presented at Nuneaton and didn't question the allegations, though Field thinks that the figure of £500 for the damage at Caludon is "beyond belief". And Buckingham didn't just wield power in his judicial capacity. In July 1451, he gathered sixty "mounted yeomen" to capture Malory. This force, as Field points out, was larger than the one Buckingham sent to quell Cade's rebellion. And Buckingham's pursuit of Malory was the "only recorded occasion" on which the Duke personally commanded such an expedition. Buckingham took Malory's case very seriously indeed.[129]

11

Watling Street

How typical was Malory? Kittredge blithely states that he is not "overmuch concerned" by the charges against the knight of Newbold Revel: might was right back then; the brigand had much in common with the knight-errant; disturbances were "of daily occurrence, and carried no stigma" for members of the gentry. Carpenter argues that the affinity system tended to contain tensions since "mindless conflict" damaged élite incomes. But her own study of Warwickshire in the fifteenth century demonstrates that the aristocracy engaged in countless conflicts. Neither Malory nor Buckingham were alone. The feud between the Verneys and the Dalbys persisted for years and involved "appalling acts of aggression". The Rous/Burdet feud saw "spiralling violence" in the 1460s. The Archers quarrelled with the Charnels and the Conyngesbys; by 1485, their feud with the Porters had lasted for almost 60 years. In the 1490s the feud between the Willoughbys and the Greys saw assaults on servants, affray and abduction. The Vernon/Savage dispute involved raiding and attacks on property. Members of the Ferrers, Pulteney and Chetwynd families were also involved in disturbances (Malory's mother was a Chetwynd). And these were only the high-level cases. Early in the fifteenth century, members of the Burdet family committed a "series of violent crimes". Later on, the Hores became well-known for their "criminal propensities"; Thomas Hore in particular was a "free-lance troublemaker". The career of Robert Arden went "spectacularly to the bad" in a "downward spiral" of litigation, debt, violence and murder.[130]

In the context of such turbulence, Malory's career seems less atypical. It was not his acts which were unusual but their consequences. Bellamy points out that during the fifteenth century, few "upper class rapists ever came to trial". Carpenter argues more generally that it was "not far off impossible to get a gentry or noble defendant into court". Outlawry held "few terrors" for the élite. Even when cases went to trial, guilty verdicts were rare and pardons easy to obtain. Yet Malory seems to have had more difficulty than other members of his class in slipping through the net. When he was first arrested, Malory should, according to Field, have been indicted at Warwick. Buckingham instead handed him over to one of his supporters, Sir William Mountford. Mountford was sheriff of Coventry, but Malory's imprisonment at Coleshill was nevertheless a "flagrant hijacking of the legal process". The fact that Malory was never brought to trial might suggest that he was able to play the legal system. But if so, he didn't do it very well. It's more likely that Buckingham himself wanted to prevent a trial taking place, hoping, as Field suggests, "to make an example of Malory".[131]

One can see things from Buckingham's point of view. Malory was no small-time rogue, and it might have been advisable to place him in a "special category" of prisoners. Buckingham followed through on his initial arrest. In March 1453 he personally set out to apprehend Malory when the latter jumped bail. And the Duke may have been active in the background some years later. Early in 1456 – after his trial had been repeatedly postponed – Malory produced a pardon. Yet the court refused to recognize it, setting no date for a subsequent trial – something which Field attributes to the "Lancastrian authorities" and sees as a further "subversion" of legal process. Malory's was indeed a special case. His extended periods of incarceration were, as Carpenter asserts, "almost unheard of". Between 1452 and 1457, a series of gaolers was ordered to keep Malory locked up under penalties ranging from £1,000 to £2,000 – sums which, as Field points out, set a "record for mediaeval England".[132]

Still, if the Duke really did want to send Malory down, it's difficult to explain why John Leventhorpe, one of Buckingham's associates, was named on Malory's bail applications in October 1452 and May 1454. Field speculates that on the first of these occasions, Malory was being encouraged "to make his peace" and that, on the second, he was being given "another chance". Was Buckingham showing magnanimity? Was another influence at work? Perhaps Malory knew something we don't know. Perhaps he swallowed the Yorkist "myth". In either case, it's tempting to look again to the affinity system for an explanation. Carpenter is clear that in Warwickshire, the expansion of Buckingham's estates in the 1430s (he acquired Maxstoke Castle in 1438) and the rivalry between Buckingham and Warwick after 1447 were the major features on the political landscape. So we might expect Malory's break with Buckingham to have involved collaboration with Warwick. Later on, Malory and Warwick were indeed connected. After being released from his first spell in prison, it is, according to Field, "very probable" that Malory participated in Edward IV's efforts to eliminate Lancastrian resistance in Northumbria – a campaign led by

Warwick. And the imputed motive – "gratitude" to Warwick – might be explained by the fact that Warwick's uncle, William Neville, Lord Fauconberg, had bailed Malory in October 1457. On this occasion, Malory didn't behave as badly as in 1453 and 1454: this is apparently the only occasion on which he "left prison legally and returned on time".[133]

But how far back did the Warwick connection go? And how deep was it? Field is clear that Fauconberg's support of Malory's bail application represents "his first certain contact with a Neville". But this connection "might have begun at any time after Warwick acquired his earldom in 1449". Warwick's hospitality was "legendary": each visitor to his quarters was encouraged to take "as much meat as he could load onto a dagger". But we don't know if barbecued beef would have bought Malory's loyalty. In any case, Field dismisses the idea that it was Warwick who commissioned Malory to have Buckingham "filled full of arrows". Malory threw in his lot with York by the end of 1450, but Warwick didn't follow suit until 1456. So it's unlikely that Neville turned Malory into a Yorkist.[134]

Malory might have been more closely connected to another affinity group – the Duke of Norfolk's, for example – than to that of Warwick. As Carpenter points out, the Dukes of Norfolk had been "overlords" of the Malory family in the past: it's possible that Norfolk was "still protecting" Malory "up to 1459". But without fresh discoveries it's likely that our knowledge will remain incomplete. We need a comprehensive account of the relation between Malory's life and his work, between the man and the age. As it stands, discontinuities are more evident.[135]

It's tempting to conclude that, in the murky world of late medieval politics, Malory was an outsider rather than an insider. He was outside because he was inside – a prisoner physically removed from the public sphere. In fact, however, Malory may well have had extensive and direct experience of the Wars. He was *hors de combat* at the first Battle of St Albans in May 1455, having been moved to the Tower some days earlier. But a few years later the situation isn't so clear. In 1459 we run up against another of those blind spots which beset accounts of Malory's life. At the beginning of the "most turbulent eighteen months in fifteenth-century English history", there is, according to Field, "no evidence of where Malory was". He was in the King's Bench Prison around January 1460 but seems to have been "illicitly at large" some months earlier. It's possible that a defaulting Malory was present at the Battle of Blore Heath in September 1459 and the Battle of Ludford Bridge the following month.[136]

Or maybe Malory sat it out in London, spent his mornings looking through the window of his cell into a courtyard where withered leaves chased each other in useless spirals; occupied his afternoons playing solitary games of dice. But Field conjures up a livelier picture. Perhaps Malory again eluded the authorities. Maybe he acquired a set of hooves. Perhaps, when he eventually made it back to London, there were "armour stains on his clothing". And maybe, in response to questions about his recent whereabouts, Malory offered his gaolers "implausible excuses about getting lost coming down Watling Street".[137]

It's an attractive idea, and one might elaborate it a little, picturing a long ride by moonlight, mist rising from the fields at dawn – not that Malory would necessarily have noticed these details (the *Morte*, as we have seen, is weatherless). Yet if he was indeed returning from Ludlow in October 1459, there might have been blood as well as armour stains on Malory's clothing – traces of an encounter with an old enemy. For a key role in the Lancastrian victory at Ludford Bridge was played by the Duke of Buckingham. And the shred of a chance that Malory fought in Shropshire (or fled – the Yorkists were defeated when Warwick's forces "melted away") suggests another, still more wispy possibility. It's not clear when Malory was finally released from prison. If he was held in the Tower he might only have been set free in late July 1460, when the Yorkist siege which had begun earlier that month was successfully concluded. At this point, Field suggests, Malory would have plunged into "the thick of things". He might therefore have been present at the Battle of Wakefield in December 1460 and that of Mortimer's Cross in February 1461 (the second was a Yorkist victory, the first a defeat which ended in the death of York himself). He might have been at the second Battle of St Albans in February 1461 and at the final, decisive Yorkist victory at Towton in March. And when York's son Edward, Earl of March, was acclaimed king by the Commons later that year, Malory – as Field rather excitedly puts it – "could have been there".[138]

But, if we go back for a moment to the summer of 1460 (this is the wisp I'm clutching at) there is another possibility – one which Field doesn't appear to have noticed. If Malory was held not in the Tower but in Newgate (and this is the last place we know him to have been) then he might well have been released at the beginning of July when the Yorkists passed through London on their way north to meet the Lancastrian forces. In which case – and yes, these are bricks with scarcely any straw at all – it's possible that Malory – out of training after prolonged confinement and shorter now of breath (by Field's calculation he might have been 45) – fought in "pouring rain" at the

FIGURE 9 Malory's war. The battles of the Wars of the Roses, numbered in chronological order (YV = Yorkist victory, LV = Lancastrian victory). Malory might have been present at battles 3–11. The route of Watling Street (see n. 137, this volume) is also shown.

Battle of Northampton on 16 July 1460 – the very date and place at which Humphrey Stafford, 1st Duke of Buckingham, saint-beater, church-burner, political wheeler-dealer, and the target of an ambush in the Warwickshire woods a decade previously, met his bloody end.[139]

CHAPTER

12

The Last Laugh

Who won the Wars of the Roses? One points automatically to Henry Tudor, crowned on the field at Bosworth in 1485. But there was another and earlier victor: by destroying the Lancastrian cause at Tewkesbury in 1471, Edward IV effectively removed the main basis of the conflict. Still, Edward's father, the Duke of York, might have viewed the idea of a Yorkist victory in the Wars of the Roses differently: he was killed at Wakefield in 1460, as was his son Edmund, Earl of Rutland. For some months, before they were removed by Edward IV after the Battle of Towton, the severed heads of York and Rutland were displayed on Micklegate Bar so that York, in the words of Shakespeare's Queen Margaret, could "overlook the town of York". The sight cheers Margaret's heart, though it "irks" the "very soul" of her husband King Henry VI.[140]

When I bought my Everyman *Morte* in 1981 I had no idea that in that Micklegate bookshop I was standing within yards of a head-spiking scene which Malory would certainly have known about and might possibly have witnessed. My point, however, is that in the flickering light of history, those who look like winners from one angle can be losers from another. Edward IV ruled for two decades with increasing authority. But his father and brother died in battle. Another brother was murdered on Edward's own instructions and his two sons were later killed (after Edward's death) by a third brother, the most notable corpse on the field at Bosworth. Edward IV himself died in 1483, apparently of "a chill contracted while boating". Winners and losers; winners as losers – and then losers plain and simple: Suffolk beheaded in 1450, Somerset killed at St Albans in 1455, Buckingham among the fallen at Northampton in 1460. Malory might well have wanted to go down in a blaze of glory, smiting and cleaving. But in 1471, in his mid-fifties, he was too old to die a hero's death. He seems to have died of natural causes – and he outlived Buckingham by more than a decade.[141]

At Northampton in 1460, Malory may well have emitted a whoop of vengeance at the death of his old enemy. By 1471, however, his laughter might have seemed hollow. Pardoned in 1462, Malory prob-ably served in the Northumbrian campaign. Field thinks he may have been abroad between 1464 and 1467. Unfortunately, the lives of free citizens aren't as carefully documented as those of state prisoners. Towards the end of the 1460s, however, Malory's name reappears in the records. In July 1468 he is excluded by name from a pardon issued by Edward IV. In February the following year, he is excluded from a further pardon. Field draws the obvious inference: "something had gone . . . awry in Malory's Yorkist allegiance". "Awry" indeed, for Malory was excluded from the royal pardons alongside no less a Lancastrian than Henry, the former King. Field thinks it "unlikely that we will ever discover exactly what Malory had done". Perhaps as early as 1467, though, Malory was back in prison. It would appear that, by "royal generosity", he was free to work. For Field, the fact that Malory was allowed to write the *Morte* shows that he did not stand accused of a "crime of the gravest kind". Still, the implication is clear: if Malory was in prison – if his name stood alongside that of Henry VI among those excluded from Edward's magnanimity – then he must have been seen as a "dangerous Lancastrian", a "real and present threat".[142]

Field looks to the affinity system to shed light on Malory's situation in the last years of his life. It is, as he points out, "natural to assume that Malory was imprisoned . . . because of something he had done as a follower of Warwick". We know that Neville's relationship with Edward had been put under strain by the King's marriage to Elizabeth Woodville in May 1464. Warwick had been negotiating a continental alliance, and in Shakespeare the failure of this project makes him imme-diately "return to Henry". But in July 1465, when Henry VI was apprehended near Bolton by Bowland (he had been on the run since the Battle of Towton in 1461), Warwick was still in sufficiently good odour to be given the task of parading the captured king through the streets of London. The timing of Warwick's U-turn remains, as Carpenter writes, "obscure": he had contact with Edward IV during 1468 but was in open rebellion by July 1469. If Warwick "was not (yet) a Lancastrian" in the summer of 1468, then Field may be right to argue that the "natural assumption" – that Malory followed his leader – is misleading. In the 1450s, Malory's links with the Yorkists became evident at an earlier point than Warwick's. Now, in the 1460s, Malory may well again have committed himself before his lord – and without reference to him. It was Malory's name and not Warwick's which appeared on the lists of those excluded from pardon in February 1469, some months before Warwick became Public Enemy Number One.[143]

It's difficult to know what to make of all this. The familiar disjunctions – the man and the work, the personal and the political, the local and the national – loom into view only to disappear like ships in fog. Field's tentative conclusion – that Malory "followed . . . different lords in turn" – may well be the only sustainable one, and in this respect he would have been no different to other members of his class. Maybe Malory, like Warwick (though at a humbler level) was solely driven by the pursuit of power. Maybe he swallowed the Yorkist myth and was then sufficiently gullible or compliant to move in the opposite direction. Or maybe he acted on his own accord – passionately but misguidedly. But unless Malory's was a case of absolute wildness there would surely have been reasons for his actions. These were difficult years for the gentry. According to Carpenter, the Warwickshire gentry found it increasingly difficult to live in "reasonable harmony". It wasn't just that levels of disorder increased but that violence occurred "between families with similar political allegiances": a landowner's attachment to his lord was becoming a "very nominal affair". By 1453, "factions were forming but had yet to harden into irreconcilable divisions". It was only after 1456 that the confrontation between York and Lancaster polarized the situation at a national level. Pressure was then exerted on the Warwickshire gentry to make "crude choices". Yet Malory's apparent willingness to make those choices – first one way and then the other – may have been atypical: Carpenter thinks it "more than possible" that the gentry "passively withdrew their support". Whilst the nobility was sucked into the "political maelstrom", the gentry did nothing – and secured their future as a self-conscious and autonomous class.[144]

For Carpenter, the "lesson of Malory's story" is twofold: first, "the actions of the late medieval aristocracy" need to be seen in the context of a political "system". Fair enough – and yet there's only so much we can do to unravel Malory's relationship with the major figures of fifteenth-century politics in Warwickshire: Buckingham, Warwick and Norfolk. And when we add in the Beauchamps, the Botellers, the Burdets and the Charnels, the Conyngesbys, the Chetwynds, the Dalbys and the Ferrers, the Greys, the Porters, the Rouses and the Savages, the Sudeleys, the Verneys, the Vernons and the Willoughbys it's hard not to conclude that this extensive and volatile kinship system must at times have been little more comprehensible to the protagonists than it is today. Carpenter's second lesson is still more salutary in Malory's case, since for her the evidence of the "more dramatic and hence better-known cases" should not be used to create some "lawless aristocratic type". Malory's career is anomalous, then. His long incarceration points to a "failure" to keep "influential friends". By the end of the 1440s, Malory had "fallen foul" of Buckingham, Grey and Norfolk. In the early 1450s, York had "no further use" for Malory. Warwick "failed to lift a finger" for him. At this point, as Carpenter acknowledges, "we enter the realms of speculation". The fact that Malory had been "patronized by nearly all the important noblemen" of Warwickshire but was "eventually dropped by them all" may point to some personal failing on his part. In the end, Carpenter concludes that Malory's fate was sealed "because he was an incompetent politician". Like other members of the "criminal gentry", Malory was "too violent too often". He was a "loser".[145]

Poor Sir Thomas. With hindsight, it looks as if he backed the wrong horse twice. Rather than being an emblem of the times, a representative of his age, Malory swam against the tide. He could have fulfilled the world-historical mission of his class by minding his own business. But he chose to be anomalous – and in doing so became infinitely more interesting. Malory didn't fit into the affinity system – that competitive little world which both fostered and undermined cohesion. It might in the end be best to revert to the older paradigm of 'bastard feudalism' and see Malory as a "thug" – Carpenter's term. He was wild: that was why he needed to be locked up.[146]

Malory was a survivor, but when the English élite fell to quarrelling like cats in a sack he paid a high price. At this point, as he might have felt, the joke was on him. But then he wrote the *Morte*. Page after page piled up as he re-told the tales he loved. Centuries later, we know about Warwick, Buckingham, Suffolk and the rest. But those fifteenth-century noblemen are silent as marble effigies compared to Malory, whose voice carries across the great deeps. So Malory can have the last laugh. But consider the life of the man who probably knighted him; spare a thought for Henry VI.

Born to Catherine de Valois at Windsor in December 1421, the future king's entry into this world was, as Wolffe records, "assisted by the presence of that precious relic, Our Lord's foreskin, known as the silver jewel, renowned for its help to women in labour, specially brought over in good time from France". In spite of these auspicious beginnings, tragedy struck almost immediately: Henry V died suddenly when his son was only 9 months old. And what a father he had been! "England ne'er lost a king of so much worth"; "England ne'er had a king until his time": so Bedford and Gloucester mourn the passing of Henry V in the opening scene of Shakespeare's *1 Henry VI*. The sky darkens, and there are only memories of a monarch whose wrathful eyes dazzled his enemies more than the "mid-day sun". By contrast, the son of the victor at Agincourt is for Wolffe "the most shadowy figure of all England's post-Conquest kings". In this case the "fatal prophecy" recalled by Exeter in *1 Henry VI* ("That Henry born at Monmouth should win all; | And Henry born at Windsor should lose all") seems a bare statement of historical fact. R. A. Griffiths sums up the reign of Henry VI as follows: "No king who loses his crown and dies in prison, and whose reign ends in civil war, can be counted a success". The understatement is devastating, for Henry's reign didn't just fail to achieve "success": it was a fifty-year disaster.[147]

It's not just the battles and the dead – St Albans (twice), Blore Heath, Ludford Bridge and Northampton; Wakefield, Mortimer's Cross and Towton; Barnet and Tewkesbury. It's not just the poisoned political atmosphere at home and the loss of empire abroad – a loss which, as Wolffe points out, left thousands "destitute and permanently embittered". The point for Carpenter is that all this flowed directly from Henry's inability to govern. "Limpness", "incapacity", "ineptness", "inertness": Henry's negative characteristics multiply, and to Carpenter's list Webster adds "indecision", "vacillation" and "obstinacy". For Carpenter, Henry's rule was from the start a mere "semblance of monarchy". By 1450 it was an open secret that there was "no king". "Positive bad rule" would have been better than "negative lack of rule": if Henry had done serious wrong, somebody could have seized the throne. But the King couldn't even engineer his own removal. He seems indeed to have been, as James I later put it, a "sillie weake king".[148]

CHAPTER
13

Connying

"Poor old Henry VI": there's a moment of sympathy in Carpenter's account of the King's first deposition in 1461. The historian's retrospective eye may be at work here, since the last years of Henry's life were the worst. After being captured in 1465, Henry was held in the Tower of London and only released by Warwick (that late convert to the Lancastrian cause) in 1470, at which point it was noticed that Henry was neither "worschipfully arrayed" nor "clenly kepte". The Tower: Henry would have known this place better even than Malory. The King had stayed here on the eve of his coronation in 1429 (the next day, as he was crowned in Westminster Abbey, the 8-year old was seen to look around "saddely and wisely"; a heretic meanwhile burned in Smithfield). And it was in the Wakefield Tower that Henry was put to death (probably by Richard of Gloucester) on the night of 22 May 1471. The official report stated that he died of "pure displeasure and melancholy" on hearing news of his son's death at Tewkesbury. But this was Yorkist propaganda: grief cannot explain the blood which flowed from the body of the ex-king when, on the day after his death, it was displayed on the pavement at St Paul's.[149]

"Poor old Henry" indeed. But the life of the young king was hardly (the pun is irresistible) a bed of roses. Gloucester out, Suffolk in; Suffolk out, Somerset in; Bedford and Gloucester raging at each other in 1433, when the 12-year-old king begged his uncles "to become friends again". Griffiths points out that this intervention reveals "a child's innocence". And that's the problem: Henry never grew up. Unmanly: this is the repeated charge. Though Henry married Margaret of Anjou in 1445 an heir was not forthcoming until 1453. Unmanly: in 1449, the King – a married man in his late twenties – was "shocked to see men and women bathing naked" at Bath. And in the early 1460s, when Henry had entered middle age, the Pope reported that he was "more timorous than a woman".[150]

"Boys", Carpenter briskly states, "grew up early in medieval England". A paragon of muscular development, Henry V won his first battle at 15. By the time he reached his late teens, Henry VI "should have been more than ready to rule". But the King was a child in this world. Henry came of age in 1437 and then, as Carpenter concedes, played some part in governing his realm. But the King was not a significant force after 1453, when he became the pawn of whoever it was – York, Margaret, Edward, Warwick – that fed and housed him. In fact, however, this had been the case from the start. When Henry V died in 1422, Gloucester became the infant king's "custodian". R. A. Griffiths's word captures the reality of Henry's life. He lived his childhood in custody and throughout his adult life remained "helpless in a political world from which he could not escape". Henry VI was probably the most incompetent monarch ever to mount the throne of England. Shakespeare's portrait of Henry VI may lack historical veracity, but the idea that he shrank from kingship is convincing. During Cade's rebellion, Henry longs to be a "subject". At Towton, he sits on a molehill and imagines being a "homely swain".[151]

On several occasions, prison walls proved no obstacle to the ingenious Thomas Malory. Henry VI was by contrast a life-long inmate, both politically and psychologically. It's not clear whether the King's descent into mental illness during the summer of 1453 was the result of an inherited condition (his grandfather, Charles VI of France, went mad) or external factors (the loss of Gascony has been cited). But it was undoubtedly serious: when he fell ill, the King was incapable of understanding that he had become a father; he had, according to Wolffe, "no sense of time or memory" and "could not stand upright" without help. It's not clear what the opinion of a contemporary psychiatrist might be: Carpenter mentions "catatonia", Webster "catatonic schizophrenia". But it may be better to think of the King's madness as a recapitulation of his childhood. As a child, Henry's life was split up and out of his control. As an adult, mad, he could be a babe again.[152]

The madness of King Henry wasn't just an internalisation of the situation at court. It was a huge stone – a great anvil, with a sword on top – thrown into the English pond, and its meanings rippled outwards. Henry was paralysed, and so was England. He was divided, and so was his realm. "Catatonic schizophrenia": it's a national diagnosis as well as a personal one. And yet, although he was in some ways a figure for the nation at large, Henry was sometimes more isolated than any of his subjects. At the first Battle of St Albans, the King was wounded in the neck by one of Warwick's archers. When captured, he begged – touchingly and with utter futility – that there "shulde no more harme be don". Henry V would have turned in his grave. And his son's lack of military prowess set a record: Henry VI was, as Griffiths points out, the "first English king never to command an army against an external foe". Even when it came to internal foes, Henry's guardians treated their ruler more as an encumbrance than a monarch. Captured at St Albans, the King was apprehended again at Northampton in 1460. On this occasion, Buckingham and several other courtiers were killed when Warwick's forces broke through (a melée at which I have placed a jubilant Malory). At the second battle of St Albans in 1461, however, the King seems to have been left under a tree. On the orders of Henry's 8-year-old son, the two knights who had served as his minders were beheaded for their negligence.[153]

Two chaperones, two battles of St Albans, twice captured: the life of Henry VI shows as pronounced a pattern of doubling as that of Thomas Malory. Two reigns, two depositions – and technically two kingdoms. At Paris in 1431, Henry was crowned King of France, the "first and last king", as Wolffe points out, of "two realms". And two major episodes of madness. It looks as if Henry born at Windsor did indeed lose all. But remember the two institutions he is credited with founding: Eton College and King's College, Cambridge (in 1440 and 1441 respectively). Even here, Henry's detractors are reluctant to applaud. Watts points out that Suffolk "played a leading part" in these projects. Wolffe argues that they were a "slavish" imitation of what had been done fifty years earlier at Winchester College and New College, Oxford. And Carpenter believes that clerics at court used Henry's enthusiasm for learning "to their own purpose". In 1451 the Commons certainly felt that the King's colleges had proved "over chargefull and noyus".[154]

But there's little doubt that Henry VI genuinely loved knowledge. He donated money for a library at Salisbury cathedral in order to encourage the increase "of connyng and of vertu of such as wol loke and studie". Alongside his more attractive characteristics – compassion and generosity, sensitivity and intelligence – the King was known for his "habit of reading chronicles and books". It didn't do any good, of course: in *2 Henry VI*, the Duke of York complains that the King's "bookish rule hath pull'd fair England down". For Shakespeare, Henry's love of reading implies reluctance to play either a sexual or a political role. The young King prefers "my study and my books" to the marriage brokered for him by Gloucester. Two plays later and shortly before being captured by Edward IV, the deposed king enters "*disguised, with a prayer-book*" – as if reading offers protection, both from other characters and from the part he does not wish to play. Imprisoned in the Tower towards the end of *3 Henry VI*, the King is "*discovered sitting with a book in his hand*". But books are of no help against Richard of

Gloucester – the man, as Henry puts it in his final speech, who "cam'st to bite the world".[155]

Yet there's still a sense in which Henry – the exemplary loser, compared even to an unfortunate like Malory – had the last laugh. Suffolk, Warwick, Buckingham *et al*: they played their part and left the stage. Fifty years after his death, however, the King was worshipped as a saint and credited, according to Wolffe, with "rescues from death by drowning, from crushings to death under cartwheels, from hangings, woundings, fatal falls, lightning strikes, fires and assaults" as well as with miraculous cures for "madness, blindness, deafness, sweating sickness, plague, epilepsy, lameness, battle wounds" and "childbirth". Perhaps the magical foreskin belatedly did its work. At Eton and Cambridge, moreover – whatever we think of Oxbridge or the public school system – Henry left us two of the most important educational institutions in the land. Eton may be best known for inculcating through sport the levels of stupidity which saw us through at Waterloo. But it didn't wholly destroy the careers of Henry Fielding, Thomas Gray, Horace Walpole, Percy Bysshe Shelley, Algernon Swinburne, Aldous Huxley, Lord David Cecil, George Orwell, Neal Ascherson, Michael Holroyd, Perry Anderson and Jonathon Porritt, though we shouldn't forget that the College also fostered Guy Burgess, Alan Clark, Sir James Goldsmith and Jonathan Aitken. And through the gates of King's, at different times, passed E. M. Forster, J. M. Keynes, J. G. Ballard, Eric Hobsbawm, Martin Bernal, Anthony Giddens, Stephen Poliakoff, Martin Jacques, Salman Rushdie, Bill Buford, Lisa Jardine and Zadie Smith.[156]

What would Malory have thought of Henry VI? The member for Wareham turned against his king in the 1450s. But Malory and Henry were born within a few years of each other and died little more than a year apart. In their different ways, they each lived out the double logic of the age. And both left monuments, though in Malory's case the cathedral was built not of stone and brick but of more durable words. One was active: a rebel, a fighter; the other was passivity itself, the inert embodiment of an institution. A man, a boy; a paradox, a nothingness; impulsive, timorous; tough, yielding; manly, feminine; a professional escapee, a lifelong inmate. But they weren't opposites: the King was mad, but he did a number of things that were eminently rational; the *Morte* is a deeply sane work of art but its author committed acts which seem crazy. Both Malory and Henry VI knew failure; they were both English to the core. Both were readers, and both had been imprisoned in the Tower of London. Indeed, between about 1467 and 1470, the former English king and the author of the *Morte* were almost certainly

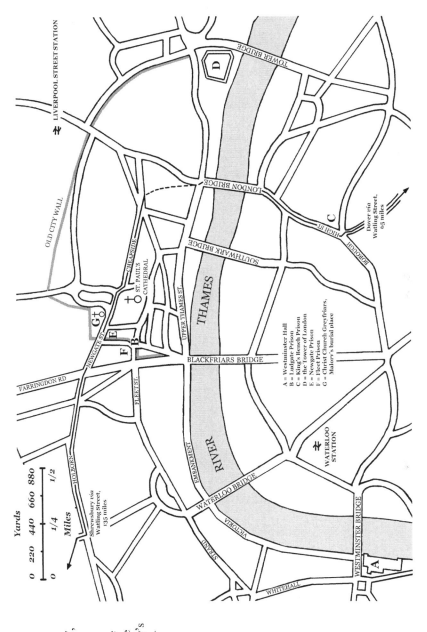

FIGURE 10
Malory's London
(for further infor-
mation, see n. 157,
this volume). The
route of Watling
Street through the
city seems to have
structured Malory's
years of imprison-
ment as much as
his time at large
(see Figure 9).

Yards
0   220   440   660   880
0   1/4   1/2
Miles

Shrewsbury via
Watling Street,
135 miles

FARRINGDON RD

HOLBORN

FLEET ST.

OLD CITY WALL

CHEAPSIDE

NEWGATE ST.

UPPER THAMES ST.

ST. PAUL'S
CATHEDRAL

LIVERPOOL STREET STATION

TOWER BRIDGE

LONDON BRIDGE

SOUTHWARK BRIDGE

BLACKFRIARS BRIDGE

EMBANKMENT

WATERLOO BRIDGE

VICTORIA

STRAND

WHITEHALL

WESTMINSTER BRIDGE

WATERLOO
STATION

THAMES

RIVER

BOROUGH

HIGH ST.

Dover via
Watling Street,
65 miles

A = Westminster Hall
B = Ludgate Prison
C = King's Bench Prison
D = the Tower of London
E = Newgate Prison
F = Fleet Prison
G = Christ Church Greyfriars,
        Malory's burial place

held in the Tower simultaneously. One can only imagine how the two gaol-birds led their days. Perhaps they grew old and shabby, splashing gravy on their tuckers and getting bits of cheap meat stuck in their teeth. Perhaps they wandered along echoing corridors, accompanied by watchful guards. They certainly read their books: both loved "connying". And one of them was writing.

The face of History is rarely blank: we sometimes see its features in all their raw particularity. It's the expression that eludes us. The motives of the Newbold Revel knight and author of the *Morte*, as Field concludes, lie "near the boundary between the little known and the entirely unknown" – which puts the 'real' Malory on the edge of darkness. He might have seen the sun rising over the Warwickshire woods in the autumn of 1459, battle-weary and knowing that he still had miles to go. He might have woken in a London dawn with his candle burnt down and a book in his hand. How can we ever know anybody – especially one who lived and died five centuries ago? But perhaps it doesn't matter. Our restless enquiries, our failure to achieve certain knowledge: this is as nothing to what Malory felt on the day he laid down his weapons at the end of his last battle, said his prayers, and prepared himself to face the universal bemusement.[157]

CHAPTER

14

Deliverance

In the previous chapter I succumbed to temptation and gave Malory a decent death. But this is pure speculation. Malory might have died in less dignified circumstances during the plague outbreak of 1471. There were thousands of fatalities in London alone, and standards of treatment were rudimentary (in one contemporary remedy the split bodies of live pigeons were applied to the victim's buboes). If Malory did die of the plague, however, one would have expected his body to end up in a mass grave. As it was, the interment seems to have been planned at leisure.

The work and the life: it's hard to make connections, though many have tried. In Book I of the *Morte*, Malory pictures the aged Uther being carried on "an horse-litter" to meet his enemies "at St Albans". It's possible that Malory thought of his own experiences at the second Battle of St Albans when he wrote this scene. But Malory didn't invent the details of Uther's last campaign: St Albans was identified as the site of the battle by Geoffrey of Monmouth. The description of Arthur being acclaimed by the Commons in Book I of the *Morte* may similarly have been informed by Malory's experiences – he might have seen Edward similarly acclaimed after Towton. Still, Edward was 19 years old in 1461 whilst Arthur is still a boy.[158]

It has been suggested that Malory's experiences during the northern campaign of 1462–4 are evident in the *Morte*. Malory might have known both Alnwick and Bamborough; he suggests in Book XXI that Launcelot's castle of Joyous Gard is located in one of these places. And the last book of the *Morte* undoubtedly contains some suggestive parallels. The description of Mordred besieging the Tower of London – particularly the anachronistic reference to the firing of "great guns" – might have been based on Malory's memories of being transferred to the Tower when the Yorkists entered London in 1460. Field thinks that Malory's account of the battle at Salisbury ("an hundred thousand laid dead", robbers stripping corpses by moonlight) is like "a view of the aftermath of the Yorkist victory at Towton".[159]

The idea that Malory used events in his own life to write the *Morte* is certainly intriguing. Elizabeth Archibald and A. S. G. Edwards have argued that the "final pages of the *Morte*" contain "insistent parallels between the collapse of the Round Table and the situation" – as Malory puts it in his disquisition on love in Book XVIII – "nowadays". I've mentioned the line in which Malory uniquely suggests that Mordred's support is drawn from "they of Kent . . . Estsex, and of Southfolk, and of Northfolk". As early as 1933, Nellie Aurner argued that this is a "clear reference to the York following in the Wars of the Roses". When he wrote the *Morte*, Malory was being held in prison by Edward IV, the Yorkist king. It might well have been amusing to suggest that England was ruled by another Mordred. If so, the earlier suggestion that Arthur prefigured Edward might have enabled Malory to deny the later and more subversive implication. But this idea makes the composition of the *Morte* seem far more calculated than is likely to have been the case. It is nevertheless worth considering a second parallel between the *Morte* and the England of the 1460s. If it was based on personal experience, Malory's account of the siege of Joyous Gard would position Arthur as a Yorkist and Launcelot as a besieged Lancastrian. In 1468, as a beset Lancastrian himself, Malory might well have identified with Launcelot. But any corresponding implication that Arthur prefigues the Yorkist monarch would again cut against connections between Mordred and Edward. And wouldn't it have been difficult for the man who in 1464 had fought in the northern campaign as a Yorkist to place his hero on the opposing side? Then and now, this side and that – the parallels are there, but they don't line up.[160]

At least, they don't line up if one assumes that Malory can only think of the conflicts in Arthur's kingdom and fifteenth-century England as a partisan. But Field argues that Malory's account of the siege of Joyous Gard discloses sympathies which point in "different directions". Many a soldier has felt more respect for the enemy than for his own officers, and feelings of ambivalence are to be expected in a conflict where the allegiances were as complex and changeable as they were in the Wars of the Roses. Perhaps, then, as Field suggests, Malory felt "sympathy for . . . both sides". Perhaps his remarks at the start of Book XXI about the "great default of us Englishmen" imply a "national guilt in which he shares". Or perhaps there just isn't any reference to contemporary events. Perhaps Malory's whole purpose in writing the *Morte* was to turn his back on fifteenth-century England, to conjure up an alternative world. The relation between the author and his work in any case remains, as Field concludes, "remarkably enigmatic".[161]

Still, it's hard to overlook the fact that rape featured both in Malory's life and in the *Morte*. One wonders what went through Malory's mind when in Book III of the *Morte* he introduced Aries the cowherd. Did he remember how he had behaved that day in the May of 1450? Did he see a connection between himself and Sir Pellinore – between the "fair housewife" of his romance and Joan Smith – or between Joan's husband and Aries? Would Malory have accepted that he had taken Joan "half by force"? Would Joan?[162]

And what of Malory's other crimes? Stealing a £22 cart may not look like a particularly expressive act. But Malory would have known the convention according to which only disgraced knights travelled by cart. In Chrétien de Troyes's "The Knight of the Cart", Arthur's queen mocks Launcelot for being reluctant to adopt so humble a means of transport. In Malory's version of the episode, one of Guenever's ladies supposes that Launcelot is riding "unto hanging". Perhaps Malory's unknightly interest in carts explains why his Guenever rebukes her maid and shows no disdain when Launcelot arrives at Meliagrance's castle. Perhaps Malory romanticized the Cosford episode. Did he remember Rowe and Dowde when he wrote about the two carters? Did he imagine himself as a fifteenth-century Launcelot? Field suggests that the scene in which Launcelot crosses the Thames on his mission to save Guenever would have been familiar to Malory, who travelled upriver to court in Westminster and back again to prison in Southwark on numerous occasions between 1452 and 1457.[163]

Identifying characters in Malory with real-life people is a risky business, of course, and the *Morte* is in no sense a *roman-à-clef*. But sometimes the connections are too delicious to resist. One might think that the last person King Henry resembles is King Arthur. The warlike monarch – the man who defeats Lucius and Mordred – is hardly a "sillie weake king". Yet Arthur has another side to his character: one sees it when he sheds tears and laments to Sir Launcelot "that ever this war began". It's worth remembering that Malory's Arthur holds a "love day" for Tristram and King Mark – just like Henry VI, who in 1458 held a famously ineffective Loveday to reconcile the Duke of York and Queen Margaret.[164]

The occasional resemblances between Arthur and Henry may be coincidental. But one character in the *Morte* is more likely to have been based on an actual person. Consider the career of Sir Gawaine. In his youth he is a hothead, and his hair-trigger reactions – as when he beheads a lady for bumping into him – cause unease amongst his peers. Gawaine doesn't initially seem to have much promise as a diplomat: in the negotiations with Lucius he is "sore grieved" by the words of Sir Gainas and cuts off his head. This starts a scuffle which is only concluded when Gawaine cleaves Sir Feldenak "to his breast". But Arthur's nephew rapidly acquires greater restraint, and is so impressed by the Saracen knight Priamus that he begs Arthur to have his opponent made a "duke and knight of the Table Round". The King takes this chivalrous suggestion as an example and magnanimously lifts his siege of a city in Tuscany. And Gawaine's commitment to peace-keeping roles is underscored when, in Book XX, he refuses to join Agravaine and Mordred's plot, reminding his kinsmen that "kindness should be remembered". Gawaine is not moved to act against Launcelot even when the latter kills Agravaine and his two sons, Florence and Lovel. It is only after Gareth and Gaheris are killed by Launcelot that he takes sides, and thenceforth acts with complete commitment. The fact that Gawaine sends Launcelot into exile confirms him as Arthur's leading knight. During the siege of Benwick, Gawaine is "overthrown" by Launcelot and suffers "such a buffet on the helmet that he fell down". When this wound reopens, the Gawaine asks on his death bed for Launcelot's forgiveness.[165]

Consider now the career of Humphrey Stafford, 1st Duke of Buckingham. He was by all accounts something of a hothead in his youth, and on one occasion at which the young Malory might have been present is said to have threatened the chained Joan of Arc with his sword. Buckingham sometimes preferred violence to negotiation: the Harcourt family knew this to their cost after one of their number killed the Duke's son with a blow on the head. But we know, too, that as a statesman Buckingham was often, in trying times, a model of restraint. When he did take sides, however, he played a judicial as well as a military role. He suffered a head injury in battle. He may have regretted some of his later actions and attempted to build bridges with those who had been his opponents. And he was slain in the service of his king.

Peacemaker and warlord, warrior and judge – the head injuries, the violence (especially towards women) – several things link the historical Buckingham and Malory's Gawaine. But where will this end? If the rape charges against Malory identify him with King Pellinore should one go on to use the fact that Pellinore kills Gawaine's father as evidence that the *Morte* obliquely locates its author within a kingdom-splitting feud? Should one comb the text for connections between Launcelot and Richard Neville, the Earl of Warwick? It's an obvious possibility: both were first knights and both turned against their kings. But that way madness lies. One can imagine that the man who wrote about Sir Launcelot identified with his own creation. But everything flips round confusingly if one begins to think of the real-life Warwick besieging the castle at Alnwick or Bamborough in the early 1460s whilst Launcelot – the fictional character he inspired – fought off attack from within the walls of Joyous Gard. And things become completely scrambled if one takes on board John Wesley Hales's suggestion that Warwick was in fact Malory's model for Mordred.[166]

The work and the life: one has to use one's common sense. Malory doesn't picture horses very vividly, but he may well have been a good judge of horseflesh. He doesn't describe the feasts in any detail, but for all we know he was a keen trencherman. The work does not reveal the life in any obvious way. It may leave out what is most important. Yet to abandon the attempt to identify connections is not to conclude that the *Morte* tells us nothing about a wider social world. One can understand why a chivalric narrative like the *Morte* rarely features ordinary people. There are crowd scenes, of course: think of Arthur being acclaimed king in Book I. The tournaments are busy places: there are "four hundred tents and pavilions" at Lonazep. The battlefields of the *Morte* are also crowded: at Salisbury "an hundred thousand" lose their lives. In the work of Chrétien de Troyes, however, there is a more pronounced sense of human bustle. When Erec arrives at the court of King Evrain, "more than seven thousand" people are concerned for his fate. Cligés is followed by "more than twenty thousand people". Chrétien sometimes gives startling numbers for what is defined as a modest gathering. One of his kings has "never before . . . been so alone", having "only five hundred" barons present in his chambers. Arthur is attended by "only three thousand knights" because "it was a small gathering". Yet it's worth reflecting that Chrétien died around 150 years before the Black Death reached Europe. Malory wrote the *Morte* when the devastation created by this pandemic was a matter of everyday experience. His was an emptier world, and one can see that in his work.[167]

I have so far mainly been using biographical evidence to illuminate the *Morte*, and the results are admittedly speculative. If we look at things the other way round, however – making the work shed light on the life – there are further points to be made. One of them is that Malory was a reader. It is a certain and undeniable fact, evident on every page of the *Morte*. Field asserts that Malory needed "ready access" to "one of the most remarkable libraries in the country". The fact that Malory fell, as Richard Altick puts it, "under the spell of the books he read" has been evident to earlier and more recent readers. In 1559, John Bale pictured the author of the *Morte* spending "hour after pleasant hour reading historical texts". In the 1920s, E. K. Chambers imagined him turning over "faded manuscripts in the window-seat of some country house".[168]

But where did Malory find these works? His life was less leisurely than Bale and Chambers imagine. I find it difficult to imagine Malory coming back to Newbold Revel after a night raising hell and curling up with *La Queste del Saint Graal.* Having examined records of book ownership at this period, Carpenter concludes that the Warwickshire gentry were "philistines of the first order". Edward Peyto's wife owned some "devotional pieces"; Thomas Littleton had a few "treatises"; William Copton owned a Langland; Gilbert Talbot a Chaucer. In such company Malory would have looked like an intellectual – if he hadn't managed to hide his light under a bushel so effectively, that is. So where, if not in Warwickshire, did Malory find his books? Matthews suggests that Malory knew the Arthurian library of Jacques, Count of Armagnac. But, as Field points out, this would have been earlier in his life and in another country. It was later, during his years in London, that Malory needed materials. And he must have had the books open before him as he wrote: according to Ralph Norris, "long passages of direct translation show that Malory had his major sources with him while working in captivity". Field reminds us that the terms of Malory's imprisonment were "relatively mild". Towards the end of his life, he seems to have been held in conditions that were "honourable and even comfortable". According to Bellamy, Newgate had "rooms with chimneys, and privies"; with money, life could be "reasonably pleasant". Yet Malory was in debt during the mid-1450s, and might not have been able to spare cash for luxuries. So perhaps, as Edward Hicks was the first to propose, Malory had access to the nearby library at Greyfriars. More recent scholars have their doubts, however. With penalties attending Malory's escape it seems unlikely that a prison governor would have been happy to see him trotting off for a morning's research. Even if Malory had been allowed out, it's doubtful whether the monks would have welcomed him into their library: their visitor's record of looking after church property was patchy, to say the least.[169]

Malory needed a "remarkable" library. But he doesn't seem to have found it in Warwickshire, in France, or in Greyfriars. For a while, Field entertained the idea that Malory was acquainted with books captured by the Duke of Bedford after Henry V's victory at Agincourt and passed down to Elizabeth Woodville, the wife of Edward IV. But why would the King lend books to a man who was too dangerous to pardon? For Matthews, the "moral paradox" of Malory is accompanied by a "bibliographical paradox". The *Morte* is built of other works, but we've no idea how Malory assembled his sources. It is a mystery, although there is one thing we know for sure:

the author of the *Morte* loved those old romances; he wanted to repeat them and to play his own variations upon them.[170]

And we know another thing from the work: Malory had been held in prison. We know this from the life, of course – the arrests at Coleshill and Colchester; the escapes; the periods in Ludgate, the King's Bench, the Fleet, Newgate and the Tower of London. Malory was for years, as Altick writes, the "hapless" victim in a "game of shuttlecock" played by London prison-keepers. Yet although the *Morte* isn't remotely autobiographical, the experiences of the Newbold Revel Malory lie concealed within its pages. For the *Morte* – the point is a surprisingly neglected one – is much concerned with imprisonment. In Book VI, for example, Ector and Lionel are cast into a "deep dungeon" by Turquine where they make "great sorrow". Launcelot subsequently smites Turquine's neck "in sunder" and Gaheris beats up the castle porter in order to obtain the keys to the cells, where other knights including Kay and Marhaus are languishing. Malory didn't need his imagination to create such scenes.[171]

It's true that Malory's treatment of the prison scenes lacks specificity: dungeons are merely 'deep' and imprisonment a matter for 'sorrow'. But he knew his subject. Arthur, Guenever and Launcelot are all imprisoned at one point or another (in Launcelot's case on several occasions). And the violence which tends to accompany the scenes of liberation (churls split to the paps, heads carved asunder, warders assaulted till blood bursts from every facial orifice) might well have enabled Malory to achieve vicarious revenge upon those who held him under lock and key. Imprisonment seems even to inform the lexicon of the *Morte*. Malory is much concerned with variations on the root word *dur* – 'hard'. Love may 'endure', though pain is more likely to do so (there are more than eighty uses of this and associated words – 'endured', 'endureth', 'enduring' – in the *Morte*). Pelleas and Nimue love together "during their life days". But such fidelity and stability is rare: in the only use of this word in the *Morte*, Dinadan complains that the sorrows of love "dureth over long". Malory likewise bemoans the fact that modern love does not "endure". *Dur.* in just three letters we see the rock of love and the sand on which it sits. In Book XVIII, Galahad has a vision of the "duresse of the world, and the great sin that our Lord found in the world". The word 'duresse' is only used twice in the *Morte*, and on each occasion it conveys in distilled form Malory's sense of our place in this world. Life is an uncertain term in an indubitable prison. We must endure its hardships with whatever firmness we can muster.[172]

Yet perhaps the most moving account of imprisonment in the *Morte* occurs when Sir Tristram, confined to a "strong prison" by Darras, falls ill and endures "great pain", to the point of contemplating suicide. At this point, Malory inserts a passage which, in the view of Edward Hicks, is the "most conclusive piece of *internal* evidence" that the *Morte d'Arthur* was written by Thomas Malory of Newbold Revel, for it has "the force of bitter personal experience". Sickness, Malory writes, is:

> the greatest pain a prisoner may have. For all the while a prisoner may have his health of body he may endure . . . in hope of good deliverance; but when sickness toucheth a prisoner's body, then may a prisoner say all wealth is him bereft, and then he hath cause to wail and to weep.

"Good deliverance" – "good delyueraunce": in the closing lines of the *Morte*, this was Malory's personal hope (see fig. 7). He too had probably wept and wailed. But the work he had delivered – in the "ix yere of the reygne of kyng edward the fourth" – would certainly endure.[173]

Part III

The Afterlife

15

The Gulph of Oblivion

The *Morte* did indeed endure: it continued to be read during centuries when whole libraries were lost forever. Perhaps surprisingly, however, the first fifteen years of the text's existence saw the most serious threat to its prospects of longevity. When Caxton printed the work in 1485, its future looked safer. But the manuscript from which Caxton set his text was the copy of a copy and therefore at least twice removed from the work penned by Malory himself. There's widespread agreement that the Winchester manuscript is closer to what Malory actually wrote. It is free from Caxton's editorial interventions (though in the 1970s, through an examination of certain "smudges and blots", Lotte Hellinga showed that the Winchester copy had been in Caxton's workshop). But the Winchester manuscript is not what Malory wrote. His manuscript and all those early copies were long ago lost in the deeps.[174]

But still: we have all 473 folios of the Winchester manuscript, sold to the British Library by the Warden and Fellows in 1976. And there are surviving copies of Caxton's *Morte*: a complete one in the Pierpont Morgan Library, New York; a second, consisting of 423 folios and lacking a number of leaves, held by the John Rylands Library in Manchester (the library of Lincoln Cathedral owns a fragment of a third). But one needs to be careful here: it might not be right to speak of the '*Morte*'. In his final colophon, Caxton writes of "thys noble and joyous book entytled le morte Darthur" (see fig. 7). Some scholars have claimed that this 'title' refers exclusively to the material presented in the twenty-first 'book' and suggested that Caxton thought of the work in its entirety as "the byrth / lyf / and actes of the fayd kynge Arthur / of his noble knyghtes of the rounde table / theyr meruayllous enqueftes and aduentures / thachyeuyng of the fangreal / & in thende the dolorous deth & departyng out of thys world of them al".[175]

It's fairly clear, however, that Caxton did in fact think of Malory's overall work as "le morte Darthur": in the final colophon he says that he has "entytled" it in this way "notwythftondynge" that it treats of Arthur's life and of the adventures of his knights. According to Field, however, the title of "le morte Darthur" is "accidentally given" by Caxton: "Malory called what he wrote *The Whole Book of King Arthur and His Noble Knights of the Round Table*". It's true that in the closing lines of Book XXI Malory writes of "the hoole book of kyng Arthur & of his noble knyghtes of the rounde table" (all but the first two words of this quotation are reproduced in fig. 7). Still, I imagine that Malory wouldn't seriously have objected to having the line from Caxton's final colophon – "the byrth / lyf / and actes of kynge Arthur" – as the title, although he might have preferred the description in Caxton's preface: "the noble and Ioyous hyftorye of the grete conquerour and excellent kyng. king Arthur / fomtyme kyng of thys noble royalme / thenne callyd brytaygne". It is a bit of a mouthful, and a modern reader would probably want it salted with capitals and served in italics. But some such title at least describes the subject matter of Malory's work in a comprehensive way. A scholar might find other reasons to raise an eyebrow at 'le morte Darthur'. Caxton's use of a lower case 'a' in 'arthur' and the absence of an apostrophe after 'D' don't need to be forgiven, of course. The problem – as French speakers like Caxton and Malory should have known – is that the French word for 'death' is feminine: the title should have been *La Morte Darthur* or, still better, *La Mort Darthur*. It's embarrassing: the most generally used title of Malory's masterpiece is (a) inaccurate, (b) French, and (c) bad French. Vinaver can only speculate that Caxton's lines were mistranscribed by an "ignorant clerk".[176]

The mistake of the "ignorant clerk" was amended in Joseph Haslewood's edition of 1816 (*La Mort D'Arthur*) and Thomas Wright's edition of 1858 (*La Mort d'Arthure*). Edward Strachey's 1868 edition was entitled *Morte Darthur*. So it was only with Oskar Summer's edition of 1889 that Malory's work was finally given the general title of *Le Morte Darthur*. For readers in the sixteenth, seventeenth and eighteenth centuries, however, all of these titles – *Le* or *La*, *Mort* or *Morte*, *Darthur*, *d'Arthure* or *D'Arthur* – were probably unfamiliar. This wasn't because Malory's readers had loyally stuck to Caxton. The Elizabethans – Spenser, for example, and Shakespeare – knew Malory not through Caxton but through Wynkyn de Worde's editions of 1498 and 1529. The first of these was entitled *The booke of the noble Kyng, Kyng Arthur, sometyme Kynge of Englonde of his Noble actes and feates of armes of chyualrye, his noble knygthes and table rounde*. The second went under a still less hypotactically organised title: *The booke of the moost noble and worthy prince Kyng, Kyng Arthur, sometyme Kynge of great Brytayne now called Englonde whiche treateth of his noble actes and feates of armes and of chyualrye, of his noble knyghtes of the table Rounde*. William Copland's 1557 edition of Malory (*The Story of Kyng Arthur, and also of his noble and Valiante*

Knyghtes of the Rounde Table) was based not on Caxton but on Wynkyn; Thomas East's 1585 edition (*The Story of Kynge Arthur, and also of his Knyghtes of the Rounde Table*) was based on Copland. William Stansby's edition of 1634 (*The History of the Renowned Prince Arthur, King of Britaine. As also, all the Noble Acts and Heroicke Deeds of his valiant Knights of the Round Table*) was based on East.[177]

Stansby's was the last black-letter edition[178] of the *Morte*. And Malory's reputation must have dwindled in the century-and-a-half which followed his death, since Stansby described *The History of the Renowned Prince Arthur* as a "piece of Antiquity revived from the gulph of oblivion". The oblivion wasn't complete: Robert Chester's *Birth, Life and Death of Honourable Arthur King of Brittaine* (1611) was indebted to Malory and, as Elisabeth Michelsson has shown, the figure of King Arthur surfaced in numerous sixteenth- and seventeenth-century court masques, commercial stage plays and civic pageants. For 200 years, however, the "gulph" continued to yawn for Malory: *The History of the Renowned Prince Arthur* was the last edition of the *Morte* until 1816. Between the English Civil War and the Napoleonic Wars – between Milton and Scott, say – Malory fell out of favour in influential quarters. According to James Merriman, Erasmus "scorned the tales of Arthur and Lancelot". In 1568, Roger Ascham saw in the *Morte* damning evidence of papistry's "standing pool": the work invited readers to take pleasure in "open manslaughter and bold bawdry". Less than a decade later, Nathaniel Baxter condemned the *Morte* as "vile & blasphemous": Malory's knights were a pack of "whoremasters". Yet the humanists of the European Renaissance and Protestant scholars in England were swimming against the tide. The intellectual élite may not have put the *Morte* on their reading lists, but Caxton's gentlemen and gentlewomen treasured the stories of Arthur. It was precisely the scenes of "manslaughter and bold bawdry" which made Malory worth reading. The *Biographia Britannica* (1748) described the attractions of Malory with masterly irony:

> As the author has not made his heroes any great commanders of their passions in their amours, nor rigorously confined them to honour and decorum, in point of fidelity and continence, his book became a great favourite with some persons of the highest distinction for a long time.

We might not share his reaction, but Ascham had seen what appealed to the old Adam very clearly. And as late as 1891 Wilfred Scawen Blunt gave another stir to the "standing pool" when he suggested that readers of the *Morte* were uninterested in the "high deeds" of Arthur's knights: what excited these thoroughly modern Paolos and Francescas was the "lost sound | Of Lancelot's steps at the Queen's chamber door". [179]

Those persons of the "highest distinction" weren't merely gentry: for princes at court, the name of King Arthur had been one to conjure with for centuries. Long before Malory was born, Henry II, Edward I and Edward III had made use of the legend set down by Geoffrey of Monmouth. In what Higham describes as a "politically astute" act of "obfuscation", Edward IV claimed descent from Arthur during Malory's own lifetime. Such claims were hardly surprising, for in myth if not in history, Arthur was the first ruler of a united nation. So it was that, the month after Caxton published the *Morte*, Henry Tudor marched to Bosworth "under the banner of the Arthurian red dragon". In the "storm of Arthurianism" which followed Henry VII's accession, genealogists constructed a royal line which went back to Arthur, and it was at Winchester – Malory's Camelot – that Arthur, Henry's first son, was born. The "storm" abated somewhat during the reign of Henry VIII: Higham points out that Arthurian motifs formed no part of the "English contribution to the pageantry of the Field of the Cloth of Gold" in 1520. But a statue of Arthur holding a round table was placed in the temporary palace built for the reception of Charles V at Calais later that year. J. J. Scarisbrick reports that when Charles visited London in 1522, a statue of Arthur with an "imperial crown" was displayed at a pageant in Cornhill. Charles was shown the round table at Winchester, which Henry had caused to be decorated with a Tudor rose and an image of himself on Arthur's throne. The wily monarch even used the story of Arthur's continental wars to shore up his claims to national autonomy during the divorce crisis of 1525–33. According to Scarisbrick, the Act of Appeals (1533) was the "foundation stone of the new order". And when the Act asserted that "this realm of England is an empire", it did so on grounds derived from Geoffrey of Monmouth.[180]

In the second half of the sixteenth century, Ascham and Baxter painted lurid pictures of the threat posed by the *Morte*. Even earlier than this, however, the notion of a historical Arthur had come under attack. In his preface, Caxton himself alluded to suspicions that "there was no such Arthur". In 1534, as Higham points out, Polydore Vergil "ridiculed the Arthurian cult site" at Glastonbury in his *Anglica Historia*. Following the Reformation, however, John Leland defended the idea of a historical Arthur in *Assertio Inclitissimi Arturii* (1544). In 1559, John Bale subjected Vergil to an Ascham-like excoriation for his "Romish lies". According to Higham, a "court cult" of Arthur continued into the reign of Elizabeth I, manifesting itself in Thomas Hughes's 1588 play *The Misfortunes of Arthur* and Edmund Spenser's *The Faerie Queene* (1590). In 1586, Raphael Holinshed conceded that much of what was written about Arthur was "beyond credit" but nevertheless maintained that this "woorthie man" existed, "a great enimie to the Saxons". Early in the seventeenth century, James I claimed an ancestry reaching back to the "royal line of . . . Arthur".[181]

In 1638 John Milton expressed his desire to "recall in song our native kings, and Arthur waging war even beneath the earth". Fascinated by the story of "Igraine pregnant with Arthur" and "Merlin's wizardry", Milton made a start on this work the following year. According to William Parker, however, "we hear no more of an epic on King Arthur after 1639". In the 1640s, Milton wrote four chapters of a prose *History of Britain*. He now expressed a doubt "whether ever any such" person as Arthur had actually existed. The idea of a historical Arthur, Milton now felt, was "monkish". Ten years later, he began *Paradise Lost*.[182]

Not all readers will view Milton's decision to write about Adam and Eve rather than Arthur with unmitigated delight. By the mid-1600s, however, the historical as well as the ideological content of the 'matter of Britain' was open to question. Daniel Defoe saw the round table at Winchester in 1726. The idea that this object was authentic, he wrote bluntly, was a "FIB". But others kept the faith. *King Arthur; Or, the British Worthy*, an opera with lyrics by Dryden and music by Henry Purcell, was first performed in 1691. This work had originally been written in 1684 to mark the twenty-fifth anniversary of Charles II's restoration. When Charles died, the opera was abandoned, resurfacing in altered form after Dryden's conversion to Catholicism and under the reign of those arch-Protestants William and Mary.[183]

Dryden found the order established by the Glorious Revolution uncongenial. But he was not alone in using the story of King Arthur to express controversial views in a coded way. In about 1702, "J. S." – John Shurley, in all probability – published *Great Britain's Glory*, in which the emphasis on Arthur's victories over the Saxons seems prompted by the Act of Settlement (1701), which provided for the crown to bypass all Catholic claimants in favour of the House of Hanover on the death of Queen Anne. But the Arthurian myth had an extraordinary malleability. In 1695, Richard Blackmore published *Prince Arthur, an Heroick Poem in X Books* – a shameless attempt to ingratiate himself with William III. Blackmore followed up with more of the same in *King Arthur: An Heroic Poem in Twelve Books* (1697). In 1700 Dryden dismissed him as a "Pedant, Canting Preacher, and a Quack".

Alexander Pope later recalled Dryden speaking cuttingly of the "ever-lasting" Blackmore. Poetic treatments of the matter of Britain were evidently no guarantee of literary quality. But Arthur hadn't quite been ejected from history, even though that history was sometimes written in the service of present political interests. John Shurley insisted on the historicity of Arthur, a king of the "Antient British Royal Blood". It was only "envious Aliens" who challenged his existence. In 1724, the anti-quarian William Stukely allowed Arthur, in Higham's words, a "minor and local role". In 1762, David Hume thought that there might be "some foundation" for the "exaggerations" of the poets. And in 1788, Edward Gibbon could not wholly identify with the "severity of the present age", which had "inclined to question the *existence* of Arthur".[184]

Within a century of Malory's death, Ascham had condemned the *Morte* on religious grounds. Caxton recommended the *Morte* to "lords and ladies, gentlemen or gentlewomen" without distinction of gender. But Ascham was less relaxed: what would happen if the *Morte* found itself in the hands of a "young gentleman" or, still more worryingly, a "maid"? Stansby must have been influenced by such anxieties: in his edition he claimed to have "corrected" those scenes in which Arthur's knights "sweare prophane". Stansby was merely paying lip-service to Puritan values, however: *The History of the Renowned Prince Arthur* was unexpurgated. Guardians of public morality were casting disapproving eyes on the *Morte* in the sixteenth century, then. But it wasn't until the nineteenth that concerns about the *Morte*'s effect on younger readers began to be acted upon by Malory's editors. In the age of Lamb's *Tales from Shakespeare* (1807) and Bowdler's *The Family Shakespeare* (1818) concerns about the moral effects of literary works upon younger readers extended beyond the plays of the bard. According to James Merriman, Haslewood's 1816 edition of the *Morte* was revised for the "eye of youth". The age-profile of Malory's readership seems to have changed in the centuries after Caxton. Medieval romance "crept under-ground for a time", as Harvey Darton writes, taking "refuge in the nursery library". The *Morte* came to be read less by gentlemen and gentlewomen than by their children.[185]

The *Morte* continued to be read. It's possible, however, that seven-teenth- and eighteenth-century readers didn't have much choice. According to William St Clair, England underwent a "cultural lock-in" during this period. New works were costly and had limited circulation. For ordinary readers, only the works of the "old canon" were acces-sible: fairy stories, tales of Robin Hood and St George – and the *Morte*. But although English intellectual life was indeed constrained during these decades, readers didn't turn to Malory as a last resort. The *Morte* wasn't reprinted between 1634 and 1816. Over the course of those 180 years, according to A. S. G. Edwards, the black-letter copies were "literally read to destruction". Malory almost disappeared – not through neglect, but because he was loved so much. In the eighteenth century, Stukely and other scholars including Richard Hurd, Thomas Percy, Thomas Warton and Joseph Ritson began to take Malory more seriously. The earliest modern painting to adopt an Arthurian theme seems to have been John Hamilton Mortimer's "The Discovery of Prince Arthur's Tomb by the Inscription on the Leaden Cross" (*c.* 1770), although according to Christine Poulson it was not until 1847 that the *Morte* became an "acknowledged . . . source" in a British painting. In the meantime, the *Morte* had become part of the literary explosion which followed the abolition of perpetual copyright in 1774. When the legislation was tightened up in the early decades of the nineteenth century, publishers ransacked the old canon in order to supply an increasingly voracious public. They weren't particularly careful with the texts they found: according to Elizabeth Pochoda, Haslewood's three-volume edition of the *Morte* is "remarkably poor". A two-volume edition of Malory also published in 1816 (Walker and Edwards's *The History of the Renowned Prince Arthur*) is also "very poorly edited". But these criticisms would have been beside the point. By the second decade of the nineteenth century, the Arthurian revival had begun: the *Morte* was reaching new readers. Many of these would never forget their first encounter and few would have cared about the editing.[186]

The vast majority of those nineteenth-century readers are nameless and silent. In this as in so much else, Sir Walter Scott was an exception to the rule. The first canto of *Marmion* (1808) contains notes referring to Malory. When Washington Irving visited Abbotsford in 1817, his host introduced him to "several passages from the old romance of Arthur". Irving remembered the "quaint-looking apartment" and Maida, Scott's staghound, lying at his feet. Scott read the *Morte* "with a fine deep sonorous voice, and a gravity of tone that seemed to suit the antiquated black-letter volume". Malory had two other notable readers early in the nineteenth century: William Wordsworth and John Keats. I imagine he would have been proud to have found such an audience. Yet this isn't to say that the Romantics took Malory to their hearts. Even in the 1840s, the subject of Arthur was, according to Kathleen Tillotson, "still strange to the ordinary reader". The presence of Malory is scarcely felt in Blake, Coleridge or Shelley. Byron despised the "monstrous mummeries" of the Middle Ages. For Merriman, the few Romantic excursions into the Arthurian legend – Scott's "The Bridal of Triermain" (1813), Wordsworth's "The Egyptian Maid" (1835) –

were "stillborn". Malory had his supporters, but they weren't uncritical fans. In 1804 Scott commented that the Tristram story had been written "without much art of combination". Robert Southey's preface to William Upcott's edition of *The Byrth, Lyf, and Actes of Kyng Arthur* (1817) claimed that Caxton's text had been reproduced with "scrupulous exactness". The fact that this edition took more pains over Malory's text than Haslewood or Walker and Edwards implies admiration as well as professionalism. And Southey confessed that the *Morte* had been "my delight since I was a schoolboy". He had read Malory in a "wretchedly imperfect copy" ("the 1634 Stansby", according to Christine Poulson) and remembered that "there was no book, except the Faery Queen, which I perused so often, or with such deep contentment". But Southey went on to echo Scott's comments about the *Morte*'s absence of "art":

> Adventure produces adventure in infinite series; not like a tree, whose boughs and branches bearing a necessary relation and due proportion to each other, combine into one beautiful form, but resembling such plants as the prickly pear, where one joint grows upon another, all equal in size and alike in shape . . . making a formless and misshapen mass.[187]

CHAPTER

16

Rah! Rah! Ree!

"A formless and misshapen mass": with enthusiasts like these, Malory hardly needed detractors. But although the *Morte* survived the "lock-in" after the Civil War and, unlike many other texts from the old canon, escaped being swept into the gulf by the reading explosion of the early 1800s – although the *Morte* appealed to traditionalists like Southey and avant-gardists such as Keats – Malory was received less as a long-lost ancestor than as a counter-example or even antithesis to Romanticism. Formless, without combination, misshapen: such responses to Malory anticipated Vinaver's sense of the *Morte*'s lack of unity by more than a century. And the Victorians followed suit: Alfred Tennyson felt that the *Morte* was "much the best" of the medieval romances but told Edward Fitzgerald that it was "strung together without art". William Morris thought Malory's book an "ill-digested collection of fragments". And Victorian historians were more reluctant to entertain the idea of a historical Arthur than Gibbon and Hume in the previous century. In *The History of England* (1848), Thomas Macaulay described Arthur and Mordred as "mythical persons, whose very existence may be questioned"; in *A Child's History of England* (1853), Charles Dickens wrote, of Arthur: "whether such a person really lived . . . no one knows".[188]

Southey was clear that the *Morte* was a "compilation": Malory had probably translated a "French compendium" of Arthurian narratives. The next editor of the *Morte* – Thomas Wright – agreed. In the introduction to his 1858 edition of Malory the *Morte* was again described as a "compilation". In the second half of the nineteenth century, however, a very different Malory began to emerge. In 1868, Edward Strachey asserted for the first time that Malory was an "author" not a "mere compiler and translator". In his view, Malory had given the Arthurian story an "epic unity and harmony, and a beginning, middle, and end". The *Morte* was not a prickly pear, then: it displayed relation and proportion; it was a deliberately formed work of art. In 1891, Strachey rewrote the introduction to his edition of 1868. The *Morte* was now, for him, "our first great work of English prose". By this time, a rising generation was adding its voice to these new claims. One of the first to be heard was Sidney Lanier, who published a children's version of the *Morte* in 1880. Lanier agreed with Strachey: Malory had managed to produce "one work, with a sort of beginning, a plot, and a crisis". The *Morte* was "the first English novel". Professional literary critics now began to sing Malory's praises more loudly. George Saintsbury returned to the figure of Malory on several occasions: in 1885 he described the *Morte* as "one of the first monuments of accomplished English prose" and in 1898 he wrote of Malory's "great and original book". The charge that the *Morte* lacked unity was again rejected when, in 1894, Walter Raleigh argued that Malory had given the "scattered Arthur legends a unity and a beauty . . . that secured for them their supreme place in English prose literature". But the most extended statement of this shift in critical perceptions of the *Morte* was delivered by Saintsbury, who claimed in *The English Novel* (1913) that the *Morte* was "one of the great books of the world". Malory was an artist not a "mere compiler": out of the "vast assemblage" of his materials, he had made "one story, and one book".[189]

Some four centuries after his death, Malory returned to the great hall of literature to claim a place at the table. Tennyson might have thought the *Morte* was "strung together" but he read Malory when "little more than a boy" (Ricks thinks he used the "3 vol. edition of 1816" – Haslewood's *La Mort D'Arthur*) and was "haunted" by Malory's work for more than fifty years. For him, the story of Arthur was "the greatest of all poetical subjects".[190] Tennyson was accompanied by countless other contributors to what James Merriman was the first to call an "Arthurian Revival".[191] In spite of the fascination with all things Arthurian, however, the *Morte* was not automatically canonized. It might have been a living work of art but for many it was an odd specimen – alien, graceless, resistant. Malory's loosely aggregative form, the interlacing, the discontinuities: the *Morte*'s seemingly accidental counterpoint was often seen more as an exercise of 'fancy' (the faculty which, for Coleridge, merely played with the counters of existing things) than as an instance of 'imagination' – that "essentially *vital*" force which "diffuses, dissipates, in order to re-create", which "struggles to idealize and to unify". Even a recent critic such as Terence McCarthy borrows Coleridge's terms when he writes that Malory "borrows and assembles *in order to re-create*" (my italics). The suggestion is that Malory gets to where the imagination goes, but by means of fancy's combinatory mechanisms. And there's no doubt that it is difficult to see the *Morte* in the light of Coleridge's formulation. It is too solid to have been created by diffusion; Malory was too practical a writer to "idealize", too enigmatic a one to "unify". The *Morte* was not accorded 'unity' until Strachey's edition of 1868, and it is probably fair to say that his view only became standard when Saintsbury published his study of the novel in 1913. By then and for several decades thereafter, literary modernism and historical events − a general smash of meaning and culture − would make 'unity' more attractive and define it more generously, in terms of the *Morte*'s 'feeling' − a pervasive sense of personal and national tragedy, of what W. P. Ker in 1905 called the "enchanted twilight" of the Arthurian world − rather than of Malory's technical abilities.[192]

The Victorians only recognized what Malory had to say to them when they saw their world coming to an end. At first, they found the *Morte* naggingly unsatisfactory. There were doubts about the relevance of the Arthurian legend: in 1842, John Sterling felt that Tennyson's "Morte d'Arthur" "does not come very near to us", seeing it (again through the lens of Coleridge) as "a mere ingenious exercise of fancy". In 1859, Elizabeth Barrett Browning found the Arthur story "too far off and flat". The *Morte* continued to be morally troubling. Southey admitted to being "frequently disgusted" by it. The "cruelties" of Arthur's knights belonged to "the history of Europe during the middle ages", he supposed. But the Grail story was too Romish for his taste. Still more problematic was the element of adultery in the stories of Launcelot and Tristram: this was not incidental; it was among the "original elements". In "To the Queen", the concluding poem of "Idylls of the King", Tennyson − the writer in whose work Malory's current flowed most strongly − saw a *Morte* "touched by the adulterous finger of a time | That hovered between war and wantonness, | And crownings and dethronements". War and dethronement were part of the historical record. Yet Southey and Tennyson were almost as apprehensive about the sexual elements of the *Morte* as Ascham and Baxter had been three centuries before.[193]

Gradually, however, as industrialization revealed its human cost at home, as acts of aggressive self-interest abroad exposed the nature of the imperial enterprise, and as the edifice of nineteenth-century liberalism tottered, the *Morte* came to stand for alternative albeit distinctly Victorian ideals. Tennyson suggested that Arthur resembled a "modern gentleman". A "simple knight", the young king is the embodiment of "courtesy", "manhood" and "knighthood". At the kingdom's zenith, the great hall at Camelot contains four "zones of sculpture". The third shows what the Round Table has achieved; the fourth represents the state to which it aspires:

And in the lowest beasts are slaying men,
And in the second men are slaying beasts,
And on the third are warriors, perfect men,
And on the fourth are men with growing wings.

Arthur is naturally a Christian: the Round Table stands for an order set above that of the "heathen hordes". "The old order changeth", Arthur tells his assembled knights, "yielding place to new". This change is secular as well as religious, for Arthur is the embodiment of just sovereignty. Rescuing the *Morte* from Malory's "wantonness", Tennyson invoked nineteenth- rather than fifteenth-century values. The King, as Tennyson's son later put it, is "pure, generous, tender" and "human-hearted". He is, in fact, an idealized version of Arthur Hallam – the "modern gentleman" who died, aged 22, of a stroke at Vienna in 1833 and who, long before "In Memoriam" (1850) or the birth of his son Hallam in 1852, Tennyson commemorated in "Morte d'Arthur", the poem which Christopher Ricks describes as his "first major Arthurian work".[194]

Tennyson spoke obliquely of his "allegorical or . . . parabolic drift" in the "Idylls", and the comment is one to which I will return. But he was more direct in the poems which eventually topped and tailed the "Idylls" – the Dedication to the Prince Consort (1862) and "To the Queen" (1873). Victoria's husband was a fan of the "Idylls": in 1860 he even asked Tennyson to sign his copy. When Albert died in 1861, Tennyson returned the compliment: the Prince was praised for his "sublime repression of himself"; he was "modest, kindly" and "wise". Albert was an "ideal knight". And now – like Arthur – "We have lost him – he is gone". But the "Idylls" didn't simply suggest connections between Camelot and Windsor. Tennyson wouldn't have pointed as quickly as I have done to the 'cost' of industrialism (although according to T. S. Eliot he didn't regard its progress with "complacency"); he certainly wouldn't have presented nineteenth-century imperialism as 'aggressive'. But this isn't to say that he thought all was right with the Victorian world. In "To the Queen", Tennyson detects the presence of a "tempest in the distance". There are "signs of storm" in "looseners of the faith", in "lust for gold" and the "groan" of "Labour". The decline of Christianity and the struggle between Capital and Labour at home is compounded by difficulties abroad. The victory at Waterloo made us "mightiest of all peoples", but even *The Times* recommended Canadian independence. Why did the voice of empire speak so "feebly"? Were we an "ocean-empire" or "some third-rate isle"? Only the "crowned Republic's crowning common-

sense" – Victoria herself – could turn these fears into "morning shadows".[195]

Tennyson's anxieties weren't limited to matters of state policy,
however. The "Idylls" might have been "allegorical" or "parabolic" but
they didn't simply involve holding up a deceased aristocrat from Saxe-
Coburg as the modern incarnation of Arthurian ideals. When
Tennyson declared that the Round Table had made men's hearts
"clean", but only "for a season", he declined to embrace the dominant
narrative of progress. As Arthur's power ebbs, he must contemplate an
awful possibility: rather than sprouting angelic wings, his knights might
make the kingdom "reel back into the beast". The point is repeated in
the concluding book of the "Idylls": Arthur has "stricken with the
sword in vain"; his wife, his friends: they are traitors to peace, "and all
my realm | Reels back into the beast". Evolution is not necessarily
ascent; a civilization can be lost as well as gained; and if, as the King
now thinks, "some lesser god" has "made the world", then Arthur's
optimistic words after his marriage to Guenever take on a wholly
different meaning. "The old order changeth, yielding place to new": in
"The Passing of Arthur", the King's farewell speech to Bedivere looks
forward to an age in which warriors will become the beasts that once
they killed.[196]

Tennyson was not by any means alone among the Victorians in
reviving the myth of Arthur. Mark Girouard points, among others, to
Kenelm Digby, who published *The Broad Stone of Honour* – a set of
"Rules for the Gentleman of England", according to the subtitle – in
1822, and Archibald Montgomerie, thirteenth Earl of Eglinton,
who attempted, not entirely successfully, to revive the medieval
tournament one rainy weekend in August 1839 – the "Eglinton Tomfooleryment", as a contemporary penny gazette captioned its image of
knights holding umbrellas whilst tilting at each other on rocking
horses. At Oxford in 1853, Edward Burne-Jones and William Morris
contemplated forming an 'Order of Sir Galahad' to perform, as
Beverly Taylor and Elisabeth Brewer write, "noble acts of charity . . .
in the East End of London". One thinks of the fresh-faced under-
graduates patrolling the streets of Whitechapel in order to identify a
suitable damsel in distress: a slender-waisted, pale-faced and flame-
haired "stunner". And it's true that the work of the Pre-Raphaelites
can tempt one to be cynical. Whilst dreaming of the Middle Ages in
Oxford, the young Burne-Jones wrote home to warn that some
"heavy calls" would shortly be made upon his father's bank balance
in order to cover outlays on twelve dozen bottles of Madeira, three
dozen of claret and two dozen of champagne – the cellarage of a

Gawaine rather than a Galahad. Yet Burne-Jones's father – a Birmingham frame maker – was, in the words of Penelope Fitzgerald, "not even moderately successful": his son's letter was a joke.[197]

According to his wife Georgiana, Edward Burne-Jones first signed himself "General of the Order of Sir Galahad" in a letter from Oxford to Cormell Price on 1 May 1853, enjoining his childhood friend to learn Tennyson's "Sir Galahad" "by heart". During the Long Vacation in 1853, Burne-Jones wrote again (now in the guise of "Edouard, Cardinal de Birmingham"): what was wanted was a "Crusade"; the task of the new Order was to wage "holy warfare against the age". In his earlier letter to Price, Burne-Jones had declared that Tennyson made him "exquisitely miserable". Yet his involvement in the Arthurian revival wasn't simply a matter of melancholy aestheticism. Even before he went up to Exeter College in 1853, Burne-Jones had been attracted to the teachings of John Henry Newman, who in an "age of materialism . . . taught me to venture all on the unseen". Newman had converted to Catholicism in 1845 and founded the Birmingham Oratory in 1849. When Burne-Jones assumed the guise of a Birmingham cardinal, he was being outlandish to amuse a friend. As it turned out, Newman actually became a cardinal in 1879.[198]

When Burne-Jones arrived at Oxford, Newman had been gone for seven years and his influence had abated. For a time, Tennyson – made Poet Laureate in 1850 – filled the gap. Burne-Jones would never forget Morris reading "The Lady of Shallott" in his dreamy chant. But "all reading men" at Oxford in the 1850s, as R. W. Dickson told Morris's biographer J. W Mackail five decades later, were "Tennysonian". For Burne-Jones, Tennyson's Galahad represented what Georgiana Burne-Jones called "the cause of celibacy". He probably also stood for the cause of Newman, who argued the case for celibacy in *Loss and Gain* (1848). Yet it wasn't easy to follow both the present laureate and the future cardinal. Tennyson's "Sir Galahad" was published in 1842, three years before Newman converted. But in "The Holy Grail" (1869), Tennyson opposed Anglo-Catholicism: the sacramental vessel does not contain wine turned into blood; its significance is, in Poulson's words, purely "symbolic". Burne-Jones produced drawings of Sir Galahad in 1856 and 1858: both, according to Poulson, embodied the "ideals of the Oxford movement". For Burne-Jones, the Grail and its contents might not have existed in any visible or material way. But they were real.[199]

Compared to Tennyson, Burne-Jones's Arthurianism seems almost introspective. Yet his Galahad represented public as well as private virtues: he belonged to a collective order – a "Brotherhood". Burne-

Jones imagined an active community – a "small conventual society", as Georgiana Burne-Jones put it, "working in the heart of London". And although the Order of Sir Galahad remained an idea, it inspired future projects. In 1855, Burne-Jones envisioned the founders of the *Oxford and Cambridge Magazine* as an "exclusive Brotherhood" who would be as enthustic as the "first crusaders". In 1857, he joined a third and more famous Brotherhood, that of the Pre-Raphaelites. In 1859 there was talk of a 'Hogarth' club. Involvement with Morris and the 'Firm' at Red House followed in 1861. By this time, Burne-Jones no longer aspired to a monastic life: he abandoned the idea of a clerical career in 1855 and married in 1860 (a child was born in 1861). Throughout his life, however, the Arthurian theme remained connected in Burne-Jones's mind with his hopes for social reform, artistic renewal and spiritual growth – for the "unseen" alternative to materialism which he had sought as a young man.[200]

Burne-Jones's passion for Tennyson didn't dwindle to the extent of Morris's. But the Laureate's enthusiasm for Low Church Anglicanism and imperialism was hard to swallow. Unlike Morris, Burne-Jones attended Tennyson's funeral at Westminster Abbey in 1892. According to Georgiana Burne-Jones, he found the event "flat and flattening". There should "have been street music, some soldiers and some trumpets, and bells muffled all over London". As it was, "I wish I hadn't gone". Burne-Jones felt that Tennyson deserved a better burial; in fact, however, the Laureate hadn't been his "prime hero" for decades. The publication of the "Idylls" in 1859 marked a turning-point: in his earliest Arthurian works, Tennyson had been "fiercely attacked"; by the time of the "Idylls", however, he was giving his readers "what they wanted".[201]

Burne-Jones had more or less parted company with Tennyson in 1859. But his enthusiasm might well have begun to cool one day in August 1855, as he scoured shops on the Strand for an image of his hero. When he entered Cornish's bookshop in New Street, Burne-Jones discovered something wholly new – the 1817 edition of the *Morte*. The struggling artist couldn't afford this work; instead, he returned to the shop day after day, reading Malory a few pages at a time. Hearing of his friend's plight, Morris bought *The Byrth, Lyf and Actes of Kyng Arthur* and, back in their rooms, they "feasted on it long". Burne-Jones took the precious volume to Birmingham, where he read it in the garden of the family home on the Bristol Road. In the summer of 1858, whilst on holiday in the country, Burne-Jones was still reading Malory (and consuming "innumerable cherries"). The encounter transformed his attitude to Tennyson, making the "Idylls" seem – as Wilfred Scawen

Blunt recollected in 1896 – a "bowdlerization". For Burne-Jones and Morris, the *Morte* was the mother lode. "The book", as Georgiana Burne-Jones reflected, "never can have been loved as it was by those two men". In the case of Burne-Jones, the *Morte* became "a part of himself . . . his own birthright".[202]

Burne-Jones's fascination with the figure of Galahad has much to say about Malory's place in English culture during the second half of the nineteenth century. Taylor and Brewer have shown that the example of the *Morte* helped to shape an "ideal of the gentleman" and an associated notion of "fair play". In troubled times, the *Morte* was becoming, in the words of Debra N. Mancoff, the "sactioned national epic". The Arthurian revival projected an age which had never existed, of course. It invoked normative standards of (male, middle class) conduct which served to shore up inequalities. In an age of change, however, the passion for Malory was also a "revaluation . . . of the contemporary".[203]

The "Tory-Radical" impulses which, in the view of Alice Chandler, were expressed in the Arthurian revival took widely different forms: the radicalism found expression in socialism and aestheticism; the conservatism could be detected in nationalist appropriations of the Arthurian narrative. "Sir Galahad", an 1862 painting by George Frederic Watts, seems at first sight to offer as solitary and meditative an image – and also as androgynous a one – as Edward Burne-Jones's earlier drawings of the same hero. In part because he didn't want to be seen as a mere illustrator and in part because he was an agnostic who believed in the theory of evolution, Watts discouraged connections between his painting and the "Idylls". As Marilynn Lincoln Board observies, Watts's image of Galahad is one of "aspiration" rather than "revelation": there is no "divine force" at work here. Unlike Burne-Jones's Galahad, Watts's painting would be "conscripted in a larger campaign to enlist the Arthurian discourse in the cause of Britain's imperialist ambitions". The fact that Galahad became, in the words of Christine Poulson, a "symbol of sacrifice for the empire" was not wholly of Watts's doing. But it was his Galahad which featured in numerous memorials for soldiers killed in the Boer War and the First World War. Burne-Jones appealed to an alternative set of values which were informed by his commitment to the "unseen" as well as his apprehensive eroticism. Watts by contrast exemplified – or was taken to exemplify – a visibly muscular and conformist Arthurianism, a king-and-country ideal of heroic manhood which could be promulgated in public schools such as Eton (where in 1897 a second version of Watts's "Sir Galahad" was installed in the College chapel).[204]

Watts's militarism *versus* Burne-Jones's anti-materialism: at the end of the nineteenth-century the former impulse often prevailed against the latter. Watts's Galahad went down particularly well in the United States: its image of "stirring, vigorous . . . young manhood" was exactly what the Reverend Ernest Dennen wanted for the Boston boys' club he opened in 1896. Dennen hoped to turn his charges into "Foursquare Men" – specimens of physical, social, intellectual and spiritual strength. A manual for the leaders of the Order recommended suitable reading matter for teenaged boys. It suggested that a committee should make use of "potted plants, flowers, crepe paper in Galahad colors, banners, flags and emblems" to decorate the annual banquet. And it set down for posterity an inspiring chant:

Rah! Rah! Rah!
Rah! Rah! Ree!
G–A–L–A–H–A–D

The Order of Sir Galahad was not the first attempt to use the Arthurian myth to discipline American youth: William Byron Forbush set up the Knights of King Arthur in 1893 and the organization claimed 130,000 members by 1922. The Watts Galahad was in the ascendant. In 1895, as the designer for a production of *King Arthur* at the Lyceum, even Edward Burne-Jones – the artist who represented the antithesis to that inflection of the Arthurian myth – played a role in promoting imperial Arthurianism.[205]

The Lyceum production was an all-star extravaganza: Arthur Sullivan composed the incidental music; Henry Irving took the role of Arthur; Ellen Terry – Watts's wife – played Guenever. Irving originally wanted Tennyson to adapt his "Idylls" for the stage, but the Laureate remained lukewarm about the project and was in any case now dead. Joseph Comyns Carr was then asked to produce a script, and it was here that problems began. Burne-Jones felt that Carr reduced Morgan and Merlin to "scandalmongering gossips"; George Bernard Shaw wrote that Arthur's speeches were those of a "jealous coster-monger"; the appearance of the Grail reminded William Archer of a "parlour-maid bringing in a *vol-au-vent*". More upsettingly – for Burne-Jones, at least – Carr put in too many "jingo bits about the sea and England".[206]

Saintsbury published *The English Novel* in 1913; I read Phyllis Briggs's *King Arthur and the Knights of the Round Table* in 1970. In the first seven decades of the twentieth century, the *Morte* survived in the work of such scholars as Kittredge, Chambers, Hicks and Baugh – and, a little later, Oakeshott, Vinaver, Lewis and Brewer. Vinaver in particular played a major role in giving the academic interest in the Arthurian narrative an enduring institutional form – a sort of research equivalent to the Order of Sir Galahad. In 1928 he established an Arthurian Society whose first Congress was held at Truro in 1930; a second Congress at Quimper in 1948 established an International Arthurian Society whose triennial conferences still take place. But Arthurianism wasn't just a scholarly matter. Between 1901 and 1970, Malory's tale was given new life in a flood of adaptations and other fiction for both younger and older readers. This detonation wasn't felt with equal intensity across all cultural forms: there was a decline in the use of Arthurian themes by British artists; in the work of poets, Malory's grip also seemed to weaken. Playwrights continued to call upon the Arthurian myth, and the 'matter of Britain' still fired the imagination of composers. The *Morte* also began to appear in the new media of radio and film. Charles Kent's *Launcelot and Elaine* (1909) was based on Tennyson. But Kevin Harty thinks that Malory might have been the main source for Giuseppe de Liguoro's *Il Re Artù e i cavalieri della tavola rotonda* (1910). In 1953 a namesake of mine – Jan Lustig – co-wrote the script for MGM's *Knights of the Round Table*, a vehicle for Ava Gardner and Robert Taylor. In the 1960 musical *Camelot* and the 1967 film of the same name, the *Morte*'s ability to draw in the crowds became evident in a way that had never been seen before. In 1964, a President's widow attempted to enshrine the memory of her assassinated husband in terms which came from Malory – via Hollywood and Madison Avenue. As Arthur and his knights galloped into the age of television, the Arthurian theme regained a prominence it hadn't enjoyed since the nineteenth century. In 1981, John Boorman, the director of *Excalibur*, explained Malory's appeal in a novel way: the author of the *Morte*, he said, was the "first hack writer".[207]

By the last quarter of the twentieth century it was evident that the Arthurian revival of the nineteenth century had become, in the words of Norris J. Lacy, an "explosion". Fascinated as I was by the story of King Arthur, I remained unaware of this wider cultural phenomenon. I simply wanted to be Launcelot, and it didn't occur to me that the original author of these tales might sometimes have felt the same thing. But even if this idea had occurred to me at the age of 8 it wouldn't have been original. A few years earlier, while undertaking research for a project which would only be published posthumously, John Steinbeck reached just this conclusion. On the morning of 26 April 1957, Steinbeck woke at dawn to see "the sun coming up over Rome". He had been worrying away at the mystery of the *Morte* for weeks: "why did Lancelot fail in his quest and why did Galahad succeed?" Then, quite suddenly, a step appeared, and then another. The *Morte* was "the first and one of the greatest of novels in the English language". But what did this mean? It seemed to Steinbeck that "a novel may be said to be the man who writes it". A novelist almost always identified with one character in the work – a person who represented "what he thinks he is" and "hopes to be". This was the "self-character". And – it was obvious – "Malory's self-character would be Lancelot". In Launcelot Malory saw his strengths and weaknesses. As Steinbeck watched "the morning sun on the brown walls of Rome", he could answer his own question. The self-character failed because this was the author's experience as a mortal; the best he could hope for was to leave behind something of himself: a son – Galahad – who embodied his "perfections" but not his "faults".[208]

Steinbeck's experience in Rome was unusual in its intensity. But numerous other readers experienced the *Morte*'s ability to fascinate. In the 1950s, as a child in Argentina, Alberto Manguel visited a bookshop near his house and leafed through *The Three Musketeers, Uncle Tom's Cabin* and – bound in green, as he later remembered – "the adventures of King Arthur". In 1961, David Jones heard how a friend had discovered her young son in tears and thought he was ill – only to discover that the boy had been overcome with grief after reading about the death of Arthur in a children's version of the *Morte*. Malory also cast a spell on older readers. Returning to England in 1962 after covering the famine in Bihar, the photographer Don McCullin began to explore the legend of King Arthur. He photographed woods around Glastonbury in "sombre, haunting colour" and began to think about questions of national identity: "what were the English and what did they represent?"[209]

CHAPTER
17

The Waste Land

In one tradition – the dominant one – the *Morte* is a deep pool whose waters supply artists (Burne-Jones and Morris, Arnold and Tennyson) with grand and sombre stories. This legacy draws its power from the darker places of the human heart, from need and desire. But the night-time Malory is not the only one. In a second tradition, the *Morte* is mined, not for dark nuggets of the soul but for its human follies, for comedy and satire rather than tragedy or epic. One sees this in a relatively recent example such as *Monty Python and the Holy Grail* (Terry Gilliam making coconut-shell sound effects for the non-existent horses which Arthur's knights pretend to ride, Michael Palin arguing the case for anarcho-syndicalism whilst piling "filth", Neil Innes as the minstrel who sings of brave Sir Robin's abject cowardice, John Cleese's Launcelot getting "carried away" at a wedding feast and murdering the guests). In this absurd iteration of the Arthurian story, the challenges become ridiculous and the loppings grotesque. Throughout it all (rehearsing his later performance as Brian of Nazareth), Graham Chapman's Arthur retains a look of saintly bafflement – an outpost of sanity in a crazy world.[210]

Yet *Monty Python and the Holy Grail* extemporises upon an established theme: Arthurian materials were parodied by Henry Fielding in the eighteenth century, by Thomas Love Peacock, George du Maurier and Mark Twain in the nineteenth and by T. H. White in the twentieth. Cervantes led the way here, though his allusions are not to the *Morte* but to *Amadis of Gaul, Don Olivante de Laura* and *Florismarte of Hyrcania*; to authors such as Feliciano de Silva, Jorge de Montemayor and Antonio do Lofraso rather than to Malory. Yet one of the writers to turn the Arthurian narrative to satirical ends was Malory himself. I'm not referring to those moments when the *Morte* becomes risible – the interminable tournaments, the childish competitiveness of Arthur's knights. These offered a richly humorous vein for Malory's successors. But the comedy in Malory isn't always unintentional: the japing and scoffing Sir Dinadan occupies a satiric space within the *Morte*, casting a sceptical eye on the ideals and customs so dear to Arthur and his court. I've mentioned the scene in which Dinadan serves fish to the exclusively carnivorous Sir Galahalt (it happens on the sixth day of the tournament at Surluse – the Queen's Club to Lonazep's Wimbledon). Modern readers are unlikely to fall off their chairs with mirth, like Guenever and the haut prince. But Dinadan's antics – on the third day at Surluse, Malory tells us that he "mocked and japed with King Bagdemagus that all knights laughed at him, for he was a fine japer" – don't just provide relief from the smiting recorded at length in Book X of the *Morte*. Bagdemagus is an ally: four books previously, his daughter released Launcelot from imprisonment by the four queens. But although we do not discover it until the start of Book XIX, Bagdemagus is also the father of Meliagrance, Guenever's future kidnapper. Dinadan's teasing may therefore have a political point and serve, if only for a time, to relieve political tensions.[211]

On the seventh day of the tournament at Surluse, Launcelot forces Dinadan to wear a "woman's garment". This incident prompts much amusement, and Guenever (whose sense of humour lacks any sophistication) laughs so much "that she fell down". But the cross-dressing relieves the tension created by the smouldering conflict between Lamorak and Gawaine. And the fact that Dinadan bestrides the gender line may well inform his subsequent conversation with Isoud. When Dinadan remarks that the sorrows of love "dureth over long" he is not only scoffing but stating a truth which the *Morte* as a whole compellingly demonstrates.[212]

By the last quarter of the twentieth century – in the years since I read the Arthur stories as a child – the Herculanean labours of the great Malory scholars were largely completed. The Winchester manuscript was edited to exacting modern standards, Malory's sources comprehensively catalogued, and the debate about the unity of the *Morte* pursued exhaustively – and, for some, exhaustingly. Yet although they stood on the shoulders of giants, Malory scholars continued to emerge. Facsimile editions of Caxton and the Winchester text were published in 1976. In 1981, the *Morte d'Arthur* entered the age of information technology – and of Margaret Thatcher – when Cedric Pickford and Rex Last employed three teenagers provided by the Manpower Services Commission to produce the world's first "computer-assisted bibliography of Arthurian literature". The youngsters spent hours inputting data on the ICL 1904 mainframe computer at Hull University.[213] Yet traditional methods had by no means been superseded. In 1983, James Spisak edited Caxton's *Morte*. P. J. C. Field issued a third edition of Vinaver's *The Works of Sir Thomas Malory* in 1990. Paperback editions of Malory were published by Penguin (1969, ed. Cowen), Wordsworth (1997, ed. Moore), Oxford University Press (1998, ed. Cooper) and Norton (2004, ed. Shepherd). In the last years of the twentieth century, a website – the Camelot Project – made available a database of Arthurian texts and images.[214] In the meantime, notes first struck in the *Morte* continued to echo when warships were named and sunk.[215] In British universities, a historical Arthur was again postulated – and again discredited.[216] Outside the groves of academe, the field of Grail studies enjoyed a rude profitability. Fewer poets and dramatists made use of the Arthurian story. But Malory's presence could be detected in the work of countless writers who adapted the *Morte* or used Arthurian materials in fantasy works for a younger audience. The *Morte* inspired numerous films, TV shows, musical works, comics, computer games and advertisements.[217] The outpouring passed me by. But even a cursory glance at contemporary culture discovers Sir Thomas's stubborn ghost time and again: he's there in the name of a lottery company; from Indiana Jones to J. K. Rowling, from Dan Brown to *Shrek*, he continues to shape the consciousness of the younger generation.

Even as a child I found Malory cropping up in the oddest places: in playground chants, fantasies of perilous quests, and dodgy notions of chivalry towards the opposite sex. Malory was there in my books as well – and not just in Briggs. What was Biggles but an airborne Launcelot? Malory was there, still more strangely, in *The Guns of Navarone*. At the start of Alistair MacLean's wartime thriller, a character called 'Mallory' hears a match being struck on "rusted metal" and applied to a cigarette "jutting out beneath the Group-Captain's clipped moustache". MacLean's Mallory turns out to be as courteous – and as brutal – as any of Malory's knights. He is also, perhaps more surprisingly, preoccupied with knightly romance – if only to notice its absence in the cat-and-mouse conflicts around the isles of Greece. Mallory knows that Corporal Dusty Miller will be a "good man to have around". But the loose-limbed and irreverent Californian, an explosives expert from the Long Range Desert Force, "didn't look like Sir Launcelot" and cannot be imagined "on a white charger, the bugle to his lips".[218]

The spelling of Mallory's name and still more his climbing abilities suggest that MacLean was recalling the twentieth-century mountaineer rather than the fifteenth-century romancer. Indeed, as if to draw attention to this parallel, *The Guns of Navarone* begins with an extended account of a cliff face ascent – one which I found particularly absorbing as a child. At the time, I didn't see anything Arthurian about this part of the story. But I wonder, now, about Malory and Mallory. Two 'l' Mallory died on Everest in February 1924. He was the darling of

Duncan Grant and Lytton Strachey, of Virginia Woolf and Rupert Brooke. One 'l' Malory was hardly a dashing socialite: he showed a greater talent for making enemies than for keeping friends. But there's something there, isn't there? Poor two 'l': when they found his body in 1999 the ravens had feasted on his buttocks. But one 'l' may have died on a mountain of his own – one made from words. The knight prisoner and the gentleman climber; a man with armour stains on his clothing and another, shivering at altitude in a gabardine jacket. Two reckless amateurs, two fine failures. The Everest expedition of 1924 and the story of King Arthur's reign: both stories evoke that perennial English fascination with causes nobly lost.

As I entered my teenage years, I was scarcely aware that the *Morte* was the source of resurfacing currents. I had no knowledge of the scholarly industry which had grown up around Malory. I didn't hear about the sale of the Winchester manuscript to the British Library in 1976; I didn't realize that Oakeshott had been "appalled" by the proposal; I certainly didn't know that Oakeshott had felt "almost undone" when his wife Noel died after a long illness. Yet the man who taught Malory in the 1920s never forgot the *Morte*. In 1975 he declared that Malory was the "representative of a Western European tradition to a degree that can be claimed of no other English author". Reviewing the facsimile Winchester in 1977, he felt that the tragedy of Arthur, Launcelot and Guenever was "almost as moving as any in literature". Oakeshott was still thinking about Malory even after I bought my Everyman edition of the *Morte* in the York bookshop that autumn morning in 1981. He spoke on Malory to pupils at Tonbridge School in 1982. Three years later, now in his eighties, he delivered a paper to the Tennyson Society at Grimsthorpe Hall in Lincolnshire. Oakeshott argued (bravely, given his hosts) that Tennyson "murdered" Malory in the "Idylls of the King".[219]

As a teenager in the 1970s, it never struck me that Malory's name is never far away when the subject is England at war. At school, my friends talked about what they had watched on television over the weekend: *633 Squadron* and *Battle of Britain*; *Reach for the Sky* and *The Dambusters*. The Lunar Rover was trundling over the surface of the Moon but the fantasies of British boys were rooted in the past. The Second World War had been over for a quarter of a century, but we were still sketching Spitfires and RAF decals in our files. This preoccupation with war – and in particular with the Second World War – is evident in Phyllis Briggs. As the campaign against Lucius begins, smiths and carpenters are hard at work throughout Arthur's "green lands". Bowmen set up their targets and practise "from sunrise to star-rise".

Forges glow, and armour is "stacked in readiness". Finally, from the coast of Kent, the fleet sets sail for France, "rolling and pitching on the blue Channel rollers". This all happens when Arthur is king, but it could just as well have taken place during the reign of George VI.[220]

It's not surprising that *King Arthur* makes us think of the Second World War, for the book was written only a few years after the conclusion of this conflict. England's wartime experiences are equally evident in Roger Lancelyn Green's *King Arthur and His Knights of the Round Table* (1953) and T. H. White's *The Once and Future King* (1958). Indeed, as John Stephens and Robyn McCallum argue, most retellings of the Arthur story in twentieth-century children's literature are a "response to the cataclysms of two world wars". Stephens and McCallum are right to emphasize the role of the First as well as the Second World War. In 1930, Edward Arlington Robinson claimed that his Arthurian poems – "Merlin" (1917), "Lancelot" (1920) and "Tristram" (1927) were "suggested by the world war". Robinson's Gawaine speaks of "a madness feeding on us all". A similar strain can be observed in Thomas Hardy's *The Famous Tragedy of the Queen of Cornwall* (1923) and Laurence Binyon's *Arthur: A Tragedy* (1923). It can also be seen in David Jones's *In Parenthesis* (1937), acclaimed by T. S. Eliot as a "work of genius", a "book about War", about "Roman Britain" and "the Arthurian legend".[221]

Nicholas Murray has argued that the War Poets "were not anti-war but 'anti-heroic'" because they "did not think . . . trench warfare was a chivalric pursuit . . . like something out of Malory". This isn't quite true. In January 1918 T. E. Lawrence found that reading Malory "relieved my disgust". But for Lawrence the campaign against Ottoman domination of the Middle East was eminently "chivalric" (at the Battle of Tafileh later that month he would win the Distinguished Service Order). Lawrence's "disgust" was prompted not by the horrors of war but by the weather conditions which had pinned his forces down in the mountains to the east of the Dead Sea. If all of Malory's readers adhered to the *dulce et decorum* myth, however, it would be hard to explain his influence on Ivor Gurney, who confided the following plan to his diary in April 1917:

> If the Bosches hit an arm off me I will get the largest pension I can and go tramping the country, sleeping rough . . . And the first walk I shall take shall be to Dymock, Newent, Ross and into Wales, to end at Chepstow after meeting names met in Malory.

That walk would have taken Gurney westwards from his birthplace in Gloucester – a long way from France, where he would later be wounded in the shoulder and gassed. Why the reference to Malory? Perhaps Gurney owned a copy of the Everyman *Morte*, in which Sir John Rhys affirmed that Malory was "a Welshman". The Welsh dimension of the Arthurian narrative – *The Mabinogion*, Geoffrey of Monmouth – was invoked with more detail in Jones's *In Parenthesis*. One might expect that Jones turned to Malory for the battle scenes: the text and notes to *In Parenthesis* make reference to Tristram fighting the Saxons, Launcelot's duel with Gawaine, Mordred's siege of the Tower of London, and the final battle at Salisbury. But Jones was also deeply interested in Malory's account of the Grail quest, specifically referring to Launcelot's experiences at the Chapel Perilous, when the earth quakes and thirty knights cry out with a "grimly voice". Jones mentions this passage in his preface, when it again becomes clear that he sees the *Morte* not as a jingoistic text but as a narrative which succeeds better than any other in evoking the "war landscape". Writing some twenty years after his experiences on the battlefields, Jones recollected daily life in "the Waste Land". It consisted of "sudden violences" and "long stillnesses", "sharp contours" and "unformed voids". It was a place of pain and death, but also of "enchantment". And, for Jones, "it is perhaps best described in Malory, book vi, chapter 15 – that landscape spoke 'with a grimly voice'".[222]

Jones's footnoted references to the *Morte* and *The Golden Bough* – indeed, the very notes themselves – make plain the influence of "The Waste Land" (1921) on *In Parenthesis*. In his own notes to "The Waste Land", Eliot mentions such writers as Spenser and Shakespeare, Webster and Middleton, Kyd and Milton, Marvell and Goldsmith. This sample of the English literary canon is accompanied by references to the Bible, to classical authors including Virgil, Ovid and Augustine, to Dante and to French poets such as Baudelaire, Verlaine and De Nerval. Eliot's intertextual salmagundi draws in the Fire Sermon and Chapman's *Handbook of Birds of Eastern North America*. Yet although he refers to Tristan and Isolde and to Wagner, Eliot never once mentions the *Morte d'Arthur*. It is an extraordinary omission – and one which can also be seen in Eliot's critics. B. C. Southam is unusual in pointing out that Eliot "probably" took the title of "The Waste Land" from Malory – but even this sounds grudging. Why ignore the *Morte*? Perhaps Eliot felt it wasn't necessary to mention so well-known a work. Perhaps the notes weren't comprehensive: they were partly written in order to bulk out the book version of the poem and Eliot himself described them as "bogus scholarship". Yet even if his understanding of the Arthurian myth had been shaped by Frazer and Weston, there can be no doubt that the *Morte* (and *The Mabinogion*) were key sources. And it's not difficult to see why the story of Arthur appealed to Eliot. He was as much a war writer as David Jones and Ivor Gurney. Although he had no direct experience of the trenches, his imagination had been shaped by mass carnage. Eliot mourned the disappearance of what he saw as a more stable order, deploring the emergence of what seemed to him a sordid and faithless society. Yet he knew that this divided and diminished world hadn't arrived all in a moment, fully formed. In "The Metaphysical Poets" (1921), an essay published in the same year as "The Waste Land", Eliot at no point argued that our "dissociation of sensibility" was exclusively a product of the Great War. It had emerged much earlier – during the English Civil War, perhaps. A division of thought from feeling could be seen in Milton; by the time of Tennyson a gulf had opened up. But 450 years before Eliot's essay Malory knew perfectly well that it took time for dissociation and discord to develop. Arthur's kingdom isn't brought down by Mordred's plot or by the new-fangled social order with which he is associated. The end is there in the beginning: seeds are sown when Arthur sleeps with Margawse; the earliest cleavings foreshadow events to come. For Malory, the corpses on the battlefield at Salisbury testify to the logic of History. The waste land is the place from which we came.[223]

Such reflections aren't evident in Eliot's only published remarks on Malory, which came more than a decade after the publication of "The Waste Land". In 1933, Oxford University Press issued a two-volume reprint of Wynkyn de Worde's 1498 version of Caxton under the title *The Noble and Joyous Boke entitled Le Morte Darthur*. In February 1934, Eliot reviewed this publication in the *Spectator*. The timing was unfortunate, since if Eliot had waited a few months he would have been able to respond to the discovery of the Winchester manuscript. Without this to consider, Eliot's review seems lacklustre. It is almost distressing to see the greatest poet-critic of the twentieth century justifying the price of the Oxford two-volume set (£9. 15s. for two leather-bound volumes) because it presents the *Morte* in "as grand a form as anyone could wish". Thankfully, remarks of greater penetration shortly follow: Eliot describes Malory as a "crude northern Homer". He sees him as "a good chronicler" and "a fine prose writer" but feels that he lacked "the poet's power over the word". And Eliot offers a nicely-turned contribution to the debate about the *Morte*'s unity, finding that the text is pervaded by a "consistent inconsequence". After a while, however, Eliot returns to the question of the *Morte* as a book – a physical object to be held and touched. And now the remarks on price and bindings take on more significance. The Oxford edition presents Malory in a handsome form – and this is all very well. But Eliot feels that a case could be made, not only for a cheap *Morte* and a scholarly *Morte*, but also for a children's edition. And the need for a children's version at last explains why Eliot is concerned by the *Morte* as a book to be held and not just a text to be read, for it was "such an edition", as he writes, that "was in my hands when I was a child of eleven or twelve". The *Morte d'Arthur* "was then, and perhaps has always been, my favourite book".[224]

CHAPTER

18

Allegorical and Parabolic

One might read Eliot's review as a belated addition to his notes for "The Waste Land": it certainly suggests that the *Morte* was as important to him as classical and Renaissance poetry, as the Fire Sermon and the work of the French symbolists. Eliot encountered these works later on. But – like Southey and so many others – he had known and loved Malory as a child. It might not have been registered in Eliot's notes to "The Waste Land", but the experience of reading the *Morte* was buried more deeply than "bogus scholarship".

Eliot's desire to make the *Morte* available to children as well as to scholars and collectors was all the more urgent because he felt that Malory's readers had been poorly served in the past. In Eliot's view, the most widely read Victorian edition of the *Morte* – Strachey's *Morte Darthur* (1868) – conformed to an "ideal of marriage" which Malory did not "set . . . before us with any power or clearness". Strachey removed the passage in which Arthur fathers Mordred upon his own sister. For Eliot, however, "the incest of Arthur is the foundation of . . . the whole book". Arthur's "unwitting sin" establishes the pattern of tragic fatality from the outset. Malory's readers needed to know that it is Arthur's "incest-born bastard who shall destroy him". Strachey hadn't simply endeavoured to make Malory "*readable* for children", then: his object was to make the *Morte* "*safe* for children". Yet this was "compulsory sterilization".[225]

Eliot's account of Strachey's *Morte* is a forceful one. Agreeing that Strachey strategically revised the text of the *Morte* in accordance with Victorian sexual norms, subsequent critics have seen this edition as "censorious" and "flawed". Strachey was admittedly in no doubt that the society depicted by Malory was "far lower than our own in morals" and didn't hesitate to omit "such phrases or passages as are not in accordance with modern manners". But it would be a harsh critic who would maintain that the removal of references to genitals and buttocks 'sterilized' Malory. And although Strachey may well have adhered to a Victorian conception of marriage, he leaves his readers – "English boys", as he imagines the majority of them – in no doubt that Gawaine beds the Lady Ettard and that Lamorak and the Queen of Orkney experience "passing great joy" in each other's arms – just as they do in Malory. In Strachey's *Morte*, Launcelot sleeps with Elaine; the latter becomes pregnant with Galahad; and Bors, when he sees the baby boy, "wept for joy" – just as in Malory. Following his return from the quest, Launcelot and Guenever "loved together more hotter than they did toforehand" – as in Malory. It's true that Strachey does not refer to Launcelot taking his "pleasance and his liking" in Guenever's bed. But the Queen and her knight clearly spend the night together. As in Malory, Launcelot injures himself whilst removing the bars to the window of Guenever's chamber, and there would be no reason for Strachey's Meliagrance to accuse the Queen of being "false" with one of her wounded knights if the blood had not been specifically shed on her bedsheets.[226]

But Eliot's principal objection to Strachey's *Morte* consisted in the fact that it removed references to Mordred's conception. This was the "foundation". In this one respect if in no other, Strachey's *Morte* was a case of "sterilization". Yet Strachey's account of the last battle leaves no doubt of Mordred's parentage. "He smote his father Arthur with his sword": Strachey's wording is the same as Malory's. In Book I, however, Strachey treats the issue of paternity more obliquely. In Malory, Arthur unknowingly sleeps with "his sister", the King of Lot's wife, and "begat upon her Mordred". In Strachey's version, Arthur is similarly unknowing but the reference to begetting is omitted. Margawse is nevertheless openly presented as Arthur's "sister". She is also a "passing fair lady" – as in Malory. And there is no doubt of Arthur's feelings: he "cast great love unto her" – just as in Malory. When, in Book X of Strachey's *Morte*, Mordred is presented as Margawse's fifth son – an addition to the four sons mentioned in Book I – one would have to be an unusually innocent or obtuse reader not to make the inference. Eliot is technically correct: Strachey's version of the *Morte* permits fornication but shrinks from an open acknowledgment of incestuous adultery. Yet "sterilization" is surely too strong a word: the narrative can still produce a sense of tragic fatality if one realizes only at the end that Mordred is Arthur's son – and then sees everything one has read in the light of this fact.[227]

Eliot was being ungrateful in his 1934 review of the Oxford *Morte*: he may not have shared Strachey's views on "modern manners" but he was indebted to his predecessor's sense of the *Morte*'s coherent narrative arc. And though Strachey's was undoubtedly a popular edition, it wasn't as if readers had been seriously disadvantaged: if they wanted to read the word "begat" in Book I of the *Morte*, there were half a dozen options to choose from, even in 1900. Eliot didn't say it in his review, but his criticism of Strachey was in part a coded attack on Tennyson, the exemplary Arthurian of the Victorian age. In 1942 Eliot would sneer at the "skill" with which Tennyson had turned the "great British epic" of the *Morte* – handled in a "'hearty, outspoken, and magnificent" way by Malory – into "suitable reading for a girls' school". This point wasn't new (Burne-Jones had responded similarly when the "Idylls" first appeared) and nor was it entirely fair: Geoffrey of Monmouth made no mention of the act of incest between Arthur and Margawse which leads to the birth of Mordred. For the first three and a half centuries, therefore, the "foundation" of the Arthurian myth was wholly absent. Eliot nevertheless has a point, and the "ideal of marriage" is even more central to the "Idylls" than it is to Strachey's *Morte*. Unlike Strachey, Tennyson goes so far as to alter Mordred's paternity: he is, as Arthur puts it, "my sister's son – no kin of mine". Tennyson is even somewhat coy about Galahad's parentage, saying only that "some | Called him a son of Lancelot". The "Idylls" isn't completely bowdlerized: Pelleas finds Gawaine in bed with Ettarre; and though for some time Arthur harbours only a "vague suspicion" about Launcelot's relationship with his wife, no reader is similarly benighted. Yet there's little doubt that Tennyson is making things "safe" for the reader, and his sanitizing activities aren't limited to sexual matters. The "Idylls" acknowledges the brutality of war, and in his account of Arthur's last battle Tennyson pictures the "splintering spear, the hard mail hewn, | Shield-breakings, and . . . the crash | Of battleaxes on shattered helms". Still more vividly, we are told of "Oaths, insult, filth, and monstrous blasphemies, | Sweat, writhings, anguish" and "labourings of the lungs". But this is the climactic conflict of the "Idylls", and Tennyson elsewhere tends to make his representations of violence more general and abstract. Manners too are less "hearty" and "outspoken" than in the *Morte*: Malory's Launcelot offers Elaine "a thousand pound yearly" to marry "a good knight". Tennyson's Launcelot is not so vulgar but also seems more calculating, promising the Maid of Astolat – but only "should your good knight be poor" – to endow her with "half my realm beyond the seas". And there is also a diminution of mystery: when Arthur is placed in the barge before setting out on his journey to Avalon, three queens are present, as in Malory. But not one of them is Morgan le Fay.[228]

It's true that Morgan's role in the "Idylls" is taken by that of Vivien, whose "sprightly talk" and "lissome limbs" seduce even the wily Merlin. But it is significant that Tennyson worried about the appearance of this "harlot", saying that the whole episode "comes in far too soon". Christopher Ricks agrees: "Merlin and Vivien" presents Arthur's court as "lamentably corrupt much too early for the moral scheme". It's also significant that Tennyson relates Gawaine's seduction of Ettarre in the ninth of his twelve idylls. In Malory, this is a jolly interlude in the fourth of twenty-one books; for Tennyson, it is the "breaking of the storm".[229]

Tennyson's prudishness seems both quaint and objectionable these days. Yet, as Eliot wrote in his 1932 essay "*In Memoriam*", it is not Tennyson's "outmoded attitude towards the relations of the sexes" that makes one "recoil". A decade earlier, in "The Metaphysical Poets", Tennyson had been a prominent instance of the dissociated sensibility. "Style" came before "content" and remained apart from it; the Laureate lacked "seriousness" and merely "decorated the morality he found in vogue". Ten years on, Eliot's attitude had markedly changed. Tennyson is acclaimed as a "great poet". In "The Lady of Shalott" there is something "wholly new". Eliot can't praise Tennyson's "metrical accomplishment" highly enough: he had "the finest ear of any English poet since Milton"; indeed, his was the "greatest lyrical resourcefulness that a poet has ever shown". Nevertheless: "The Princess", "Maud", "Idylls of the King" – each of these works is in essence a series of shorter poems. "For narrative", as Eliot wrote, "Tennyson had no gift at all". And this was not some failure of experience – a lack of stories to tell. Tennyson may not have felt "violent passion for a woman", but his poetry showed plenty of "emotional intensity". The problem was that "melancholia" impeded "dramatic action". "In Memoriam" was unique; elsewhere, Tennyson's "real feelings" never found complete expression.[230]

Eliot's scornful references to the "Idylls" in the 1942 essay – "suitable reading for a girls' school" – suggest that his feelings of the 1930s had cooled. But this isn't quite true. Eliot certainly thought that in Tennyson's hands Malory's "original ore" had been "so refined that none of the gold is left". Yet his estimate of "In Memoriam" remained high, and he repeated the claim that Tennyson had "the finest ear for verse . . . of any English poet since Milton". One can't deny that the "Idylls" has some wonderful moments. Launcelot's admission of his sinful nature deepens the picture:

> . . . all of pure,
> Noble, and knightly in me twined and clung
> Round that one sin, until the wholesome flower
> And poisonous grew together, each as each,
> Not to be plucked asunder.

Tennyson's account of the last tournament – a "wet wind blowing", and thoughts going round and round in Launcelot's "sick head" – is pathologically as well as meteorologically evocative. But Arthur's final meeting with Guenever is more troubling. One can accept that Arthur is grief-stricken and does not "greatly care to live". But has Guenever really "spoilt the purpose of my life"? The monologue in which Arthur shows Guenever "the sin which thou hast sinned" is sickeningly holier-than-thou. And the Queen's posture during this disquisition – "grovelled with her face against the floor" – makes us collaborators in an act of moral sadism.[231]

Yet the most serious problem is not Arthur's "denouncing judgment" of his wife, not even his comparison of her to a "new disease". It is the idea that Guenever's beauty has been a "kingdom's curse". How can the "shame" of one woman bring "sword and fire"? Modern readers probably find Guenever's yearning for "warmth and colour" – for Launcelot, in other words – preferable to Arthur's pallid and tepid chastity, in which the "maiden passion for a maid" is used to "keep down the base in man". They may also find the idea that adultery brings down a state incredible. And it won't do to blame Malory rather than Tennyson: in the *Morte*, the private realm influences the public one but does not determine it as exclusively as it does in Tennyson. Nor does Malory point the moral so sternly.[232]

Some of Tennyson's effects might have been an unintentional result of the protracted composition of the "Idylls". The focus changed as he wrote: the early poems about true and false love gave way to reflections on history and the state, and Tennyson then unwisely brought these strands together. Yet Eliot's point remains: Tennyson had, like Strachey, reduced fifteenth-century vigour to nineteenth-century sterility. And it's here that Tennyson's cryptic distinction between the allegorical and the "parabolic" becomes relevant. When he wrote of his "parabolic drift" in the "Idylls", Tennyson may simply have meant that his poem had the quality of a parable – a tale whose meaning is indirect. But I suspect he was also – "drift" – thinking in terms of movement through space. In this sense, the "Idylls" might be parabolic because, like an object moving forwards under gravitational attraction, its meanings follow the path of a parabola. Allegory is by contrast a linear phenomenon: it involves replacing one thing by another at a higher level of meaning (or seeing an earlier event as a figure for a later one). It was an allegorical reader – the Bishop of Ripon – who suggested that the three queens who accompanied Arthur on his journey to Avalon stood for "Faith, Hope and Charity". Tennyson was unpersuaded. The Bishop was "right" and "not right". The three queens "mean that and they do not". Then came something more heartfelt: "I hate to be tied down to say, '*This* means *that*', because the thought within the image is much more than any one interpretation".[233]

The thought within the image: it was not about lines but arcs; it was not allegorical, it was parabolic. But what then did Tennyson mean when, in the concluding section of "Morte d'Arthur", he spoke of the King as a "modern gentleman"? And what did Hallam Tennyson mean when he wrote that his father had infused the old legends with the "spirit of modern thought"? Was the 'old' order merely a figure for the 'new', 'lower' for 'higher'? That would be allegory pure and simple. "The Round Table: liberal institutions": Tennyson jotted down this note in about 1833, and it seems – even bearing in mind the telegraphic nature of such memoranda – as mechanical as the Bishop of Ripon's reading of the three queens. One can see the shape of a parabolic reading more clearly by asking a simple question: was Tennyson saying that Arthurian England was better or worse than Victorian England? If the answer is 'better', then the "Idylls" becomes an exercise in nostalgia. This is certainly an aspect of the Victorian fascination with the Middle Ages, but it doesn't square with the text. Tennyson's point is that the Round Table is not an 'organic' society. But if the answer must then be 'worse', Tennyson looks like a Whig historian and his worries about historical degeneration become incoherent. Arthurian society is *both* 'better' *and* 'worse' than Victorian society. 'This' doesn't mean 'that': our thought must instead move forwards and backwards in criss-crossing arcs; it must be parabolic and not allegorical.[234]

Tennyson's notion of parabolic meaning is inherently dynamic. For Eliot, however, Tennyson's melancholia was fundamentally static. Yet the contradiction is only apparent. If we attend to the melancholy, scene replaces narrative, emotion forestalls action and auditory intensity gives way to silence. Seen parabolically, thought moves this way and that; the image of one age appears in the glancing reflection of another. In geometry, a parabola is a section through a cone. On this earth, however – in the flight of an arrow, for example – the trajectory is determined by gravity. Everything falls back to earth; the movement and the stillness are aspects of each other.

According to Eliot, Tennyson's readers regarded his verse as a "message of hope . . . to their rather fading Christian faith". Eliot finds something more "interesting" and "tragic". In the end – Eliot surely got it right here – it's not about ideas. Tennyson was distressed by the notion of "a mechanical universe". But he couldn't commit himself to a countervailing notion of progress because "his feelings", as Eliot puts it, "were more honest than his mind". And so, "temperamentally",

Tennyson became "opposed to the doctrine that he was moved to accept". Grand narratives of perfectibility – the reality of social change – the solitary and gloomy reaction: all these responses to time's parabola were possible, but the tendency of the curve led, with a cadence as inevitable as a line of Tennysonian verse, from left to right and through flight to fall. The experience, the passion: for Tennyson it wasn't sexual but theological. Tennyson's poetry was "religious" not "because of the quality of its faith, but because of the quality of its doubt". In an acutely "time-conscious" age, Tennyson moved this way and that. In the end, only the words held fast. Like Burne-Jones, Eliot felt that Tennyson had given his readers "what they wanted". By "looking innocently at the surface" of his work, however, one could glimpse an "abyss of sorrow". In the penultimate paragraph of his essay, Eliot imagined Tennyson "among the Great in Limbo, the most instinctive rebel against the society in which he was the most perfect conformist". He was, Eliot concluded, "the saddest of all English poets".[235]

19

Eliot the Harper

Eliot's image of the "compulsory sterilization" to which Strachey subjected Malory's text suggests that the *Morte* has a primal fecundity, a primitive virility. Rewriting Malory according to the neutered values of their day, Strachey and Tennyson passed on to succeeding generations a *Morte* shorn of its force and deprived of its foundations. Eliot's point applies equally to subsequent versions of the *Morte*. In Briggs, for example, a veil is cast over Mordred's parentage. The "sterilization" deplored by Eliot wasn't challenged by those adapting Malory until the end of the 1950s, when T. H. White insisted that incest is a "vital part of the tragedy" (in the same decade, John Steinbeck also resolved that in his own version of the *Morte*, "I will not clean it up"). Both Steinbeck and White wanted to recover an original, earthy *Morte* – an impulse which Eliot would have applauded. White in particular also saw the Arthurian narrative in relation to modern life, with comparisons by no means to the advantage of the latter. Whilst Briggs removed challenging subject-matter in deference to the prevailing moral climate, White used Malory to inveigh against new, and to him repugnant, values. He insists that the love of Launcelot and Guenever does not belong to a "story of the present" – one in which "adolescents pursue the ignoble spasms of the cinematograph". Guenever is not "promiscuous"; her beauty is not that of a "film star". She is a woman who wanted to live and to love "while there was still time".[236]

As the 'permissive society' emerged, White (like Malory before him) expressed his view of love "nowadays". Eliot would have liked this approach: he was no advocate of a promiscuous modernity. Nor was he a prude: Eliot wanted the incest, he wanted the adultery. He also wanted to leave Victorian poetry behind: for him, a modernist work like *In Parenthesis* got closer to the *Morte* than the "Idylls of the King". Yet Eliot's affection for his childhood edition of the *Morte* remains difficult to account for if the text he read was indeed *The Boy's King Arthur*, Sidney Lanier's 1880 retelling of the *Morte* for younger readers.

According to A. S. G. Edwards, however, this "may well have been the form" in which Eliot encountered Malory.[237]

One can understand why Edwards suggests that the young Eliot read Lanier's version of the *Morte*. Beverly Taylor and Elisabeth Brewer note that *The Boy's King Arthur* was in part written to console the defeated South in the aftermath of the American Civil War. Lanier didn't openly favour slavery, of course. But his evocation of the age of chivalry might well have appealed to the traditionalist in Eliot – who was, of course, a Southerner. With its handsome scarlet boards, its embossed black lettering and its gold-leaf image of a hand with a sword emerging from the depths, *The Boy's King Arthur* is a pleasure to hold in one's hands, and Eliot was certainly sensitive to the sensory aspects of the reading experience in his 1934 review of the Oxford *Morte*. Lanier divides the *Morte* into six parts, which is both simple and effective, and provides brief but lucid explanations of archaic words such as 'assayed', 'maugre', 'wote' and 'weened'. This too is something which the adult Eliot might well have applauded: his review raised no objections to a modern-language version of the *Morte* and seemed to suggest that a certain amount of simplification was acceptable.[238]

There was, however, one thing which Eliot insisted on, even in a children's *Morte*. The story had to rest on its "foundation" – Arthur's incestuous union with Margawse. It was "such an edition" that Eliot had read as a child. But *The Boy's King Arthur* is a thoroughly sanitized *Morte*. Launcelot is presented as a "sinful man" but Lanier has nothing about the adulterous relationship with Guenever: there are no secret visits to the Queen's chamber and no blood-stained sheets. And the fact that Mordred is Arthur's incestuously conceived son is completely dispensed with: when Mordred declares that he will marry Guenever, the Queen is described simply as "his uncle's wife".[239]

It seems unlikely that Eliot would make such definite stipulations about a children's *Morte* if he did indeed encounter Malory in *The Boy's King Arthur*, as Edwards suggests. What, then, was in his hands when he was a child of 11 or 12? Who introduced Eliot to the work which became the foundation of his most famous poem? If Lanier's case fails, the second candidate is James T. Knowles, who published the earliest children's version of the *Morte d'Arthur* – *The Story of King Arthur and His Knights of the Round Table* – in 1862. But Knowles is an even less likely contender than Lanier: *The Story of King Arthur* is dedicated to Tennyson and Knowles claims at the outset to have followed a "rule laid down in the 'Idylls of the King'", meaning that he has "suppressed and modified" the text "where changed manners and morals have made it absolutely necessary to do so". This prefatory boast would from Eliot's point of view have been as off-putting as the assertions made in Strachey's introduction to his 1868 edition. The question of the *Morte*'s morality was indeed a perplexing one. In the end, however, an editor could only amend "manners", concealing or softening acts which Malory had more openly depicted. But Strachey felt that Tennyson enjoyed greater freedom: his version of the Arthurian narrative could address "morals" as well as "manners", altering underlying values and not merely their expression in behaviour. In the "Idylls", Strachey wrote, Tennyson had "shown us how we may deal best with this matter for modern uses".[240]

Knowles's enthusiastic adoption of Tennysonian suppression tends to rule him out of contention. And the example of Tennyson was also embraced in the work of a third candidate: B. Montgomerie Ranking, whose *La Mort d'Arthur* appeared in 1871. Indeed, Ranking's wasn't really a children's Malory: including material from *The Mabinogion, La Mort d'Arthur* was actually a compilation of the sources used in the "Idylls". Tennyson had indeed shown abridgers and adapters how they might "deal best" with problematic material: Ranking followed the Laureate in ignoring the details of Galahad and Mordred's parentage. That was not quite true of *The Story of King Arthur*. Following the *Morte* more closely than Ranking, Knowles was to some extent constrained by the "manners" of his original. His Galahad is accordingly presented as the son of Launcelot. The adulterous nature of Launcelot's relationship with Guenever is also delicately apparent. Everthing is above board when the Queen holds Launcelot in "great favour". After the quest, however, we learn that Guenever shows "such favour" to Arthur's leading knight that "in the end brought many evils". Still more significantly, Mordred only appears in the latter stages of Knowles's narrative, and is described as "King Arthur's son by Belisent".[241]

Knowles was making the *Morte* "safe", although the reference to Belisent was a nod to those in the know. In Tennyson's "Idylls", Bellicent is the parent (with King Lot) of Modred and a "loyal sister" of Arthur. In this renaming, the Laureate attempted "to avoid", in the words of Alan Lupack, "the suggestion of incest associated with Morgause in Malory's version of the story". More straightforward techniques of "sterilization" can be seen in *La Morte D'Arthur* (1868), the fourth contender for the honour of having sown a seed in the mind of the young T. S. Eliot. In his preface to this work, Edward Conybeare points to Malory's "occasional coarseness" and reveals almost apologetically that he has "taken liberties with the text" which may seem "unjustifiable". Conybeare was writing three decades before Eliot was introduced to the work of Malory and more than six before he reviewed the Oxford *Morte*. But Eliot would probably have found the approach adopted in *La Morte D'Arthur* "unjustifiable". It is true that Conybeare's Launcelot returns from the quest and begins again to "resort unto" Guenever, though the word 'hotter', which is both suggestive and oddly contemporary in Malory's *Morte*, is removed from *La Morte D'Arthur*, in which Launcelot and Guenever "loved together more than before". It's not that Conybeare alters details of the plot to make Malory safe. He simply closes the door at an earlier point, as when Guenever, held captive in Meliagrance's castle, takes Lancelot by the "bare hand . . . and so she went with him to her chamber". It is a cue to the imagination. But the line might well confuse: how can hand-holding justify Meliagrance's allegation that Guenever is a "false traitress"? *La Morte D'Arthur* took more "liberties" with its original than the more well-known edition published in the same year – Edward Strachey's *Morte Darthur*. 'Modred' kills Arthur in single combat, but is nowhere – not even at the end – presented as the the King's incestuously conceived and illegitimate son.[242]

It seems unlikely, then, that Eliot read either Lanier or Knowles, either Ranking or Conybeare. We are left with a last contender: Mary Macleod's *The Book of King Arthur and His Noble Knights* (1900). Eliot said that he read his children's version of the *Morte* "when I was a child of eleven or twelve" – that is to say (being literalistic) between 26 September 1899 and 25 September 1901. *The Book of King Arthur* was published in 1900. It is therefore possible that Eliot was given Macleod's book for his birthday in 1900. Or perhaps he received it as a present at Christmas that year. *The Book of King Arthur* doesn't instantly stand out as a high octane version of Malory. In spite of the vividness of Eliot's language in his 1934 review, however, this is not what we are looking for. Indeed, Macleod treats the relationship between Launcelot and Guenever with more circumspection than Conybeare. She cuts out the Knight of the Cart episode leaving no Meliagrance to accuse Guenever of falsity. Macleod nevertheless quietly raises the stakes, presenting Launcelot's relationship with the Queen as an instance of chivalric failure – of "worldly desires" rather than knightly ones – and not of mere sexual transgression. Moreover, while Lanier and Ranking conceal Galahad's parentage and Knowles only briefly acknowledges it, Macleod relates Launcelot's rescue of Elaine from a room "as hot as any furnace" in order to set the scene for her subsequent statement that Galahad is the "son of Sir Lancelot of the Lake and the Lady Elaine".[243]

Peter Ackroyd describes the young Eliot as a "dreamy, bookish boy". It wouldn't be surprising if so studious a lad appreciated

Macleod's *Morte*. It was a beautiful book, profusely illustrated by Arthur George Walker, who had collaborated with Macleod when she adapted *The Faerie Queen* in 1897 and who in 1915 went on to produce the statue of Florence Nightingale which stands near the Crimean War Memorial in London. But it was also a more scholarly version of Malory than any other children's *Morte* produced in the nineteenth (or, indeed, the twentieth) century. *The Book of King Arthur* came equipped with a twelve-page introduction by John Wesley Hales of Trinity College, Cambridge and King's College, London. An editor of Spenser and Milton and an expert on Langland, Hales communicated to "young students" Kittredge's then-recent suggestion that the author of the *Morte* was the Malory of Newbold Revel. And Macleod herself was no common or garden children's author. She wrote academic articles on English calendar customs and was President of the Folklore Society (her 1938 presidential address was entitled "Syncretism in a Symbol"). As Arthurian writers, James T. Knowles and Andrew Lang rank somewhat below T. H. White or Roger Lancelyn Green, though the reputation of both has been preserved by their sheer productivity. But Mary Macleod stands alongside Phyllis Briggs and Jessie Weston in the "forgotten tradition" of Arthurian literature by women.[244]

We know roughly when Eliot held that children's version of the *Morte* in his hands. Unfortunately, the 1934 review does not reveal where this seminal experience took place. It might have been in New Hampshire, where Eliot's family holidayed each year. One imagines late afternoon sunlight streaming through the windows of a room and a boy with his head bent over a book. But it is summer: there are rock pools to explore and birds to watch. If my imagined Eliot was turning the pages of a book, it was, perhaps, Cory's *Birds of Eastern North America* (1899). Or perhaps Eliot did his reading back in St Louis: Sencourt recalls that "he would often curl up in the window-seat behind an enormous book". A children's *Morte* would have been a good companion on a Sunday morning in November.[245]

So it may have been in that place – in late 1900 or early 1901 – that Thomas Eliot finished his book. He read of a man standing "among a great heap of dead men" – the very words of Malory – and then of Mordred piercing "the helmet and brain-pan" . . . of his 'father'? No, alas, not there, not in that late scene. In the equivalent passage in *Morte Darthur*, even Strachey went further than Macleod – Strachey, Eliot's much-criticised sterilizer of the *Morte*! And yet Eliot nowhere suggested in his 1934 review that this last-minute communication of Mordred's parentage established the tragic fatality which he admired in the *Morte* itself. One needed a "foundation": the act of incest between Arthur and

Margawse had to be recounted before Malory's cathedral of words could rise into the air. And in this respect, Macleod's claim is more convincing than those of her competitors. When the kingdom enters its critical phase, she reminds readers that Mordred is the "youngest son of Arthur's sister". This is a selective truth, as is the earlier description of Mordred as Arthur's "nephew . . . the son of King Lot's wife". Mordred is indeed Arthur's 'nephew' as well as his 'son', but in the previous quotation these two words are placed so closely that a reader's eye might easily stumble onto that which remains unstated. Why is the "son of King Lot's wife" not the 'son of King Lot'? Here again the truth lies beneath and between the words on the page. We only need to cast our minds back a few pages, to the scene in which Arthur meets the "wife of King Lot of Orkney", who is "a most beautiful woman" and also "his own half-sister". Merlin almost immediately predicts that "King Lot's wife would have a child who would destroy Arthur". Macleod does not state that Mordred is Arthur's son by his half-sister. But the details point silently in one direction only.[246]

One can understand why the young Eliot might have been drawn to *The Book of King Arthur*. Macleod didn't talk openly about incest or bastardy, but her *Morte* had not been sterilized. Indeed, the influence of Tennyson was entirely absent from this text, making it unique among nineteenth-century children's versions of Malory. But it's not just that we now have reasons to identify Macleod as the most likely author of the children's *Morte* which Eliot read in 1900 or 1901. When Eliot wrote on Malory in 1934 or when he was at work on "The Waste Land" more than a decade earlier, it's possible that a very specific image from his childhood came into his mind. Almost a third of *The Book of King Arthur* book is devoted to the Tristram story, and Macleod works hard to give this section a coherence which, according to most of Malory's critics, the 88 chapters in Book X of Caxton's *Morte* signally lack. Yet Book X is the mid-point of the *Morte*: its swirling and seemingly purposeless action offers fragmentary anticipations of the final scenes.

One of the most significant of these foreshadowings occurs in Chapter 26, when Malory describes how news is brought to the court at Camelot from Tristram at Tintagil. There are "goodly letters" for Arthur and for Launcelot, and they write "goodly letters" in reply. Back in Cornwall, King Mark is "wroth" with Tristram and sends his own letters "privily" to Arthur and Guenever. Mark wants to make Arthur suspicious about the relationship between Launcelot and the Queen. But Arthur puts "all that out of his thought". Mark's malice nevertheless causes a stir at court, and Malory's language is significant. Arthur is "wroth". But Guenever is "wroth out of measure". Meanwhile

Launcelot is so "wroth" that (rather uncharacteristically) "he laid him down on his bed to sleep". After this depressive nap, Dinadan suggests that Launcelot shouldn't try to refute Mark's accusations: comedy would be a more effective gambit. This isn't surprising: Dinadan's affection for Tristram has already led him to conduct a series of practical jokes which culminate in King Mark being chased through a "great forest" by Sir Dagonet, King Arthur's fool. In response to Mark's renewed plotting, Dinadan proposes to make a "lay" and send a harper down to Tintagil to sing it. It will, he promises Launcelot, be the "worst lay that ever harper sang". In Chapter 31, the harper duly sings before King Mark. His lay is the "worst" not because it is of inferior quality but because it gives the most comprehensive account of Mark's villainy "that ever man heard". When the harper has finished, Mark is "wonderly wroth". Yet the Cornish king preserves a courtly mask, telling the harper to "hie thee fast out of my sight" but ensuring his safe conduct "out of the country".[247]

I have already noted that Dinadan is at one point compelled to wear the clothes of a woman. His ability to cross the boundaries of gender seems to have a political corollorary, for Dinadan is the most significant intermediary between Cornwall and Logres. If one person can represent the mid-point of the *Morte*, a stable centre amidst swirling conflicts, it might well be Dinadan. At first, however, it's difficult to see the full significance of the "worst lay" episode. In the ensuing chapter, with a particularly abrupt "now turn we", Malory devotes his attention to the tournament in Surluse. In Chapter 50, with another "now turn we", Malory "beginneth the treason of King Mark" against Tristram. But the end of this story is left hanging: at the end of Book X, Tristram goes into exile in England with Isoud; in the final chapter of Book XII he fights Sir Palomides, who begs forgiveness and agrees to be baptized. This, as Caxton's *explicit* makes clear, is the end of the "*second book of Sir Tristram*" (the "*first book*" begins in Book VIII of Caxton; the second book "*followeth*" Book IX). But Malory provides "*no rehearsal of the third book*", turning instead to "*the noble tale of the Sangreal*". So Mark's treason begins but does not seem to end. Most scholars would see this as an instance of Malory's literary deficiencies. Yet the suspended ending of the Tristram story is itself significant: the line of Malory's narrative may well be both dispersed and curtailed, but straws are in the wind. Malory clearly wants to contrast the figures of Arthur and Mark. Both are kings; both are hapless thirds in their respective erotic triangles. But while Mark jealously broods over Isoud, Arthur sweeps his suspicions under the carpet and tries not to think about "all that". Mark is malign but knows the truth; Arthur is benign but lives a lie. And whilst Mark's attempt to revenge himself on Tristram is never completed within the narrative, it's clear at Lonazep that the Round Table is fatally divided. It feels like nothing's happening. But only small buildings collapse in a moment.[248]

At first sight, the gathering at Lonazep looks like business as usual. Tristram sees the "questing beast" drinking at a well and deduces that Palomides can't be far behind. When Tristram's contingent reach Castle Lonazep there is the customary banter: Tristram is impressed by the "tents" and the "marvellous great ordinance" but Palomides thinks the armaments at the Castle of Maidens were equally impressive and Dinadan observes there was "as great a gathering" at Surluse. In the days that follow, Dinadan's moans about the "great buffets" he has received make Arthur and Launcelot laugh "that they might not sit", reminding us of happier days. Yet something is wrong. On the second day, Arthur addresses Isoud in terms which make one suspect that he (or Malory) has forgotten that they were introduced to each other the previous day. On the third day, Tristram "unknowingly" knocks the King off his horse. And throughout the tournament, Guenever suffers from a "sickness" which prevents her from watching the action.[249]

There are reasons for these mishaps: Isoud's presence at Lonazep brings Palomides into conflict with Tristram; Tristram's feats of arms make Launcelot's kinsmen envious. But such differences can be resolved: when Arthur's knights come together in individual combat, the dynamic is reassuringly centripetal. We need to look elsewhere to see the forces – more slowly acting but in the end more fatal – which are tearing the kingdom apart. The root problem is not adultery; it does not lie in the relationship between Tristram and Isoud or Launcelot and Guenever. It's not incest – that long-ago story whose consequences will only become evident at the end of the *Morte*. It's more like miscegenation – the violation of some ancient and barely comprehensible taboo. We have known since Book IX that Sir Lamorak thinks Morgawse (previously 'Margawse') is the "fairest queen". Shortly before the episode of Eliot the harper, we discover that Lamorak and Morgawse have slept together with "passing great joy". For the wife of King Lot, the consequences are immediate: Gaheris comes to the bedside, "and . . . gat his mother by the hair and struck off her head". On this occasion, Lamorak escapes: Gaheris will not kill him "by cause thou art naked". But by the time that Tristram and his supporters reach Lonazep, we know that Lamorak has fallen victim to the vengeance of Morgawse's sons. Gawaine, Agravaine, Gaheris and Mordred set upon Lamorak in a "privy place" and, after a fight lasting three hours, Mordred gives Lamorak "his death wound behind him at his back".

This news is narrated only at second hand, but Alan Lupack rightly notes that it has "ominous . . . implications for the larger Arthurian tragedy". Gareth refuses to "meddle" in the re-ignited feud between the families of Lot and Pellinore. But the strongest forces are now centrifugal: the court is separating into factions. Mordred needs more time to plant the charge that will bring down Camelot's fair towers. The assassination of Lamorak is an early and telling coup, however, for Lamorak is surely a substitute for Arthur – Morgawse's earlier lover.[250]

It is on May Day that Arthur proclaims "a jousts before the castle of Lonazep". To quote the line again is more clearly to hear the sadness in its brave trumpetry. Arthur will bring together "all the knights of this land" to fight against Ireland, Scotland, "and the remnant of Wales, and the country of Gore, and Surluse, and of Listinoise". Only two chapters later, however – even before the tournament starts – we discover that Lamorak has been "feloniously" slain. If one counts each chapter of the *Morte* and calculates the mid-point of Malory's work, it comes in Book X, Chapter 13 – the point at which Dinadan's practical joke results in King Mark running away from Sir Dagonet. But a numberical approach fails to identify two more important hinges in the narrative, both of which also occur in Book X. Malory's critics are united in finding the author of the *Morte* prolix and undisciplined at this point. But each of these episodes suggests that Malory did not in fact "bungle his structural problem", as E. K. Chambers once claimed. Lamorak's murder in Book X, Chapter 54 of the *Morte* is a tipping point. It casts a shadow over the second half of the *Morte* because it shows how quickly feuding between rival clans can split a kingdom. There is, however, an earlier and less obvious pivot in Book X, Chapter 31 – the "worst lay" episode. Lonazep involves violent action, revealing that the stability of Arthur's kingdom rests upon the thinnest of edges. But the actions of Dinadan and the appearance of Eliot the harper might be seen as the *Morte*'s contemplative centre. We may remember the letter which the Maid of Astolat holds in her hand and the letter that Gawaine composes on his death-bed. To a greater extent than anywhere else in the *Morte*, however, Book X in general and the "worst lay" episode in particular involves acts of reading and of writing, letters sent and received – for "goodly" and for wicked ends. This correspondence preserves courtly forms, just as tournaments follow the rules of chivalry. Yet, like the tournaments, the letters which pass between Camelot and Tintagil simultaneously conserve and subvert the Arthurian order. Writing – and reading – sustains this world and undermines it irreparably.[251]

Macleod sees the importance of the "worst lay" scene: she places it at the end of the Tristram story, where it immediately precedes her account of the quest for the Grail. The episode therefore provides an upward impulse before the inevitable downturn. It is, in effect, the last time that Arthurian society is able to renew itself. After this, the story is one of dispersal and death. When the harper finishes his song, King Mark is "wonderfully wroth". And Arthur Walker, Macleod's illustrator, went so far as to picture the scene in an illustration whose title is drawn from Mark's angry words to the harper: "how darest thou be so bold as to sing this song before me?" When he looked at this picture as a boy, it's possible that Eliot found the text which he held in his hands

FIGURE 11 Eliot the harper. A. G. Walker's illustration in Mary Macleod's *The Book of King Arthur and His Noble Knights* (p. 314). Reproduced by kind permission of the Syndics of Cambridge University Library (1900.8.384).

suddenly transformed into the strangest of mirrors. For the harper in the court of King Mark went by his own name – Eliot.[252]

It wasn't a matter of plot or character or even of Malory's motifs, though some of these would later turn up in "The Waste Land". Macleod's version of the *Morte* might have given the young Eliot an unforgettable vista. For the first time, he could see an entire civilization – the culture whose collapse was later commemorated in what is widely regarded as his finest poem. But how did Eliot respond to the "worst lay" episode in particular? What did he think in 1900 when he read *The Book of King Arthur* or in 1934 when he recalled his childhood reading in the *Spectator* review? If Walker's illustration gave Eliot an early vision of the vocation of a poet, which aspect of this image appealed most strongly? Was it the fact that a singer in the age of Arthur could play as effective a part as a knight (more so, since swords are less subtle than songs)? Such a conception of poetic prowess might well have appealed to the bookish boy as well as to the mature intellectual. Perhaps the "worst lay" episode gave Eliot an insight into poetic freedom: the harper can tell truth to power and get away with it, since his right to safe passage is respected even by so conniving a ruler as Mark. Or maybe the message – to the older if not the younger Eliot – was one of humility: perhaps the singer was merely a medium, and never owned his song. King Mark finds Eliot "bold", but the harper's response to his question – which appeared directly below the illustration – emphasizes obedience rather than defiance:

> "Sir", said Eliot, "wit you well, I am a minstrel, and I must do as I am commanded by those lords whose arms I bear. Sir Dinadan, a knight of the Round Table, made this song, and bade me sing it before you".[253]

In the "worst lay" episode, it is Dinadan and not Eliot the harper who is the 'author'. And if, as is likely, the young T. S. Eliot wondered about the connections between himself and his namesake, he might also have thought about Dinadan – in many ways the strangest figure in the *Morte d'Arthur* as well as the most modern. Dinadan – Sir Dinadan – is a knight, a card-carrying member of the Arthurian ruling class and not some court fool. His japes bring laughter to the hall at Camelot; without him, the faces of Arthur's knights and ladies would remain forever fixed, like portraits in an empty hall. But this comic gift goes deeper: Dinadan is a "scoffer" as well as a "japer", and his scoffing reveals his weariness with the courtly ways of Arthur's world, his reluctance to obey the chivalric code unquestioningly.[254]

Did Eliot identify with Dinadan's scepticism? Might he have seen Dinadan as a representative of 'tradition', with the 'individual talent' supplied by Eliot the harper? It's impossible to tell. But it is difficult not to read "The Waste Land" in the light of the "worst lay" episode: the poem mocks a corrupt order and seems designed to make some modern Mark "wonderfully wroth". "Disruptive, shocking . . . scandalizing . . . anarchical": Steve Ellis puts his finger on the "sheer heady power" of "The Waste Land". It was a poem about depression and loss, but it also raged and mocked and – like Dinadan – scoffed. Dinadan's antics had deeper meanings, and so had Eliot's. Norris J. Lacy suggests that readers pursuing the quest motif in "The Waste Land" are on a "wild goose chase". "A few references to the Fisher King, the general symbol of the wasteland . . . a couple of allusions to the story of Tristram and Isolt": as Alan and Barbara Lupack observe, "the actual Arthurian content of the poem is slight". Beverly Taylor and Elisabeth Brewer point to a series of absences: "there is no quest, no hero, no Grail city or castle, no lance or cup". But that's the point: to look into the "heart of light" may be to find only "silence" – an empty chapel with no windows. This is disappointing and even absurd, but it is also tragic. Eliot writes about April rather than May as the "cruellest month", yet his sense of spring's fatality came not from Tennyson but from Malory.[255]

It would be hard to say – as Burne-Jones had of the "Idylls" – that Eliot gave his readers "what they wanted" in "The Waste Land". Indeed, Eliot's poem might usefully be read as an inversion of Tennyson's. It goes without saying that Eliot was no supporter of mass democracy. This was the man who, in 1928 – the year after he took British citizenship and converted to Anglicanism – described himself as a "classicist in literature, royalist in politics, and anglo-catholic in religion". Eliot's interest in the figure of the maimed king, and more particularly in what might be done to heal him, articulated an elitist politics: if the waste land is to flower, change must be introduced from above. Tennyson also saw problems at the top of his society: the "Idylls" was about nothing if not about elite corruption. But whilst the political views of the two poets might have begun similarly they ended in very different places. Tennyson didn't think much about the lower orders, assuming that they were mainly happy with their lot. His greatest fear was of regression – a return to the values of the past. Eliot rather liked the past, in contrast: he was worried by a lowering of values and standards, not by a reversion to the old order.[256]

In part, Eliot's references to Tennyson in the 1920s involve rejection and reversal. But the relationship between Eliot and Tennyson was also a strangely doubled and mirrored one. Several critics have noted that Eliot was deeply influenced by Tennyson in his youth, though he probably read Malory before turning to the "Idylls". Nancy Hargrove has further demonstrated that, far from rejecting the example of Tennyson, Eliot called on the work of his predecessor as part of a "general method". Most intriguingly, James E. Miller sees the 1932 essay on "In Memoriam" – and specifically Eliot's observation that Tennyson had by some "strange accident" expressed "the mood of his generation" whilst expressing "a mood of his own" – as an oblique comment on "The Waste Land" and evidence of "deep identification". Eliot's line about the "surface" and the "depths" – and the sense of movement between – is for Miller a "surprising and revealing" insight: Eliot is "talking indirectly about himself". It's true that Eliot would not (at least after his conversion) have been persuaded by Tennyson's Anglicanism, evident in the treatment of the Eucharist in "The Holy Grail". He probably shared Burne-Jones's interest in the Oxford Movement and Newman's emphasis on the "unseen", though he was too much of a loner to have dreamed of an Arthurian brotherhood. For Eliot as for Burne-Jones, the Grail was not simply a vessel; nor was the taking of bread and wine merely symbolic. "The Waste Land" was no idyll: Eliot subjected Tennyson's melancholic scenes to a process of fragmentation – broken lines for a broken time – which magnified intensity. And yet although his waste land came from Thomas Malory, it came by way of Alfred Tennyson. John Ruskin's words are as appropriate a response to "The Waste Land" as to the "Idylls":

> on the whole, these are much *sadder* ages than the early ones; not sadder in a noble and deep way, but in a dim wearied way, – the way of ennui, and jaded intellect . . . the Middle Ages had their wars and agonies, but also intense delights. Their gold was dashed with blood, but ours is sprinkled with dust.[257]

The Book of King Arthur provided – by way of Malory – a complex image of the poet's task. And the resonances didn't end with the idea of the poet as principled sentinel. For Dinadan's intercession ultimately fails: he puts King Mark in his place, but the rifts already evident in Arthurian society cannot be repaired. Writing can right the wrongs that writing in part has caused; truth can be heard, and for a time violence can be circumvented. But writing – and reading – will also articulate what once was tacit. Writing will foment resentments; it will deepen wounds. In the end, writing won't help Arthur, Launcelot or Guenever. It won't defeat King Mark – or Mordred, or Gawaine. It won't save

Dinadan. And after the episode of the "worst lay", Eliot the harper is never heard of again.

It's not surprising that Terry Pratchett imagines young Arthur, in the London churchyard, pulling the sword from the stone "without bothering to read the inscription". Malory's Arthur reads and writes letters at various points in the narrative but his literary capacities are indeed incidental to his kingship. One is rather surprised when Gawaine writes Launcelot a letter, and Launcelot himself is clearly no penman. In a number of cases, Malory associates literacy with malice: Morgan is a "clerk" of necromancy; Mark excels in counterfeit letters; Mordred becomes king after forging letters which report that Arthur has been "slain in battle".[258]

I've suggested that Book X of the *Morte* shows us a society in which literacy becomes an instrument of destruction as well as of creation. The fact that this insight is itself contained within a book is ironic. And yet (as I suspect Thomas Malory and Thomas Stearns Eliot both knew), the irony is a doubled and redoubled one. Dinadan is no Tristram, though it's possible that Eliot identified with the former as a type of the modern poet who is able to rupture established forms and to twist his native tongue to various tasks. But I think Eliot also wanted, if only indirectly, to retain some identification with Tristram as well as Dinadan: the "individual talent" needed to sustain "tradition" as well as to break with it. What, then, should we make of the connection between the poet of "The Waste Land" and the japing author of the worst lay? We've seen that Dinadan's literary efforts have only a limited and temporary effect. But Malory's point in Book X – and here again we see the architectural qualities of the *Morte* where we least expect to find them – is a sharper one. The tournament at Lonazep is overshadowed by news of Lamorak's death at the hands of Mordred. But many of Dinadan's actions – not the initial mockery of King Mark, but certainly the later orchestration of the worst lay episode, together with the description of Dinadan as a "scoffer and a japer", the practical joke on Galahalt, and the sceptical speech to Isoud about the merits of love – all these occur after and in the light of something which Malory discloses in Chapter 25 of Book X. It's at this point – before Surluse and Lonazep – that we are told how Mordred and Agravaine "cowardly and feloniously . . . slew Dinadan" during the quest for the Holy Grail. Long before the murder of Lamorak, then, the vengeance of clan Lot has been set in motion. All of Dinadan's efforts on behalf of the Arthurian order fall under the shadow of his death. Malory may have identified with Launcelot, but it is possible that Dinadan was also a "self-character".[259]

20

Merry England

I have argued that the influence of Malory isn't only evident in major works like "The Waste Land" and the "Idylls of the King". It's also present in in numerous adaptations and in the more general cultural landscape. But the word 'influence' hardly conveys the pervasiveness of the *Morte*. Take *The Wind in the Willows* as an example. It would be easy to argue that Kenneth Grahame's imaginative wellsprings were primarily classical. The central chapter of *The Wind in the Willows*, "The Piper at the Gates of Dawn", describes an encounter between Pan and his uncomprehending worshippers, the Rat and the Mole. The final chapter goes by a positively Homeric title: "The Return of Ulysses". Yet Grahame quietly strikes other notes. One of these can be heard as the animals finish their supper in "great joy and contentment". I'm reminded of Malory's reference to "joy and mirths" at court and to the knights riding out in "great joy and delights".[260]

That echo may well be coincidental. But Grahame published *The Wind in the Willows* in 1908, when the Victorian enthusiasm for things Arthurian remained intense. In 1906, J. Comyns Carr followed *King Arthur* with a further play, *Tristram and Iseult*. The following year saw the publication of *The Story of Launcelot and His Companions*, the third episode in Howard Pyle's Arthurian cycle. And in 1909, Vitagraph brought out a film, *Lancelot and Elaine*. Grahame came at the material less directly. But no account of Toad would be complete unless it noted his resemblance to Launcelot. Toad is a Launcelot *manqué*, of course. But Grahame's "Terror of the Highway" is an obvious case of 'bobaunce'. And critical reactions to Launcelot remind one of Toad: Terence McCarthy describes him as an "overgrown adolescent"; Mark Lambert argues still more suggestively that his love for Guenever is a case, not of "theft or fraud", but of "reckless driving".[261]

Grahame's most sustained reworking of the *Morte* comes in the chapters which surround "The Piper at the Gates of Dawn". In the final lines of Chapter 6, Toad is sentenced for reckless driving and becomes a prisoner in the "remotest dungeon of . . . the stoutest castle in all the length and breadth of Merry England". The story of his imprisonment is taken up in Chapter 8. Having been given a steaming plate of bubble-and-squeak by the gaoler's daughter, Toad cheers up and thinks of "chivalry . . . and deeds still to be done". He imagines that his female attendant feels a "growing tenderness" for him (in fact, she merely wants a pet). This scene is based on Malory's description of Launcelot's imprisonment by Meliagrance in Book XIX of the *Morte*. There's no bubble-and-squeak in the *Morte*, though Launcelot receives "his meat and his drink" from a "lady" who, as Malory tells us, "wooed him, to have lain by him". Seeing how the land lies, Launcelot purchases his release with a kiss. Toad lacks his precursor's sexual charisma but, with the assistance of the gaoler's daughter, escapes from prison in the garb of a washerwoman. But if we jump to the conclusion that this act of cross-dressing severs all links between Toad and his Arthurian counterpart, we should remember that Launcelot elsewhere disguises himself in a "maiden's garment".[262]

I was familiar with *The Wind in the Willows* when I read *King Arthur* in 1970. But I doubt if I thought about Kenneth Grahame when Phyllis Briggs described Launcelot procuring his release. Had the similarity between the two passages been pointed out to me I might have explained it in terms of the shapes that stories create: heroes must be imprisoned because their freedom would otherwise be illimitable, and they must be released, for otherwise they would not be heroes. But whether or not there is a wider case to be made about imprisonment and narrative, there's no doubt that Grahame is indebted to Malory in Chapter 8 of *The Wind in the Willows*. The same is true, more intriguingly, when Grahame refers to "Merry England" in Chapter 6. The words gain prominence because they are the final ones of the chapter. As the *Oxford English Dictionary* notes, the phrase 'merry England' – an England "characterised by the robust cheerfulness of its people" – is "freq. humorous or ironic". That's certainly true in *The Wind in the Willows*: it is hardly merry England for poor old Toad. But was the usage "humorous or ironic" in the third source cited by the *OED* – a reference in the *Morte d'Arthur* to "oure noble knyghtes of mery Ingelonde"?[263]

The reference to "mery Ingelonde" occurs during the account of Arthur's campaign against Lucius and, with the final tragedy some way in the future, it seems unlikely that Malory means the line in anything other than its straightforward and literal sense. And yet, I don't think the line can be taken at face value. A first-time reader may not notice it, but everything in the *Morte* is touched by the shadow of events to come. "Oure noble knyghtes": Malory is speaking here of Arthur, Launcelot and Gawaine – each of them on the same side, the representatives of a unified order. The fact that they are "oure" knights is extremely suggestive, for that collective pronoun will be less accessible if we look forward to Malory's remarks in Book XXI on the "great default of us Englishmen". In that book, Joyous Gard becomes a place of "dolour", and by this time it would seem that "mery Ingelonde" has in the same way been transformed. But this, of course, is an instance of a familiar logic, for it is in May, "when every heart flourisheth", that Arthur's kingdom is brought down by "anger and unhap".[264]

Yet Grahame's reference to "merry England" can't possibly be a conscious allusion. *The Wind in the Willows* was published nearly forty years before Vinaver completed his edition of the Winchester manuscript, and the phrase "mery Ingelonde" appears in that version of the *Morte* and not in Caxton. Grahame is clearly making use of the *Morte* in Chapter 8, so it's only a minor point. One nevertheless feels let down – until one realizes that the wonder lies deeper. As John Steinbeck observed, Malory's words are "alive even in those of us who have not read them".[265]

I wouldn't have known that Malory had written about 'merry England' when my father read *The Wind in the Willows* to me at bedtime, and Briggs doesn't use the phrase in her retelling. As a child, however, the word 'merry' was already lodged in my mind. The family knew that 'Lustig' meant 'merry' in German, though I wondered from an early age (knowing the word 'lust' whilst being vague about its meaning) whether this wasn't euphemistic.[266] My point, however, is not that Malory found his way into my own lexicon but that he is present in the national one. The *Morte d'Arthur* changed the language we speak. When Malory describes Dinadan as a "scoffer", he is, according to the *OED*, the first to have used this word. And there are seventy-eight other instances in which the *Morte* provides the earliest evidence of a word coming into English: examples include 'adulterous', 'communal' and 'courage'; 'daffish', 'lamentably' and 'manhandle'. Still more fittingly, Malory is the first known source for the word 'unhappiness'.[267]

But what of Malory's role in the development, not of the English language, but of English literature? For Richard Altick, Malory is the "first master of English prose narrative"; Muriel Bradbrook asserts that the *Morte* stands at the "centre of English literature". Larry O. Benson sees the *Morte* as part of the "permanent canon of English literature"; for P. J. C. Field, Malory is the "first major prose writer of English fiction". These views – formed between the late 1950s and the early 1970s – are not unprecedented. Towards the end of the nineteenth century, as we have seen, critics such as Strachey, Raleigh and Saintsbury were speaking of Malory as a master of "English prose".

Earlier still, Scott remarked on Malory's "excellent old English". The *Morte*, as Scott observed in *Marmion*, was "written in pure old English" and "told with a simplicity bordering upon the sublime". Readers in the 1800s were drawn to Malory, but didn't think of him as 'central', 'permanent' or 'major'. In the 1930s, Eliot remembered being fascinated by Malory as a boy. As shining examples of 'English literature', however, he would have cited other names (Spenser, Shakespeare, Milton or Donne) before that of Malory. It was only in the second half of the twentieth century that the *Morte* was widely recognized as a great work. Its prominent place within 'English literature' was generally acknowledged. Less commonly mentioned was the text's contribution to a notion of 'Englishness'.[268]

Any idea that Malory's writing is fundamentally 'English' would be rejected by several critics. C. S. Lewis followed Southey rather than Strachey when he argued that Malory had "no style of his own"; for Derek Brewer likewise, Malory dissolved into his sources. Vinaver's verdict was particularly forceful: in 1929 he argued that Malory "invented little"; in 1947, he still thought that, of the "great prose writers of all time", Malory was "perhaps the one who 'invented' least". The Arthurian stories had their source in ninth-century Wales; three hundred years later, Geoffrey of Monmouth's tales whetted the appetite of the Normans, who dished them up in mainland Europe. After a further three centuries (now richly marinaded) those legends were served again in England. But one cannot say that the story of Arthur had at last come home: in P. J. C. Field's view, the *Morte* is a monument to French "cultural hegemony".[269]

It's a bit of a let-down: the work which became a "foundation text for English readers" was actually, as Andrew Lynch observes, "a latecomer" in the field. One might respond to these observations by identifying episodes in the *Morte* which have no known source (the tale of Gareth or the healing of Urre, for example). But Malory himself isn't of much help here: he claims to have had the story of Gareth from another "book" and mentions a "French book" after Urre is healed. Still: we know that 'Ingelonde' was central to Malory's design. Arthur may claim to be descended from the Romans but he is first and foremost king of "all England". Malory was no cartographer but his tale took place (as Edmund Reiss puts it) in an "English world". And it wasn't just a matter of changing the signposts along the grassy path of romance, for Malory systematically anglicised his sources. In doing so he was creating an English readership.[270]

But what did 'English' mean in 1470? Eric Hobsbawm suggests that the "modern sense" of the word 'nation' is "no older than the eighteenth century". Moreover, the idea of a specifically *English* nationalism "sounds odd to many ears". This, for Tom Nairn, is the "English enigma". One can be vehemently Welsh, Scottish or Irish – but such identities emerged in resistance to a more powerful and also more amorphous nation. Our leaders once persuaded us that we were citizens of 'Great Britain' or the 'United Kingdom'. In the last half century, however, the 'great' and the 'united' have begun to seem less self-evident. The question of England meanwhile became a *point de repère* in academic studies, works for a wider audience and discussions in the media. But whose England? Written as German aeroplanes rained bombs on British cities in the autumn of 1941, George Orwell's reflections on national identity bore little resemblance to Malory's. His England was a place where the beer was "bitterer", the coins "heavier" and the grass "greener" – a country of commoners with "mild knobby faces" and "bad teeth". In this landscape the nearest thing to a tournament was the spectacle of "old maids biking to Holy Communion through the mists of the autumn mornings". On the evidence of the *Morte d'Arthur*, Malory had little interest in alcohol or money, and none at all in physiognomy, dentistry or meteorology. Absurd as it sometimes seems, however, the image of Arthurian England which Malory created has, against all odds, maintained its potency. It's not about ideology. One sees it, rather, in Malory's attitude to his subject matter. There is a gentleness of attention here, a kind of watchful reticence. It's impossible to pin it down – but the very ineffability is part of it, for 'England' is a matter of feeling rather than thinking.[271]

157

CHAPTER

21

Style

It may be true that nationalism in its 'modern' meaning – the sense of the nation as a political entity – didn't exist until the eighteenth century. But 'modernity' didn't happen overnight. According to Hobsbawm, nationalism was in essence a consequence of the French Revolution. Yet the events of 1789 were a reaction to the *ancien régime* – an order which would have been recognizable to those who lived at the end of the Hundred Years' War. Malory didn't predict that nations would one day consist of citizens who voted for their political representatives, of course. His England had no common culture: what mattered to him was the system of affinities. During Malory's lifetime, however, failure at home and abroad sharpened the sense of nationhood as much as earlier triumph: modern meanings are coming through in York's comments on the loss suffered by the "English nation" as a result of Suffolk's French campaign. Malory's knights don't think of themselves as English in the way we might do now, but Kenneth Hodges is nevertheless right to see "proto-nationalist sentiment" in the *Morte*. And Hodges goes further: the fact that Malory "imagined" England suggests that it was already a "modern nation". Hobsbawm sees the danger of projecting present meanings onto the past, even (or especially) when the words have remained the same. But this obscures the connections which run through time. Higham argues that the *Historia Brittonum* articulated a notion of 'Britishness' as early as the ninth century, when the story of Arthur was an "aspect of nationalist rhetoric". The notion of Britishness may have been "constructed outside Britain" and even when it took hold remained an "élite phenomenon". But one can nevertheless speak of "national identity" a thousand years ago and more.[272]

We are touching here on the longstanding debate between 'modernists' (historians who, according to John Kerrigan, believe that nations were "constructed over the last couple of centuries to provide a focus of loyalty for populations deracinated by industrialization") and 'primordialists' (who feel that nations "grow out of long-established . . . mentalities, ethnically and dynastically configured"). Hobsbawm is a modernist. Like many (but by no means all) Arthurian scholars, Hodges and Higham are primordialists. There are merits in both positions, merits too in their criticisms of each other. But it's surely true – obvious, even – that the English are not unique in having forged complicated relationships – ones with sufficient stability to have been described and disputed, enough solidity to have fought and died for. In one tradition, trumpets blare for King and Country. Agincourt, Trafalgar, Waterloo: the story here is one of success, often achieved against the odds; of progress upon approved Whig lines; of freedom and independence. In another and more thoughtful tradition, however – one which Raymond Williams records – English 'culture and society' thought expresses resistance to the governing order and proclaims human values in the 'long revolution' of democratic socialism. It's not the battles which are celebrated, but the people: the Peasants' Revolt, the Diggers and the Levellers, Ned Ludd, Tom Paine and the Tolpuddle Martyrs, the Chartists, the suffragettes, and those who fought the Fascists on Cable Street. Yet perhaps both these discourses are merely alternatives to another and earlier vision. We see it in Malory's remarks on the "great default" of the English, that "there may no thing please us no term": that discontent, and the sadness it breeds, is the oldest narrative of all.[273]

Malory's sense of the failure of "us Englishmen" is fundamental to the story of Arthur. That failure is central even when (as in Geoffrey of Monmouth) Arthur is British rather than English. At the beginning of *The History of the Kings of Britain*, Geoffrey describes how the Britons, living in the "best of islands", forfeited their lands through "arrogance". A similar sense of insufficiency and loss pre-dates even the 'matter of Britain': in *De Excidio Britanniae* (c. 540), Gildas never mentions Arthur but berates his fellow Britons for their ingratitude, haughtiness and disobedience. Unhappiness, disaffection, an unparalleled ability to screw things up: the picture may not appeal to those on the left or the right of the political spectrum and yet, from Gildas the Briton to Malory the Englishman, these seem to have been prominent components of the national character. And the idea that we can speak of such national continuities is strengthened by the fact that past times can sometimes seem uncannily contemporary. In Book X of the *Morte*, Dinadan tells Tristram of the tournament at Surluse, saying that it compared favourably with Lonazep: there was at Surluse, he says, "as great a gathering as is here, for there were many nations". "Nations": it is the only use of this word in the *Morte*, and Malory nowhere refers to England as a 'nation' in the singular. The plural suggests that Arthur's England is fundamentally divided. We are not just at the centre of

Malory's narrative but at the heart of his purpose. That being so, it's entirely appropriate that it is Dinadan who finds the word to describe a new reality.[274]

There's little doubt that the *Morte* contributed to what Caroline Eckhardt calls the "discourse around the growth of English national identity". Malory was a self-consciously English writer addressing an English readership. But it's more than this: Malory's crucial move was to make Arthur the King, not of 'Britain' (as he was for Geoffrey of Monmouth) but of England – 'Ingelonde'. Previous writers created a body of work which came to be called the 'matter of Britain'. Malory's subject was the matter of England. It was serious, it was substantial; it was the primary issue, the immediate instance. But it was also a problem, a question everywhere implied: what was the 'matter' of this island nation, the marrow in its bones? And also: what was the matter with England?[275]

Malory was a product of his age: his views didn't spring fully formed out of his own head. Noting that Arthur is "king of England, not of Britain", Felicity Riddy adopts a primordialist position: for her, Malory is writing from a specifically "English point of view". His handling of the French sources isn't simply a matter of "translation" but of "narrative perspective". Malory was writing during the "worst political crisis England had known since the Norman conquest". He was also concerned by the "larger failure of Englishness" represented by the loss of the French dominions in 1453. In the ensuing years, the English upper classes turned inward, warming themselves by the glowing coals of failure. They settled down to read a myth of their former greatness, and it was called *Le Morte d'Arthur*.[276]

For Riddy, the *Morte d'Arthur* "sustains and is sustained by the ideology of aristocracy". Yet although Malory's sense of the nation must have been inflected by particular loyalties, he wasn't merely an "ideological mouthpiece", as Jeremy Smith would have us believe. To the extent that Arthurian romance was, as Elizabeth Pochoda puts it, a courtly society's "advertisement for itself" it could indeed be described as propaganda. But the propaganda of those who feel themselves to be losers is quite different to that of the victors. For Pochoda, the "central paradox" of the *Morte* is that what began as "establishment myth" turned into "exposé". Hodges would agree that the *Morte* does not promote "simple national unity". In spite of initial appearances, Malory's imagined England is an unstable and ambiguous place.[277]

I may have exaggerated the differences between primordialists and modernists. Malory's critics incline to primordialism but few of them would reject the strictures of a modernist like Hobsbawm. Nor would

Hobsbawm be unable to accept the arguments of primordialists. Indeed, he makes some of these arguments himself, writing, for example, that an "élite literary or administrative language . . . can become an important element of proto-nationalist cohesion". Elements of a national identity – of an English identity in this case – have pre-modern sources in élite language, élite literature, and presumably also in an élite text like the *Morte*. Hobsbawm suggests that we can see "something close to modern patriotism" in the plays of Shakespeare. If so, the case for another Warwickshire writer becomes stronger – and Malory's 'patriotism' is at least as sad and as wise as Shakespeare's.[278]

Alan Lupack opens a recent discussion of the *Morte* by observing that "no romance has been more influential or more adapted and reworked". I have only been able to trace a few salient instances of the *Morte*'s remarkable afterlife in the work of the Romantics and Victorians. My discussion of Malory's prominence as a reference point for twentieth-century writers has been equally selective. We can nevertheless see that for Phyllis Briggs and Edward Arlington Robinson, for David Jones and T. S. Eliot, it was the predicament of nations at war which underlined the relevance of the *Morte*. And it is not clear what is at stake in the representation of Arthur and his knights unless we turn from the *Morte* to the Arthurian legend as a whole. After the English Civil War, as Higham argues, Arthur was superseded by Alfred as the "founding father" of the "Anglo-centric British state", the "quintessential English hero-type". English liberty was Anglo-Saxon in origin: this, according to Higham, was the "mantra of late-Victorian historiography". The kingdom was ruled by the House of Hanover from the accession of George I in 1714 to the death of Victoria in 1901. After the outbreak of war in 1914, however, the "entire Anglo-Saxonist/Germanist historical enterprise" began, in Higham's view, to founder. King Alfred didn't immediately vanish from the scene in August 1914. The Germanist consensus endured long enough to be further damaged by the outbreak of war in 1939. In the following decades, the loss of "world empire and . . . political and economic leadership" was disorientating. Notions of a Saxon Englishness lost their appeal; we wanted instead to see ourselves as British. Before he was finally "consigned to the margins of academic history", we needed King Arthur once again. This shift of sensibilities found its most complete expression in John Morris's *The Age of Arthur* (1973). For Morris, Arthur was a British warlord who resisted the Saxon hordes. This was Dark Age history but Morris was also, as Higham points out, telling his own story and that of the "European conflicts which had framed his world".[279]

Born in 1913, Morris read history at Jesus College, Oxford. He was a peace campaigner during the 1930s but fought in the Second World War. From 1948 until his death in 1977, he taught at University College, London. Like the subject of his book, however, Morris ended up on the margins. Indeed, his Wikipedia entry – there is nothing in the *DNB* – notes that the publication of *The Age of Arthur* "severely damaged" his reputation in the eyes of his peers, for whom the veneer of scholarship crumbled on closer inspection. As a child, I read *King Arthur and the Knights of the Round Table* and not *The Age of Arthur*. I wonder in retrospect, though, if my interest in Arthur was part of the shift described by Higham. A new Arthurianism is certainly detectable in Briggs's retelling of the story, in which allusions to the Second World War are plain. The young Arthur is crowned king of the "fair rolling lands of England". When invasion looms, however, it is the "rolling green lands of Britain" which are threatened. It is the "British fleet" which sets sail for France, the "British army" which enters Rome in triumph.[280]

But what is 'Britain' – or 'England'? I come back to Malory and to what J. A. W. Bennett calls the "specifically English qualities" of the *Morte*. When, in the late 1950s, Muriel Bradbrook argued that the *Morte*'s principal concern was the "masculine bond" she wasn't simply making a point about gender: Malory's lack of interest in the "artifice of courtly etiquette" differentiated him from the French romancers and established a national contrast. For Elizabeth Edwards, Malory's "coyness or prudery" about matters erotic and his oblique treatment of Launcelot and Guenever's adultery is distinctively English. Terence McCarthy takes the idea a stage further: with its scenes of "sophisticated infidelity", French romance is "basically feminine". In the *Morte*, by contrast, we see a "soldierly preference for . . . affairs of state".[281]

The idea that French romance is "feminine" is rather strange, since McCarthy presumably means only to suggest that (male) French writers were more interested than Malory in writing about adultery. Still, McCarthy invokes a familiar contrast: Englishness is 'masculine'; it is natural rather than artificial; it is seen on the battlefield rather than the boudoir. The idea that the *Morte* has comparatively little sexual content would have surprised Tennyson and Ascham. Yet this makes the point about national character all the more strongly: the notion that sexuality is un-English is an enduring instance of a typically English hypocrisy. The point in all this, however, is not that there's no sex in Malory – or not as much as in the French romances. It's that Malory saw sexuality in tragic terms. This isn't to say that the *Morte* always represents love as doomed: it may sometimes be fun and occasionally it lasts. In general, however, the pattern is a more sombre one – and this, too, belongs within the field of Englishness. Acts of incest and adultery structure the *Morte* – a text which has been variously described as "one of the finest tragedies in English literature", "perhaps the first true tragedy in English" and "one of the most finely conceived . . . tragic stories in the English language".[282]

When concepts like 'tragedy' are in the air, the critical waters rapidly become muddied.[283] But the status of the *Morte* as both a tragic narrative and a peculiarly English one depends less on ideas about literary genre than on something which looks like crudity but turns out to be a kind of finer feeling. This quality is present in the characters but can also be found in the words Malory uses, the things he makes us feel. For Bradbrook, Malory presents us with "earthly men and women" who want to enjoy "the good life of earth". If they lack the artificiality of courtiers, it is not because they are unacquainted with passion but because they know that life is short. Desire is a serious matter and should not be spoken of glibly. And this, for Bradbrook, is why Arthur's knights are characterized above all by their "taciturnity". Field likewise notes that in Malory the "wordy and sentimental" speech of characters in French romances gives way to a characteristic "brevity". It is the "terse, even elemental" speech of Malory's knights which makes them English.[284]

It's possible that I'm dealing here less with the typical than the stereotypical, less with what the English are than with what they'd like to be. But the tensions inherent in 'Englishness' – in the sensibility I'm trying to describe – become more evident when one turns from characters in the *Morte* to the character of Sir Thomas Malory. The *Morte* is indeed drawn more to the exploration of external rather than internal space, to cleaving rather than clipping. And this undoubtedly suggests a lack of interiority on the part of its author. Critics draw attention to Malory's deficiencies: Brewer writes of his "incapacity for abstract thought"; Lambert is clear that he is "not important as a thinker"; for McCarthy, the *Morte* "is not an intellectual book"; and, according to Field, Malory's mind was "strikingly unacademic". These are modern versions of the "sublime simplicity" which Scott found in Malory and which others find in the English character.[285]

John Burrow points to the irony that the "greatest Victorian poet to exploit the legends of Arthur was christened Alfred". Anglo-Saxon Alfred writing about British Arthur – the conformist ego conjuring a repressed precursor – it is positively Freudian. Tennyson was Malory's greatest nineteenth-century interpreter and in this respect if in no other, a case could be made for Eliot as Tennyson's twentieth-century equivalent. But the ironies of influence are sweeter still: the writer who is so often seen as incoherent, stupid, narrow and literalistic – a writer of 'prose' and no more – was a lifetime fascination for two great poets. When it comes to writing one should listen to writers. But critics too are writers. And although the scholars point to the *Morte*'s inconsistences and limitations they see something else as well. The *Morte* is mechanical, derivative – but according to C. S. Lewis, Malory's prose is "as musical, as forthright, as poignant, as was ever heard in England". For Derek Brewer, Malory lacks "conscious artistry" but nevertheless manages to create an unparalleled "richness of feeling". The "simple declarative sentences" of the *Morte* are "primitive", but P. J. C. Field goes on to assert that Malory "calls forth the strongest degree of evoked emotional response . . . in any English author of major literary status".[286]

Realistic; practical; down-to-earth: this, for Mark Lambert, is the "ale-and-roast-beef" account of Malory as a "good English writer". But that version of Englishness only gets us so far. Something more interesting is going on in the *Morte*: Malory manages to create a "particular country of the mind". His techniques are simple in themselves, but their cumulative effect is one of complexity. We read the *Morte* and "glimpse unnamed patternings . . . under the surface of the world we know". It's in the gap between emotion and articulation – at the point when words fail – that the English tragedy unfolds and feeling soars. And the source of this "strange magnetism", as Eugène Vinaver wrote in 1929 – some years before he had heard of the manuscript to which he was to devote years of his life – lay in the "mysterious power of style".[287]

Conclusion

I began this book with observations about the form of the Arthurian narrative; I'm ending it with reflections on style. And not just the fact of style, as if it was a pint of beer or a loaf of bread. That would leave us with the roast beef Malory ('paratactic', 'factual') and miss Vinaver's point. Between 1969 and 1981 – in the years between reading Phyllis Briggs and Thomas Malory – my understanding of 'style' was bound up with fashions in such things as shoes, satchels, shorts and shirts. To have 'style' – to be 'stylish' – wasn't a matter of brushing one's hair and being tidy: quite the reverse. Style flouted convention: it was about wildness and waste. I could see that in Sir Launcelot more clearly than in Mick Jagger. But how can so personal and idiosyncratic an understanding of style be of any assistance when it comes to the mystery of Thomas Malory?

In "The Metaphysical Poets", Eliot introduces a familiar distinction between style and substance. Tennyson was a case of 'dissociation' because his technical facility exceeded his intellectual capacity: ideas and feelings didn't work together as a sinuous and simultaneous experience. I don't know if Eliot would have said that Malory felt what he thought, like Donne. But there's no doubt that Malory's current ran deep in Eliot's mind. He was never a prominent reference point, like Tennyson or Milton. But in 1922 a note was struck in "The Waste Land". Malory was obliquely present when Eliot wrote about Tennyson in 1932. One needed to know the "Idylls" in order to see the greatness of "In Memoriam", but Tennyson's adaptation of the *Morte* exposed his conformism. Then, in 1934, there is Eliot's admission that he read the *Morte* at the age of eleven or twelve and that it was "my favourite book". This disclosure was made in a minor piece of work. But the pattern is visible, and it persists: Malory was present in 1937 when Eliot wrote the introduction to *In Parenthesis*. He was there again when Eliot returned to the "Idylls" in 1942. Tennyson had turned the *Morte* into suitable reading for a girls' school – unlike David Jones. In the case of another monument of literary modernism, Eliot might not have been so complimentary. But here again the *Morte* was in the wings.[288]

On 16 June 1904, Leopold Bloom visits a maternity hospital in

Holles Street in order to attend Mrs Purefoy's confinement. Full well has foetus formed, but no bouncing bantling is bare breast bound. For the action of the 'Oxen of the Sun' chapter in *Ulysses* proceeds by means of an extended chronological parody of English narrative styles, from alliterative poetry and medieval travel writing to Bunyan and Pepys and then, by way of Fielding and Dickens, to journalism and cheap romance. At an early point in this bravura passage we encounter "Sir Leopold" and, in a version of Ector's lament in Book XXI of the *Morte*, are told that he is "the goodliest guest", the "meekest man and the kindest . . . the very truest knight of the world". In Joyce's novel, Bloom is and isn't Ulysses; now, in cameo, he is and is not Sir Launcelot.[289]

The Malory passage in 'Oxen of the Sun' begins with the familiar Pentecostal scene: "And whiles they spake the door of the castle was opened and there nighed them a mickle noise as of many that sat there at meat". To those whose are attuned to Malory's style, there are several reasons to find this sentence ham-fisted.

(1) In Malory, pavilions, prisons, chapels and chambers have doors. But when castles have doors, these lead into chambers located within. Malory would never have written of the main entrance as "the door of the castle".
(2) The word "nighed" is used on only one occasion in the *Morte* and is therefore uncharacteristic.
(3) The word "mickle" is used on eight occasions in the *Morte*, but always as a synonym of 'much' and not of 'great'.
(4) Malory's knights go "to" or "unto" their meat, but nobody ever sits "at" meat.

Joyce isn't completely incompetent. For the kind Sir Leopold, the cries of pain in the hospital "dureth overlong". This is a nice touch, as is the line about Bloom speaking "full gently". But the reference to a "franklin" doesn't come from the *Morte*. And the hospital sister's request that the men in attendance should "leave their wassailing" strikes another false note: there is no wassailing in the *Morte d'Arthur*.[290]

In *Ulysses*, Joyce gives us a petit bourgeois version of Malory. The style of the original must stretch to fit the subject, of course. But if it is to make the point it should not be torn. Joyce appears to think that Malory's style is cluttered: he doesn't see the spareness. But still, the mash-up in *Ulysses* at least serves to underline the *Morte*'s extraordinary ability to survive. Modernists rejected the work of their Victorian forbears, and Eliot told Virginia Woolf that *Ulysses* "would be a land-mark, because it destroyed the whole of the 19th Century". But it certainly didn't destroy the fifteenth century. Malory remained as important to Eliot, and perhaps even to Joyce, as he had been to Tennyson and Burne-Jones. As far as I know, Eliot never discussed Bloom's translation into Launcelot. But he knew the 'Oxen of the Sun' chapter: Virginia Woolf reported him saying that Joyce's parodies "showed up the futility of all the English styles". In *The Implied Reader* (1974), Wolfgang Iser developed this idea, arguing that Joyce shows us the "latent comedy" of style. For Iser, style contains an "ideology" which reduces "reality". The comedy consists in exposing the "naiveté" of those writers who assume that their style captures reality. In fact, according to Iser, style offers a distortion of reality rather than "reality itself".[291]

In the case of the *Morte*, one can see where Iser – and perhaps both Joyce and Eliot – might go with this notion. The comedy would consist in the fact that the style of the *Morte* is shaped by an "ideal of Christian knighthood" which is incapable of dealing with "love and procreation". We couldn't be further from Vinaver's observation about style's "mysterious power". For Iser (and for Iser's Joyce), style represents a false fixity which must be avoided: *Ulysses* sets "both object and observer in motion". But Iser is surely wrong to present style as a "problem" and to argue that it "fails to achieve its ends". Iser insists that things are relative and reality is complex – but these are platitudes. Of course style involves judgements which are "historically precondi-tioned". For Iser, there is the world of reality and the realm of literature and the latter provides a misleading account of the former. But this way of looking at things is hardly complex or relativistic or dynamic. To describe Leopold Bloom as "meekest", "kindest" and "truest" is not necessarily to show that Malory's style is either problematic or insuffi-cient. It is to provide a description which draws our attention to the ways in which Bloom both resembles and is different to Launcelot – a description which moves us as much by the differences as by the simi-larities. One need not conclude that style and substance are forever sundered, that appearance and reality can never coincide, that past and present are wholly different, or that any of these terms are either 'good' or 'bad'. One might instead think parabolically. Style constitutes rather than concealing reality.[292]

In 1907, Henry James described another and more famous literary son of Warwickshire as a "monster and magician of a thousand masks". One could trace his successive plunges "into Romeo and into Juliet, into Shylock, Hamlet, Macbeth, Coriolanus, Cleopatra, Anthony, Lear, Othello, Falstaff, Hotspur". But "the man himself" was "positively nowhere". Shakespeare sank into the sea of himself: all that remained was "the lucid stillness of his style". Something similar may go for Malory. Perhaps we see only the masks: Arthur and Guenever, Mordred, Dinadan, King Mark, Tristram, Morgan, Launcelot, Pelles, Palomides, Dagonet, Gawaine. Perhaps, in the end, there is only Malory's 'style'.[293]

In the end, Malory seems to have been more interested by the ways in which human relationships break down than by those in which they are maintained. I wonder whether or not the stories we tell are compatible with the idea of progress. To fail to be what we ought to be: the story grips the artist-sadist and gives the masochist-reader sweet pain. At any rate, the *Morte* is an important text because it presents human relationships as serious and problematic. "There may no thing please us no term": Malory's account of the "great default of us Englishmen" may be resigned or anguished. It seems to point to loss and to failure, to troubles and anxieties. But it looks at things in the face. There are no answers here; even the questions remain tacit. But when it comes to national and to sexual identity, it's the ability not to have an answer – not quite, not yet – which is important. It means that we are still thinking.[294]

So much to tease out; so many threads left untouched. The British Library declined to grant me permission to view the Winchester manuscript, although I have looked at Caxton's *Morte* in the John Rylands Library. But I couldn't end this book without trying for a closer connection – even if it seemed embarrassing, like writing a fan letter or asking for an autograph. This at any rate was why, one November morning, I found myself driving southward on the M6 through Warwickshire – the "centre of England", as Catherine Carpenter reminds us. I came off the motorway at Junction 1 and headed for Lutterworth. Then, for a few miles, I drove along the A5 – the road which follows the route of Watling Street and down which Malory may have ridden on his way to Ludlow in October 1459 or on his return from Northampton in July 1460. May have ridden, and then again may not, for the open-air Malory – the Malory of woodland ambushes and raids on lonely abbeys – might well have spent ten of the last fifteen years of his life in gaol.[295]

You drive through Pailton, along the old Coventry road. Then, as you leave Stretton-under-Fosse, you see a sign for a turning on the left: "Prison Training College". You turn into the avenue leading to Newbold Revel and there is another sign: "No public admittance". You come to a barrier and push a button to activate the intercom. You state your business and are directed to a car park on the right. In the reception area, you are asked for the registration number of your car. You wait for your appointment and your mouth goes dry; you feel as if you have come for a job interview. No GPS system could ever show it, but in terms of longitude and latitude you know that there's a high possibility that you are standing – now, right now – where Thomas Malory once stood.

"Prison Training College": the irony of that sign is probably lost on those who work here. But it's so sharp it almost makes me wince. Poor Sir Thomas! The likely birthplace of the "knyght presoner" is now the site of Her Majesty's Prison Service College. Since 1985 Newbold Revel has been the principal training centre for the officers who staff the modern version of an institution whose medieval ancestor did so much to change the life of Malory – the service, in fact, which was in all likelihood indirectly responsible for the composition of the *Morte d'Arthur* in the first place. I'm not sure that life always beats art. But when it does, the victory is total.

So there I was: at 9.30 on a November morning, I was standing where Malory once had stood. But not just him, for the Malory family owned Newbold Revel for only around 150 years of its thousand-year known history. On the eve of the Norman Conquest, the manor belonged to Lewin, a Saxon nobleman. William the Conqueror then gave the estate to Geoffrey de Wirce, who was succeeded, over the next century, by the Mowbrays, the de Wappenburys and the Revells, which latter family gave their rather upbeat name to the distinctly downbeat 'Fenny Newbold'. Sir Stephen Malory (Thomas's great-grandfather) gained the manor in 1383 on the death of his father-in-law, Sir John Revell. When Malory's wife Elizabeth died in 1479, Newbold Revel passed to a grandson, Nicholas. In 1538, Nicholas's daughter Margery sold the manor to Thomas Pope.

I had come to Newbold Revel as a ghost-hunter. But even if one thinks exclusively of the property-owners – leaves aside all the other family members who were born or died here, the servants who took out the night-soil in the morning or banked the fire at night, the visitors, the very cats and dogs – the spirit of Sir Thomas Malory must compete for attention with a dozen others, many of whom made a far more visible contribution to Newbold Revel as it appears today. Thomas Pope sold the estate to William Whorwood, whose daughter sold it to Sir William Stamford. Stanford's grandson sold it to Elizabeth Alderford, whose son Edward sold it in about 1640 to Sir Simon Clarke. Newbold Revel was later purchased by Sir Fulwar Skipwith, whose family – which included a second Fulwar, as well as Thomas, Selina, a second Selina, and a distant relation, Grey Skipwith – held the property until 1862, when it passed into the hands of Charles Ramsden, who then sold it to Edward Wood, a merchant and landowner from Scotland. The Woods were succeeded in 1898 by Colonel A. H. Heath, a Staffordshire ironmaster. In 1911 the mansion was sold to Leopold Bonn, an Austrian banker. When Bonn died, Newbold Revel was bought by the British Advent Missions and used to train missionaries. In 1939 the mansion was requisitioned by the Air Ministry and played a supporting role to Bletchley Park in signals intelligence, apparently specializing in Japanese Morse code. After the war, the Sisters of Charity of St. Paul bought Newbold Revel and it became a college for Catholic teachers. When the college closed in 1978, Newbold Revel was acquired by British Telecom and allowed to fall into disrepair. Then, in 1985, this leaky-roofed edifice came into the hands of the Home Office's Prison Department.[296]

I'm pretty sure that the idea of his old home being inhabited by trainee prison guards would have made Sir Thomas's hackles rise. And he might not have been particularly amused by the thought of nuns wandering his demesne. Yet Malory was entirely familiar with the idea of gentry property-holding, and until the middle of the nineteenth century Newbold Revel was owned by members of the social class to which he had himself belonged. But still: what about the later upstarts – *nouveaux riches* like Wood or foreigners like Bonn? Everything we can infer about Malory's attitude to social change suggests a deep ambivalence. He probably wouldn't have minded the idea of his old home being used by the RAF, though. Those clever young linguists working late into the evening weren't knights in armour. But in a way they belonged to a Round Table: they had sworn an oath; they were dedicated to the cause of the nation. And then there were the students – generations of them poring over their books and mugging up for exams. Malory might well have thought that there were worse ways to make use of his house.

Except, of course, it wasn't his house by then. The medieval manor, which itself replaced a still older Saxon dwelling, was long gone. When William Dugdale visited Sir Simon Clarke at Newbold Revel in 1637 whilst gathering material for *The Antiquities of Warwickshire*, he would have found a sixteenth-century mansion. But this was completely rebuilt in the century that followed. Later on, Edward Wood's grandson added a gymnasium, a swimming pool, and facilities to entertain visiting cricket teams. Colonel Heath put in mahogany doors and Italian mantelpieces, adding a cushioned dancing floor to celebrate his son's coming of age. The Sisters of St. Paul converted the stables into lecture rooms, building accommodation blocks for their students as well as a library and a chapel. And the prison service itself made extensive alterations and additions. But none of these changes has much affected the Queen Anne building of brick with its architraves, its balustrade and its stone dressings. A floor plan of the house was published in 1717, and at that point Newbold Revel had assumed the basic appearance – "provincial baroque", according to Andor Gomme – which it has preserved to this day. Gomme is confident that the "bones" of the sixteenth-century house "still partly survive, buried in the present mansion". And within that shattered skeleton – in the cellars, perhaps, or in the substantial chimney stack at the northern corner of the house – it's possible that fragments of the medieval or perhaps even the Saxon building remain. This is not quite Theseus' ship, with every plank and nail replaced so that it contains no particle of the vessel which set sail from the builder's yard one sunny day in

Figure 12 Newbold Revel. The photograph was taken from the south. The medieval hall would have occupied the area to the right in the image and faced south-east. The original chimney stack would have been located near to the northern corner of the building. Reproduced by kind permission of the Acting Head of College, Prison Service College Newbold Revel, and the Chief Press Officer for the National Offender Management Service.

Greece. But there's nothing at Newbold Revel – not a single window to look through or a stone to touch – nothing to see or feel of which one can say with conviction that Malory touched or saw this too.[297]

They were very kind, my hosts that day at Newbold Revel. Dot met me in reception and showed me the 'Blue' and 'Green' rooms before leading me through a series of passageways to the library. Catherine sat with me over a cup of coffee and talked about her work for the prison service. Then Andrew from the Works Department took me on a more extensive tour. We located the enormous chimney stack, but the hearth was boarded up and contained, according to Andrew, nothing older than an ancient stove – a relic, perhaps, from the days of the nuns or the missionaries. We went down into the cellars – an intricate series of vaulted chambers made out of brick – but found only electrical cables, heating ducts and workshop paraphernalia. Andrew took me outside to see two lead rainwater pipes bearing the inscription '1673'. I started to think that it was out here and not inside the house that one could stand, if only for a moment, in the shoes of Sir Thomas. I began to feel it on the terrace, from which I could gaze across a lake where three swans drifted on the breeze and a heron stood motionless in the reeds. I felt it more strongly as we followed a leaf-strewn path leading to a couple of fishponds, in one of which a large carp swam languidly a few inches below the surface.

And I felt it still more later that day, as I wandered round St. Edith's church at Monks Kirby. Unlike Newbold Revel, the building is of Malory's era. His mother might be buried here; so might his three sisters; so might young Robert Malory, who died, as Dugdale reports, "in his Fathers life time". Malory might have worshipped here; so might Joan Smith, the woman he is said to have raped: this was their parish church. Inscriptions on the gravestones in the churchyard – Liggins and Mason, Stennett and Whitwell, Cryer and Paybody – date back only to the 1730s. And the interior is mainly Victorian, with a plaque on the north wall recording the names of parishioners who died in the First World War: Bishop and Busby, Plant and Harris, Izzard and Lea, Southam and Wright. But near the door on the south side of the church there is another plaque with a translation of the original charter in 1077, which records a gift of land to the "Abbot and monks of Saint Nicholas at Angers" from Geoffey de Wirce, whose worldly wealth had come "from William the most worthy King of the English". The only testament to Thomas Malory – one can't expect the Church of England to memorialise a raider of abbeys – is a small and rather shabby framed document which hangs high up on a pillar near the entrance and gives the text of Malory's epitaph:

Conclusion

Dominus
Thomas Mallere
Valens miles obiit . . .
14 March 1470
de parochia
Monkenkyrkby
in comitatu
Warwici

But in a little chapel to the north of the altar stand a pair of tombs. One is dated 1347 and the other 1380. On each of these monuments lies the carved effigy of a lord and his lady, four pairs of hands clasped in prayer, eight marble eyes sightlessly awaiting the Resurrection.[298]

It's not difficult to conjure up images of a possible life. I can think of Malory wandering through bluebell woods in the springtime or netting a carp in the fishpond one summer's evening. I can picture him standing in the doorway at Newbold Revel, his face illuminated by the sinking autumnal sun. I see him on a frosty morning, leaving the kitchen with a hunk of bread in his hand. For some reason it is the boy and not the man that I am thinking of now. I imagine young Malory, one Christmas morning, walking from Newbold Revel to Newbold-on-Avon to see the mumming play. St George kills the Turkish Knight, but Father Christmas revives him with his bottle of "hocum slocum aliquid spam". Then St George kills the Turkish Knight again, and this time a Doctor administers "galvanic drops". "Arise, arise", cries St George:

Go back to thine own land, and tell
    What old England has done for thee.
Tell 'em we will fight
    Forty thousand men like thee.

In 1899, the text of the Newbold Mumming Play was printed in a scholarly journal with a commentary by W. H. D. Rouse. Alluding to Rouse's article in *From Ritual to Romance*, Jessie Weston described the Newbold play as a "symbolic representation of the death and re-birth of the year": one example among numerous other survivals of an ancient theme which Weston thought she could detect in all versions of the Grail myth from Chrétien de Troyes onwards. If Malory did indeed see the Newbold play, its jocular rusticity had no influence at all on the *Morte*. But if Weston is right (and she probably wasn't) then both works – one of 'high' and the other of 'low' culture – have a common and ancient root.[299]

Conclusion

I have tried to show Malory then and Malory now. But it's tempting to wonder what Malory would think of us. How would he view Britain's membership of the European Community or its military interventions in Afghanistan and Iraq? What would he have thought about Margaret Thatcher or Tony Blair? How would he have viewed the word 'Britain'? Would he have bemoaned the fact that since the 1960s the term 'English' has become, in the words of Raphael Samuel, "widely and publicly despised" as being "self-enclosed and inward-looking"? Or instead of engaging in a debate about national identity would he have donned his crusader costume, bought tickets for the match, and chanted for 'Ingerland' with the crowd? St George and the Turkish knight: that curious combination of cosmopolitanism and xenophobia. If Malory turned his eyes on us I am not sure he would see anything particularly surprising. He made a significant contribution to the idea of 'England'. But he was also one of the first to contemplate what, five centuries later, Tom Nairn and others would look forward to as the 'break-up' of Britain. It's not that nothing changes; it's that so much remains. But if that's true at a national or historical level, I am not sure how things stand in the personal case and the local instance. I remember buying my copy of *Le Morte d'Arthur* that crisp morning in York so many years ago. I remember the evening when I read *King Arthur* one summer's evening. I wanted to be Sir Launcelot; I longed to meet Guenever. I am the same person now as I was then, but it all seems so long ago.[300]

Notes

1   The Simmons edition of 1893–4 is said to have started the "Beardsley look" (Gillon 1972: vi) and featured nearly 600 designs by Aubrey Beardsley, whose "androgynous phantoms" include nymphs with bejewelled nipples and fauns with elegantly diminutive penises (Lacy ed., 1996: 114). At one point – confirming Brewer's view that the illustrations are "not very Malorian" – Pan appears to Tristram (1981: 6). Fitzgerald reports that Edward Burne-Jones, an early admirer of Beardsley's and a lifetime devotee of the *Morte*, was "bitterly disappointed" by Beardsley's illustrations, which he found "slovenly" (1975: 248).

2   "More complete": Vinaver 1947: vi. Vinaver's assessment has been disputed: Spisak (the editor of a scholarly edition of the Caxton text) argues that the Winchester text is no more "authentic" than Caxton (1985a: 9). Matthews puts the point more strongly: Caxton's text is "much better" than the Winchester manuscript: "more accurate, fuller, and . . . graced by Malory's own revision of the Roman War episode" (2000: 101). For Finke and Shichtman, preferences either way betray a misguided conception of authorship (see 2004: 160). Wheeler and Salda accept that the Caxton edition "fell out of favour" after the publication of Vinaver's edition in 1947. But, as they point out, the Caxton version continued to have "a classroom use" and also retained its place "in the hearts of many who call themselves Malorians" (2000: xi). My use of the Dent Everyman edition isn't entirely eccentric: Taylor and Brewer claim that it is "the version of the *Morte Darthur* most widely known to nineteenth- and twentieth-century readers" (1983: n. p.). My copy is the 1978 reprint. A searchable version of the Everyman text is available at www.gutenberg.org, and I have found this useful on a number of occasions. Gwenyvere: the spelling of the name in *The Works of Sir Thomas Malory*. Tennyson has 'Guinevere' and modern scholars generally refer to 'Guenevere'.

3   "Ĥit": Malory 1978: XXI. 7.

4   Malory's forbears: King Arthur is not mentioned in the *De Excidio Britanniae* of Gildas (*c.* 540). There may be a reference to Arthur in *Y Gododdin* (*c.* 600) although this might be a later interpolation. Arthur

made his first unquestionable appearance in the *Historia Brittonum* (*c.* 830), a work once attributed to Nennius. But it was only in the late 1130s, with Geoffrey of Monmouth's *Historia Regum Britanniae*, that Arthur achieved prominence. Geoffrey is likely to have been Malory's earliest source, although he didn't necessarily read the text we know. Malory knew Wace's translation of Geoffrey into Norman French (*c.* 1155), which contained the first reference to a Round Table. He also knew Layamon's translation of Wace (*c.* 1200), the first account of Arthur's reign to be written in English. It's not clear that Malory knew the romances of Chrétien de Troyes (*c.* 1160–90), "the inventor of Arthurian literature" (Kibler 2004: 1). Nor does he make direct use of the first cycle of Arthurian tales – the works attributed to Robert de Boron (*c.* 1180–1205). Malory's earliest literary source is likely to have been four of the five works by various authors (*Estoire del Saint Graal*, *Estoire de Merlin*, *Lancelot*, *Queste del Saint Graal* and *Mort Artu*) which together comprise the 'Vulgate' or 'Launcelot-Grail' Cycle (*c.* 1215–35). He also knew another and less unified cycle, the prose *Tristan*, which introduced the figures of Palomides and Dinadan. Malory used the alliterative *Morte Arthure* (*c.* 1360–75), a work in the Anglo-Saxon poetic tradition drawn from material in Wace. He also referred to the stanzaic *Morte Arthur* (*c.* 1400), a poem based on the Vulgate. According to Field, this "completes the list of the books that Malory is known to have used" (1978: 33). For the suggestion that Malory's English sources were more extensive, see Kennedy 1981. On the development of Arthurian literature before Malory, see Bruce 1928; Loomis 1959, 1963.

5   "Old": Briggs 1957: 184.

6   Knight suggests that the *Morte* has two movements, the first "episodic" and the second "polyphonic" (1969: 35). McCarthy sees a tripartite division into "Rise", "Glory" and "Fall" (1988: 7). Benson favours a five-part structure (1968: 92). Most famously and controversially, Vinaver's edition of the *Morte* is arranged into eight separate tales – the 'works' of Malory – since, according to Vinaver, Malory did not write "a single book" but "a series of separate romances" (1947: vi). Vinaver explains why he reached this conclusion in the 1970 preface to *Malory*, the book he had published as a young scholar in 1929, some years before the discovery of the Winchester manuscript. He claims that he initially thought of the *Morte* as "a single unified epic" (1970: n. p.). In 1929, however, Vinaver actually insisted that the "mass of stories" translated by Malory were "unconnected with each other" (1929: 110). After the publication of Vinaver's edition, the question of the *Morte*'s unity preoccupied a generation of critics. Brewer argued that the *Morte* displayed an "essential unity" (1963: 61). Lewis declared himself to be "on Mr. Brewer's side" but noted that Malory

lacked a modern conception of textual unity: his "matter" was "one" and "many" (1963: 20, 22). In 1963 Vinaver sought common ground with Lewis: one could speak of the *Morte* as a "whole book"; within this, however, Malory had intended to produce separate works (36). In *Malory's Originality*, Lumiansky offered a sustained critique of Vinaver's position. Lumiansky accepted that Vinaver's eight-book arrangement was "more effective" than Caxton's but argued that Malory intended to write "a single unified book" (1964a: 3). The essays in the collection bore out this central point: Wright argued that a system of "cross reference" unified the *Morte* (1964: 50); for Rumble, the text contained deliberate "chronological overlapping" (1964: 164); Moorman suggested that Malory made the quest for the Grail an "integral part" of the *Morte* as a whole (1964: 186) and Guerin saw Vinaver's eighth book as "the climactic . . . conclusion of a unified epic-romance" (1964: 269). Moorman subsequently made the larger claim that Malory had intended to write "a single, unified history of Arthur's reign" (1965: xi). In 1967 Vinaver acknowledged that the idea of the *Morte* as one book was "precious" to many readers and again allowed that, in one sense, the *Morte* was indeed a "whole book" (xliv, xlvi). He nevertheless maintained that the work lacked "unity of composition" (xlv, xlvi). In 1971, Pochoda attempted to terminate the unity debate: the question of whether the *Morte* was one book or many was "boring" and "barren" (14). Lambert took Pochoda's hint, writing of the unity question: "in this tourney I do not ride" (1975: x). But discussion continued into the 1990s. See, for example, Evans 1985; Sklar 1993: 323 n. 2; Archibald and Edwards 1996: xi–xiii; Meale 1996; Nolan 1996.

7 "Rightful": Briggs 1957: 11; "Scotland": 14.
8 "Rightful": Briggs 1957: 180; "go back": 177.
9 "What": Hodges 2005: 7. "All true": Finke and Shichtman 2004: 1. "From Henry II": Higham 2002: 226.
10 Arthur as a figment: for most contemporary scholars, the absence of Arthur from the *De Excidio Britanniae* is crucial because Gildas was writing not long after Arthur was supposed to have reigned: Malory tells us that the Siege Perilous was filled "four hundred winters and four and fifty" after Christ's passion (Malory 1978: XIII. 2); Geoffrey of Monmouth writes that Arthur passed his crown to Constantine "in the year 542" (1984: 261). "*Idea . . .* nationality": Higham 2002: 3–4; "foundation myth": 120. "Historical . . . readers": Burrow 2009: 232–3. For Higham and Burrow, myth can be seen as a kind of history. In a "postcolonial reading", Finke and Shichtman work on the assumption that history is a kind of myth: for them, Arthur is a "potent, but empty, social signifier" (2004: 9, 2).
11 "I love . . . queen": Briggs 1957: 18. In Malory, Arthur's declaration

to Merlin ("I love Guenever") in III. 1 is preceded by the even more
definite statement when Arthur first sees Guenever that "ever after he
loved her" (I. 18). In his "Roman de Brut", Wace's description of the
relationship between Arthur and Guenever contains a world of
meaning: "Arthur cherished her dearly . . . yet never had they a child
together" (1962: 54).

12   "Whoso": Briggs 1957: 11; "raised": 17; "in the cool": 133.

13   "Stung": Malory 1978: XXI. 4. The adder makes its first appearance
in the stanzaic *Morte Arthur.*

14   Tournaments and cricket matches: for T. H. White, medieval tournaments were "like cricket in many ways"; Launcelot is "a sort of
Bradman, top of the battling averages" (1958: 333). White presents
Malory as an old gent in the pavilion at Lord's, delving into an
"ancient Wisden" and boring listeners with stories of long-forgotten
matches (517).

15   "Pricking . . . last": Spenser 1916: I. i. 1–6. "Deficient": Lewis 1979b:
101.

16   On parataxis in Malory, see Field 1971: 38; Allen 1985: 237; Sklar
1993: 309; Smith 1996: 104–7. "Bright": Chambers 1922: 6. On
Malory's representation of space, see Cooper 2004a: 104; Mahoney
2005; Elizabeth Edwards 1996: 37–9. "No seasons": Parins 1988, 311.

17   "Overgoverned": Malory 1978: I. 6; "we will have": I. 7; "shooting":
III. 3. Elizabeth Edwards discusses those moments in the *Morte* when
knights enter a world of "pastoral economy and civic organization"
(1996: 42). When Tristram goes mad, he associates with "herdmen
and shepherds" (Malory 1978: IX. 17). When Launcelot, likewise
mad, runs through the streets of Corbin, young men throw turves at
him (see XII. 3).

18   "Smells . . . brothers": Briggs 1957: 21. "Kings": Malory 1978: V. 1.
"Work . . . thread": Briggs 1957: 40; "common . . . Camelot": 18;
"peasant . . . beard": 19; "woefully . . . man": 28.

19   "Sick": Malory 1978: IX. 20; "waxed . . . flesh": IX. 7. In Chrétien,
it is Yvain (and, in *The Mabinogion*, Owain) who, following a period
of madness in the woods, becomes unrecognizable. "She leapt":
Malory 1978: IX. 20. Argus appears in Book XVII of the *Odyssey*.
"Alas . . . helm": Malory 1978: II. 18; "Alas": XI. 13; "alas": XVI. 3;
"smitten . . . side": XVI. 2.

20   "Riding": Malory 1978: VI. 13; "hair": VII. 29. On the lack of refer-
ences to hair colour in the *Morte*, see Field 1971: 84. "Upon . . . not":
Malory 1978: XX. 8; "there was never": VII. 34; "alas . . . flatling":
IX. 5; "alas . . . best": X. 5; "alas . . . done": XII. 8.

21   Launcelot's divided identity: I am here indebted to Lambert (1975:
67), Riddy (1987: 55–6, 163–4) and Scala. As Scala writes: "In a
society in which identity must continually be performed in order to

be assured, Lancelot has to take ironic measures to maintain his reputation. Disguise, therefore, cannot simply be read as a covering over of who Lancelot 'is' but an endeavour to establish, confirm, and experience that identity. In other words, he can prove he is Lancelot only be temporarily denying that he is Lancelot in order to perform and therefore assure his identity as 'Lancelot'" (2002: 385).

22 "Man": Robinson 1930: 370.

23 "So sore . . . saddle": Malory 1978: X. 69.

24 "Misfortune . . . side": Malory 1978: XVIII. 11; "great": XVIII. 12. "Cleft": Briggs 1957: 42; "steel": 170; "grievous": 180; "split": 183. "That it went": Malory 1978: I. 15; "great": II. 10; "so hard": IV. 3; "cleft": V. 8. Burrow contrasts Geoffrey of Monmouth's "convincing" account of war with Malory's "chivalric rough-and-tumble" (2009: 237). And it is true that Malory has Lucius spectacularly despatched by the King himself whilst in Geoffrey the emperor is most undramatically killed by "an unknown hand" (1984: X. 11). Geoffrey nevertheless enjoys a good cleaving: Corineus splits Suhard's head "in two halves from top to bottom"; Gawaine cleaves Marcellus Mutius "through helm and head to his chest"; and Arthur cuts Frollo's head "into two halves" (I. 13, X. 4, IX. 11). But it's only with Chrétien de Troyes that head injuries become a motif in Arthurian narrative. Erec delivers "three blows in quick succession" which shatter Yder's helmet and slice through "one of the bones in his head" (2004: 49). Erec subsequently strikes the Count of Limors "on top of the head, so that he sliced through his brains and brow" (96). Cligés beheads one Saxon with his own sword and, in combat with a second, severs "his head and half his neck from the body" (168). Yvain strikes a demon "such a blow that he severed head from trunk" (365). Chrétien's Launcelot is neither as brutal nor as unarguably supreme as Malory's, but even he sends the head of one knight flying "on to the heath" (243). And Launcelot's victory over Meleagant is still more bloody than the equivalent scene in Malory: Guenever's kidnapper has his right arm chopped off, his belly slashed and the nosepiece of his helmet knocked into his mouth before being beheaded (see 294). Instances of piercing are particularly vivid in Chrétien and possibly more frequent than those in the *Morte*. Erec plunges his lance "a foot and a half" into the body of a robber and then pulls it out "with a twisting motion" (72). With greater strength but less refinement of cruelty, Cligés gets "six feet of his lance" through the body of a third Saxon during the encounter mentioned above (168). Percivale handles his lance so skilfully that he pierces the Red Knight "through the eye and brain", his weapon emerging from the back of his opponent's cranium "amid a gush of blood and brains" (395). In a discussion of "formulaic repetition" in the *Morte*, Lambert writes that

"lopping off an arm is less impressive than lopping off an arm and shoulder, and cutting through the helmet to the teeth is a more impressive feat than either". For Lambert, "the differences between these feats have no thematic or rhetorical meaning; we cannot see any significant pattern in the sequence of blows" (1975: 46–7). Finke and Shichtman go further. For them, physical violence in the *Morte* "provides the structure for an elaborate structure of exchange that determines sociopolitical hierarchies" (2004: 177). It also "escapes these authoritative discourses and creates a perverse kind of carnival in which the official gods of violence are subverted". For Finke and Shichtman, such anarchy is "figured by the archaic imago of the fragmented body, including representations of castration, mutilation, dismemberment, dislocation, and the bursting open of the body" (178). The 'Gotcha!' headline appeared in the *Sun* on 4 May 1982, two days after the *Belgrano* was sunk by H. M. S. *Conqueror* with the loss of 323 lives.

25   "Traditional": Reiss 1966: 185. "Fair . . . paps": Malory 1978: VI. 10; "clave . . . navel": VI. 11. In Chrétien, it is Erec rather than Launcelot who achieves this double victory: he strikes the first giant "in the eye, right through the brain, so that . . . the blood and brains spurted out"; the second receives "such a blow on the top of the head" that he is "split into two halves" (2004: 91–2).

26   "Best": Malory 1978: II. 19; "breast": V. 6, V. 8; "shoulders": II. 4, VII. 6; "brows": II. 10; "canel bone": IV. 27.

27   Galahad severing a knight's arm: see Malory 1978: XIII. 13; "through": VIII. 7; "ointment": VII. 22.

28   "Unintentionally": Field 1971: 109. "Sir Uwaine . . . fog": Twain 1986: 139–40. "His ribs": *Orkneyinga Saga*: 30.

29   "Genytours": Malory 1978: V. 5; "summer": XI. 6; "sunbeam": XIII. 7; "ye": XV. 2; "water . . . clereness": XVII. 13; "bright": XVII. 15; "still": XVII. 16.

30   "They": Malory 1978: XIII. 7; "remnant . . . home": XVIII. 1. On violence towards women in the *Morte*, see Fries 1985; Elizabeth Edwards 1996; Hodges 2005: 35–6, 45–6; Radulescu 2005, 128. "Lightly . . . court": Malory 1978: II. 3; "misadventure . . . done": III. 7; "always": III. 15; "swapped . . . man": VI. 17.

31   "Awk . . . shameful": Malory 1978: VIII. 25; "grovelling . . . head": VIII. 26.

32   "The country": Malory 1978: X. 52; "such": XIX. 9; "brainpans": XX. 8.

33   "We": McCarthy 1988: 7. "Unwearying": Field 1971: 145. "Morte": Malory 1978: XIX. 13. It is difficult to see why Malory has "lost" his source (presumably a version of Chrétien de Troyes's "The Knight of

the Cart"): Book XIX of the *Morte* appears to use material from this source (see Walsh 1985, Spisak 1985b, McCarthy 1996).

34 "Two . . . problem": Chambers 1922: 4–5. The "overgrowth" of the Tristram sections should probably be attributed less to Malory than to his source: according to Field, the prose *Tristan* is "a mere succession of incidents" (1978: 32). On the "wilderness" of the Tristram materials in the *Morte*, see Shaw 1963: 117. See also Ker 1905: 23; Reiss 1966: 110; Vinaver 1967: xlix; Benson 1968: 92. McCarthy puts the case with surprising delicacy when he suggests that the Tristram section "varies . . . in quality and relevance" (1988: 20). Some attempts have been made to argue that the Tristram materials do not disturb the 'unity' of the *Morte*: see Rumble 1964; Moorman 1965: xxvii, 76–7. I put this argument more strongly in Chapter 19.

35 "Begat": Malory 1978: XXI. 1; "on her": I. 20; "all . . . sea": I. 27. According to Higham, the idea that Mordred is "the product of incest committed by the unwitting Arthur and his scheming sister" is a comparatively late development (2002: 220). Mordred – or 'Medraut' – first appears in the *Annales Cambriae* (*c.* 954), which mention a battle against Arthur at Camlann in 537 AD. The "long slide into villainy" only begins with Geoffrey of Monmouth's *History of the Kings of Britain* (*c.* 1136), in which Mordred becomes "the archetypal figure of evil" (2002: 209). The Massacre of the Innocents: see Matthew 2. 7–16. Field argues that Arthur's actions either derive from a lost source or represent an earlier vision of Arthur on Malory's part (see 1998: 89–92). "False": Malory 1978: X. 39.

36 "Third . . . necromancy": Malory 1978: I. 2. "Die here": Briggs 1957: 47. "Ah": Malory 1978: XXI. 5. Kibler suggests that the "malevolent side" of Morgan's character only emerged "in the *Lancelot-Graal*" (2004: 506 n. 8). In Chrétien, she is Morgan the Wise – a healer whose "ointment" cures Yvain of his wounds and his madness (332). The "Merlin" attributed to Robert de Boron was apparently not among Malory's direct sources. But in this narrative Morgan has the same parentage as in Malory, is "sent away to study in a nunnery" and learns "secret arts" (2001: 103). Morgan's motives in the *Morte*: there are immediate sources of resentment. Her father (the Duke of Tintagil) is killed by Uther Pendragon's forces. Uther then sleeps with her mother (Igraine) and "begat on her . . . Arthur" (Malory 1978: I. 2). Having reached manhood, Arthur sleeps with her sister Margawse (later 'Morgawse'), his own half-sister and "begat upon her Mordred" (I. 19; see also II. 10). Margawse's husband, King Lot of Orkney, is later killed by Pellinore, one of Arthur's knights (II. 10). Morgan's desire for revenge is compounded by ambition. After Lot's death, she uses her lover Accolon in an attempt to usurp Uriens, her husband, and Arthur. When Arthur defeats Accolon, Morgan's conspirator is

forgiven but dies of his wounds (see IV. 12). Morgan now has the death of a lover, a brother-in-law and a father to hold against Arthur. But her actions have deeper sources. Like the "counterfeit" Excalibur which she gives to Arthur, Morgan is "brittle, and false" (IV. 8). She hates Arthur because she is by nature opposed to goodness. Alongside revenge, ambition, envy and sheer bloody-mindedness there is also jealousy: Morgan is "an enemy to all true lovers" (VIII. 34). This helps to explain the plot against Launcelot in Book VI. Morgan is also "jealous" of Tristram's relationship with Isoud, and the Cornish knight makes things worse by killing Morgan's new lover, Sir Hemison (IX. 40). Morgan feels "sorrow out of reason" when she sees Hemison's corpse, although Malory makes it clear that she "loved Sir Launcelot best" (IX. 42, IX. 40). Sexual as well as political failure is involved: Morgan loses family members to Camelot but cannot gain lovers at Arthur's court and has to put up with relative nonentities. She is "as fair as a lady" but Alisander – the next object of Morgan's passion – would rather "cut away" his "hangers" than sleep with her (I. 20, X. 38). Morgan even repels potential allies. Gawaine and his "fair brethren" avenge the death of their father King Lot by killing Pellinore but Gawaine knows that Morgan "did never good, but ill" (X. 21, IX. 24). If Morgan's actions are merely destructive, however, it's difficult to explain the plot against Launcelot in Book XI. Morgan imprisons Elaine, the daughter of King Pelles, in the Castle of Corbin because she is "the fairest lady of that country" (XI. 1). And it is Dame Brisen rather than Morgan who enables Pelles to fulfil his wish "to have had Sir Launcelot to have lain by his daughter" (XI. 2). Morgan nevertheless makes possible the birth of Galahad, the fairest flower of Arthurian knighthood. And although Morgan hates "true lovers", her meddling might in another context be seen as an attempt to maintain courtly values. Morgan is not, like Mordred, a conspirator: surprisingly, the *Morte* does not record a single meeting between them. Morgan may be guilty of "false treason", but she is first and foremost "a queen, and a king's sister, and a king and queen's daughter" (IX. 24). "Gentle . . . enemy": Heng 2004: 849. Heng argues that Morgan's "otherness" points to the presence of "submerged discourses" in the *Morte*. Morgan enjoys "extraordinary autonomy": she "selects whom she will love" (847).

37   "Lily . . . Englishman": White 1958: 460. "Has come": Briggs 1957: 130.

38   "Haut": Malory 1978: XVIII. 8; "great": XVII. 22. On Malory's resurrection of dead knights, see Lewis 1963: 22; Brewer 1963: 41; Moorman 1965: 4–10; Meale 1996: 6; Field 2002: 28. On chronological inconsistencies in the *Morte*, see Vinaver 1947: xxxii; Benson 1968: 91–2, 100–1; Knight 1969: 20–4; McCarthy 1996: 85–6.

39 "Duke": Malory 1978: XIX. 11; "died": XIX. 11.

40 "By whom": Malory 1978: XIII. 4; "best": XIX. 10; "much better": XI. 4. On Urre's healing, see Kelly 1985; Benson 1996: 229.

41 "Delivered": Malory 1978: XI. 3; "fifteen": XII. 9; "wild": XII. 1; "Sir Galahalt": X. 40; "Sir Galahad": VIII. 26.

42 "Hardly": Lewis 1963: 24. "Almost": Field 1971: 81. Vinaver argues that Malory "disliked" the interwoven structure of medieval romance and tried to "disentangle" it (1947: lii, lix). On 'interweaving' (or 'interlacing') in Malory, see Lewis 1963: 7; Wright 1964: 13–17; Moorman 1964: 186; Reiss 1966: 30; Benson 1968: 100–1; Knight 1969: 50–1; Ihle 1983: 3, 102–9; Archibald 1996: 136; Cooper 1996: 186; 2004: 105; Hodges 2005: 2; Norris 2008: 152.

43 "A greater . . . best": Briggs 1957: 131. Ihle suggests that the parallel passage in the *Morte* – "I know well I was never the best" (Malory 1978: XIII. 5) – was Malory's invention (1983: 142), but in Chrétien de Troyes a similar line ("I don't count myself among the best") is put into Gawaine's mouth (2004: 480).

44 "Forbidden . . . achieve": Briggs 1957: 125; "achieved": 138; "vision . . . samite": 133. *OED* defines samite as "a rich silk fabric . . . sometimes interwoven with gold". "Little": Vinaver 1959: 547. "Fed": Malory 1978: XI. 4; "made whole": XI. 14; "seen": XI. 2; "healed": XII. 4; "achieve": XI. 4. Bryant observes that Chrétien's Grail is introduced "in a most downbeat way" and might be just a fish platter; it was the author of the works attributed to Robert de Boron who transformed the Grail into "the vessel used by Christ at the Last Supper, given to Pilate and passed on by him to Joseph of Arimathea, who uses it to collect the blood that flows from the crucified Christ's wounds" (2001: 4, 7).

45 "Holy": Malory 1978: XIII. 18; "half . . . sin": XIII. 18; "enter": XVII. 15; "four": XVII. 16.

46 "Flaxen-haired": Briggs 1957: 133. "Soon": Malory 1978: I. 3. "Tapestried . . . chimney": Briggs 1957: 9. "Pulled": Malory 1978: I. 5. "Twinkled . . . letters": Briggs 1957: 11.

47 "Thick forest": Briggs 1957: 30. "Little leaved": Malory 1978: VI. 6. "Curveting": Briggs 1957: 33 (compare Malory 1978: III. 12). "Pressed . . . knight": Briggs 1957: 138; "frightened": 16.

48 "Vaulting": Briggs 1957: 24; "dreamer": 121; "swell": 39.

49 Kay's sharp tongue: this trait seems to have been introduced by Chrétien de Troyes; Robert de Boron's Kay is mendacious as well as malicious. "Questing . . . lion": Malory 1978: IX. 12. The beast is 'questing' because it makes "such a noise as it had been the noise of thirty couple of hounds questing" (or 'barking') (IX. 12). "Good": Malory 1978: X. 47; "laughed": X. 48; "the joy": X. 56. According to

Lacy, Dinadan's "amused scepticism" first appears in the thirteenth-century prose *Tristan* (1996: 116).

50 "Individual . . . brief": McCarthy 1988: 117. Percivale and Bors: Robert de Boron's Perceval is "not wise or worthy enough" to achieve the Grail and is something of a clodhopper, as is Peredur in *The Mabinogion* (2001: 143). The Perceval of the Vulgate Cycle is, according to Matarasso, a case of "plain stupidity"; Bors is "a plodder" (1969: 18). Reaction rather than action: Lambert writes that "we believe in Lancelot's importance less because of what we see Lancelot do, than because of the narrator's attitude toward what Lancelot does" (1975: 40).

51 "Resort . . . quest": Malory 1978: XVIII. 1; "prove . . . heartily": XVIII. 7; "noblesse": XIX. 13; "so well": VII. 34; "alas . . . battle": XX. 13.

52 "Fair housewife . . . maidenhead": Malory 1978: III. 3. "World": McCarthy 1988: 57. "Do": Malory 1978: IV. 21; "wellnigh . . . arms": IV. 22; "loved no more . . . days": IV. 23. On Pelleas and Nimue, see Hodges 2005: 57. "Fair . . . needle": Malory 1978: XI. 1; "skipped . . . naked": XI. 3. On Elaine as a "proto-novelistic figure" who cannot be fitted into polarized stereotypes, see Sklar 2001: 65. On Malory's "frankly desiring women", see Cooper 2004b: 300.

53 "Hot": Malory 1978: XVIII. 9; "good . . . yearly": XVIII. 19. "Generosity . . . vulgarity": McCarthy 1991: 158. Batt suggests that men rather than women in the *Morte* "lack . . . volition in sexual matters" (2004: 809–10). Launcelot in particular is "the object of feminine . . . manipulation" and his passive role in Galahad's conception is a "reversal of normative gender expectations" (811, 813). Batt reads this reversal – unspecifically and therefore not wholly persuasively – as the symptom of a "crisis in masculinity" (813).

54 "Housewife": Malory 1978: III. 3; "ladies": III. 15; "went . . . plesaunce": XIX. 6; "abed": XX. 3. The tension between the direct reference to adultery in Book XIX and Malory's reticence in Book XX is complicated by Launcelot's admission in XVIII. 20 that he has not confessed for fourteen years and during this time has loved the Queen "unmeasurably", doing deeds of arms for her sake and not for God's. Kennedy argues that Malory's treatment of his sources "eliminates all but one instance of actual adultery" (in XIX. 6) (1992: 9). Launcelot's confession reflects the fact that love between he and Guenever has "grown slowly"; for Kennedy, however, that love is not yet sexual (260). Kennedy later maintained this line of argument (see 2001: 22) but it has been challenged by Radulescu (see 2004: 287, 291), Hodges (see 2005: 23, 104) and Archibald (see 2012: 315). McCarthy argues that Malory does not tell us what Launcelot and Guenever were doing "because he knows we will misunderstand"

(1991: 165). Nevertheless, most critics agree that the relationship between Launcelot and Guenever is a sexual one and that the explicit reference to adultery in Book XIX is synecdochic. It is worth noting that, although Dame Brisen's crafts make events unfold differently, Launcelot is ready to accept Guenever's invitation to "come to her chamber that night" (Malory 1978: XI. 7). And there is no doubt that the relationship is adulterous in Chrétien de Troyes's "The Knight of the Cart": Guenever wants to be "quite naked" with Launcelot "in order to enjoy him fully" (2004: 259). Still, though Chrétien has the Queen drawing Launcelot "into the bed beside her", he adds a line which supports McCarthy's point: the lovers feel "joy and wonder", but Chrétien will "let it remain a secret for ever, since it should not be written of" (264–5).

55   "Bobaunce": Malory 1978: XV. 6; "pride": XVIII. 15; "to help": XV. 5; "recluse . . . pride": XV. 6; "turn": XXI. 9.

56   "Read": Malory 1978: XXI. 10; "loved . . . draughts": XVIII. 1. On the "privy draughts" phrase, see Kennedy 1992: 286. McCarthy argues that the *Morte* concerns the "public consequences" of "private behaviour", as if Malory was familiar with the modern distinction between public and private (1988: 50). McCarthy later asserts that "personal identity is of little or no importance" in Malory and that "one's public identity and one's real identity are the same thing" (1991: 149). This is why, in the case of Launcelot and Guenever, "the doors marked 'private' remain unopened" (151). I tend to agree with Elizabeth Edwards when she argues that the *Morte* enables us to see the *emergence* of a distinction between the public realm (the court, the forest) and "the space of privacy, which is both physically the bedroom of the lady and the private emotion in the psyche of the lover" (1996: 48). But Pochoda has argued persuasively that, at least in the case of the sovereign, a distinction between public and private had been established by the beginning of the twelfth century (see 1971: 41–8). For Pochoda, the relation of public and private was "at the center of fifteenth-century political theory" and of the *Morte*, in which "an attack on the king as a private individual necessitates catastrophe for the entire structure" of the Round Table (73, 132). Reponses to this issue depend on whether one adopts the paradigm of 'modernism' or 'primordialism'. "Kings . . . beaten": Malory 1978: XIX. 12.

57   "Most . . . end": Lambert 1975: 64–5. "And there": Malory 1978: XI. 8; "arse . . . thigh": XII. 3; "brast": XVIII. 17; "brawn": XIX. 6. In his account of Launcelot's injury, Malory modifies Chrétien de Troyes's original: here, Guenever's lover cuts "the end of his little finger to the quick" and severs "the whole first joint of the next finger" (2004: 264).

58   "Bebled . . . her": Malory 1978: XIX. 6. Chrétien de Troyes's

Guenever is more quick-witted if less dignified than Malory's: when Meleagant seizes on the bloodstained sheets as "clear proof" that she has slept with a wounded knight, the Queen claims that "my nose bled last night" (2004: 266). The scene in Meliagrance's castle is one of several in which parallels between Launcelot and Tristram come to light. When the wounded Tristram sleeps with the wife of Segwarides, the blood stains on "both the over sheet and the nether" enable Segwarides to conclude that his lady has slept with "a wounded knight" (Malory 1978: VIII. 14). Both Launcelot and Tristram endure episodes of madness; both have their injuries tended to by fair maidens. Tristram escapes from Sir Andred by leaping from a window (see VIII. 34); Launcelot escapes from the castle of King Pelles in the same way (see XI. 8). "Lady": XVIII. 21.

59 "To do": Malory 1978: III. 15. "All": Briggs 1957: 36; "work": 40; "I . . . do": 143.

60 "Loved . . . knights": Malory 1978: VI. 1. "In": Briggs 1957: 43; "loved . . . knighthood": 120; "met": 126.

61 On Arthur's lack of centrality, see Pochoda 1971: 17; Riddy 1987: 41–3; Lacy 2005. In the "Idylls", Tennyson attempts to explain Arthur's detachment: Launcelot is "the first in Tournament" but Arthur is "mightiest on the battle-field" (1969: 1497). Launcelot tells Elaine that the King is "mild . . . at home, nor cares | For triumph in our mimic wars". At the Battle of Badon, however, Arthur, in his element, stands "High on a heap of slain, from spur to plume | Red as the rising sun with heathen blood" (1629). Yet the Arthur of the "Idylls" remains an impalpable figure: after his final interview with Guenever, the King is described as a grey figure "moving ghostlike to his doom" (1740). Kennedy argues that Malory's Guenever "offers no sign that she reciprocates [Arthur's] passion" and "creates the impression that the King stopped loving Guenevere soon after they were married" (2001: 15). It's true that Guenever experiences "great sorrow" when Arthur departs on his continental campaign (Malory 1978: V. 3). But the King and Queen are clearly not sleeping together at Camelot when Guenever invites Launcelot to come to her chamber "that night" (XI. 7).

62 "Such . . . enow": Malory 1978: XX. 9. "Sorry": Briggs 1957: 174; "great": 171.

63 "Bounty": Malory 1978: XVIII. 19. "Some": Briggs 1957: 160. "Nigh": Malory 1978: XVIII. 15. In some ways, Guenever's haughtiness towards Launcelot makes more sense in Chrétien de Troyes than in Malory. In "The Knight of the Cart", the Queen rebuffs Launcelot when he appears at Meleagant's castle. This is a "joke", though Launcelot doesn't find it amusing: Chrétien has explained that carts were used to transport criminals who had lost their "feudal rights",

and the Queen's point is that her champion was momentarily reluctant to ride in such a vehicle even for her sake – a "sin" for which her lover instantly craves pardon (2004: 259, 211, 262). In the same scene in Malory, Guenever rebukes one of her ladies for suggesting that the knight in the cart "rideth unto hanging" (Malory 1978: XIX. 4). The Queen's subsequent *froideur* is due not to snobbery or jealousy but because "better is peace than ever war" – an astute remark, except that Guenever then makes conflict more likely by arranging for Launcelot to visit her "the same night" (XIX. 5). Briggs is not alone among Malory's adapters in making Guenever prone to rage: Tennyson's Guenever writhes upon her couch and clenches her fingers "till they bit the palm" on hearing about the token which Launcelot wears for Elaine (1969: 1638). When Guenever later tells Launcelot that he might have shown more "grace" to Elaine, her "wrath" is like the sea, "yet working after storm" (1657).

64 "Quite": McCarthy 1991: 169. "Not": Archibald 2012: 317.

65 "Not wholesome": Malory 1978: III. 1; "virtuous . . . stability": XVIII. 25. These lines precede Malory's version of the "Knight of the Cart"; in Chrétien de Troyes, a similar complaint ("today very few serve love . . . Now love is reduced to empty pleasantries") immediately follows that episode (2004: 295).

66 "Old love": Malory 1978: XVIII. 25; "disports": Malory 1978: XX. 3; "his pleasance": XIX. 6. "No reference": Archibald 2012: 315. "True lady": Malory 1978: XX. 11; "lycours lust": XVIII. 25; "unstableness": XVI. 5. On the theme of instability, see Kennedy 2001: 39–41.

67 "Out": Malory 1978: XIII. 20; "out": XVIII. 20; "out": XVIII. 19; "for . . . him": XI. 7; "wroth": XIX. 5; "wroth . . . pan": XXI. 4; "we": I. 7. On the phrase 'out of measure', see Field 1985: 233; Radulescu 2005. "For their harness": Malory 1978: XXI. 4; "common . . . fangle": XXI. 1. 'Default': "failure of something"; "absence (*of* something wanted)"; "want, poverty" (*OED*, sense 1); "a failure in being perfect; an imperfection, defect, blemish, flaw" (sense 2); "failure to act; neglect . . . failure to perform some legal requirement or obligation, *esp.* failure to attend in a court on the day assigned" (sense 3); "failure in duty, care" (sense 4). The now more familiar sense of a "failure to meet financial engagements" came later (sense 7).

68 "By the seaside": Malory 1978: XXI. 4. The distance from Salisbury to Totton, at the head of Southampton Water, is 17 miles. Strachey delicately observes that geographical relationships in the *Morte* are "often impossible to harmonise" (1868: xi).

69 "To get": Malory 1978: II. 1; "at that time": VIII. 1. "To gete . . . Englond": Malory 1485: II. 1.

70 "North . . . Logris": Malory 1978: VIII. 39; "the realm": IX. 37; "the

realm . . . land": X. 51; "out": XII. 5. "Can": Higham 2002: 181. In Robert de Boron, by contrast, "Logres" is, according to Bryant, "thought of as a city" – probably London, since it is in Logres that Arthur takes the sword from the stone (2001: 105 n. 17).

71 "All": Briggs 1957: 14. "All": Malory 1978: X. 52.

72 "Some": Malory 1978: XXI. 12; "over": IV. 1; "some": XX. 18. "Go back": Briggs 1957: 177.

73 "No tribute . . . them": Malory 1978: V. 1.

74 "First": Geoffrey of Monmouth, 1984: I. 1. In Geoffrey, Julius Caesar accepts that the Britons "come from the same race" as the Romans, since both "are descended from Trojan stock" (IV. 1). The Britons themselves justify their refusal to pay tribute to Rome because "a common inheritance of noble blood comes down from Aeneas to Briton and to Roman alike" (IV. 2). Arthur's defiance of Lucius' ambassadors is based on more specific grounds than in Malory: "Rome ought to give me tribute", Arthur asserts, because "my ancestors [Belinus and Constantine] once captured that city" (IX. 16). Malory does not take up Geoffrey's notion that Guenever is "descended from a noble Roman family" (IX. 9). "Lineage": Higham 2002: 124.

75 My Ladybird book: Peach 1965.

76 "Fiendly": Malory 1978: XI. 1; "fair": XI. 2; "over": XI. 1; "king . . . Armathie": XI. 2. The curious placelessness of Castle Corbin would seem to come from the Vulgate *Estoire del Saint Graal* rather than Malory himself (see Lupack 2007: 440).

77 "Aramathie . . . achieve the Sangreal": Malory 1978: XIV. 3; "of the eighth . . . Jesu Christ": XIII. 7; "of the eighth . . . degree": XIII. 7. *OED* defines 'degree' in sense 3a as "a 'step' in direct line of descent . . . both upward to a common ancestor and downward from him", dating this usage from 1300. The first and most elaborate account of the Grail's journey westwards from the Holy Land is in "Joseph of Arimathea", part of the Arthurian cycle attributed to Robert de Boron.

78 "Fulfilled": Malory 1978: XVII. 19; "see": XVII. 20. "Great": Matthew 27. 60. "Great": Malory 1978: XXI. 1; "signs . . . done them": XVII. 20. "The people . . . them": Briggs 1957: 141.

79 "First . . . land": Malory 1978: XVII. 3.

80 "Made jousts": Briggs 1957: 43. "I am": Malory 1978: X. 2; "better": X. 55.

81 "We hear": Lewis 1979a: 43. Freud introduced the term 'reality principle' in "Formulations on the Two Principles of Mental Functioning" (1911). While the pleasure principle – the desire for immediate gratification – is said to dominate mental life in childhood, the reality principle involves a "renunciation of pleasure" which can be seen in

religion, art and science: "a momentary pleasure, uncertain in its
results, is given up, but only in order to gain along the new path an
assured pleasure at a later time" (1953–74: XII. 223).

82 "A man": Tennyson 1969: 504. "He had": Briggs 1957: 39. "Broad
. . . curls": Tennyson 1969: 358. Although there is no purple in
Malory, the alliterative *Morte Arthure* has the Romans making use of
"silk and purple" (Armitage 2012: 48). Malory mentions only the
silk (1978: V. 6).

83 "Lord": Malory 1978: XX. 3; "unhappiest": XVIII. 22; "stark dead":
XXI. 12; "courteoust . . . measure": Malory 1978: XXI. 13.

84 "Coldtongue": Grahame 1961: 8. "Bread": Ransome 1970: 31; "ices
. . . icing": 308. "Pike": Chrétien de Troyes 2004: 89. "Boars' heads":
Briggs 1957: 23; "capons": 32. "Cold": Chrétien de Troyes 2004: 100;
"venison . . . displeasing": 390. In Simon Armitage's translation of the
alliterative *Morte Arthure*, the knights are served "meat in pastry that
would melt in the mouth" (2012: 9).

85 "Black pudding": Briggs 1957: 47.

86 "Constant": Lewis 1979a: 120; "the poet": 213.

87 "A jousts . . . sea": Malory 1978: X. 52.

88 "Lusty . . . forgotten": Malory 1978: XVIII. 25. According to
Lumiansky, the May passage is not found in Malory's sources (1964c:
226).

89 "Kind . . . privy hate": Malory 1978: XX. 1; "the month": IV. 22.

90 "Great . . . glad": Malory 1978: X. 52; "get": II. 1; "this land . . .
against": X. 52; "under . . . king": VIII. 1.

91 "Run": Pochoda 1971: 109. "Winter . . . summer": Malory 1978:
XVIII. 25.

92 "Maying": Malory 1978: XIX. 1. "Usual": Lewis 1979a: 213. "Passing
well . . . queen": Malory 1978: XIX. 1; "dolefully": XIX. 2; "a child":
XIX. 3; "ditches . . . sunder": XIX. 4.

93 "Queen": Briggs 1957: 161–2. "Herbs": Malory 1978: XIX. 2;
"carved": XIX. 10. "Steel": Briggs 1957: 170.

94 "Flourisheth . . . world": Malory 1978: XX. 1; "the tenth": XXI. 2.

95 "Succour": Malory 1978: III. 15. "Rushing . . . fire": Acts 2. 2–3; "of
every nation": 2. 5; "Parthians": 2. 9–11. On the Pentecostal theme
in Malory, see Plummer 1985.

96 "Again": Malory 1978: XIII. 6; "cold earth": XXI. 4. Tennyson
ending the "Idylls" in winter: the last tournament takes place in
"Autumn-tide" (Tennyson 1969: 1711); Arthur's final battle occurs on
"that day when the great light of heaven | Burned at his lowest in the
rolling year" (1745); in the final line of the poem, Arthur is carried to
Avalon as "the new sun rose bringing the new year" (1754). "Born":
Malory 1978: I. 27.

97   "Fine": Oakeshott 1963: 2. "Thrill . . . empire": Dancy, 1995: 59. "Bedside . . . fat": Oakeshott 1963: 2–3.

98   "More than once": Oakeshott 1963: 6. On Oakeshott teaching Malory, see Dancy 1995: 43; on the Winchester Bible, see 86. "No manuscript": Dancy 1995: 65; "remarkable": 66.

99   "Salmon": Dancy 1995: 66.

100   "Skimmed": Oakeshott 1963: 5. The articles: see Oakeshott 1934a and 1934b. "More complete . . . wrote": Vinaver 1947: vi.

101   "Lively": Dancy 1995: 63. On Oakeshott's contribution to the democracy/dictatorship debate, see Dancy 1995: 63; on Oakeshott as a lecturer to working men, see 62; on Oakeshott's support for the Republicans in Spain and on *Men without Work*, see 69.

102   "People . . . existed": Dancy 1995: 68.

103   For Vinaver's account of the *Morte*'s textual history, see Vinaver 1947: lxxxix–xci. "*Explicit*": the term "used by scribes in indicating the end of a book" (*OED*). "Thys": the Winchester manuscript of the *Morte d'Arthur*, folio 70v (compare Malory 1990: I. 180). "Stirred . . . deeps": Oakeshott 1963: 6.

104   "Cathedral": Lewis 1963: 28. "Self-effacement": Field 1971: 5.

105   "Chosen . . . Friday": Malory 1978: XXI. 13. "Praye . . . nyght": Malory 1485: XXI. 13 (folio ee62).

106   "Was always": Matthews 1966: 39. "Most": Field 1996: 115.

107   "First . . . felon": Archibald and Edwards 1996: xiv.

108   "Five rings . . . arrows": Field 1993: 101.

109   Dugdale's 1656 map was made long after Malory rampaged through the Warwickshire countryside. Yet in spite of rural depopulation, the rise of sheep pasturing and the thinning of woods for iron-making, Malory would have recognized the landscape it depicts. At the same time, the map is familiar to a modern eye: it was based on a survey carried out with a theodolite and printed by means of copper-plate engraving. Christopher Saxton had published a map of Warwickshire in 1579 as part of his *Atlas of the Counties of England and Wales* – "the first national atlas", as Tooley points out, "of any country in the world" (1979: n. p.). A larger version published in 1583 is described by Lynam as "the most authoritative map of England" before Dugdale (1947: 20). Saxton's surveying was assisted by a letter from Elizabeth I which instructed Justices of the Peace to conduct him on request "into any towne, castle, highe place or hill to view the countrey" (Tooley, n. p.). Saxton's maps were engraved on copper-plate and surveyed by compass and crosstaff, but the scale is inconsistent and no roads are marked – a disadvantage which also applies to John Speed's county maps published in *Theatre of the Empire of Great Britaine* (1611). Speed was known for his "very rare and ingenious capacitie" in decorative cartography. According to Arlott, however, he carried

out "little original surveying" (1954: 7). William Smith is thought to have produced a map of Warwickshire in 1602–3, but "almost nothing is known about his cartographical work" (Delano-Smith and Kain, 1999: 87). Henry Beighton produced an "excellent" one inch to the mile map of Warwickshire using original surveys in 1722–5 (87). "Divers": Field 1993: 116; "swords": 113. A langue-de-boeuf is "a kind of spike or halbert, with a head shaped like an ox tongue" (*OED*, sense 2, dated from 1450).

110 "We now know": Matthews 1966: 7. "Strangely": Carpenter 1980: 31. "Like": Field 1993: 1. "Must": Field 2004: 359. Hicks suggests that Malory was "something like 21" when he was at Calais in 1415 (1928: 13). Carpenter also thinks that Malory was in Calais at this time (see 1980: 32). If he was born in 1394, however, the rapist and would-be assassin was a man in his mid-fifties. "Complete": Field 1993: 121.

111 "Buryed": Dugdale 1656: 56. "HIC": Matthews 1966: 33. Matthews's source is a 1915 book by Charles L. Kingsford. Using B. L. Cotton Vitellius F. xii, folio 284r and a register of sepulchral inscriptions in Greyfriars church compiled by J. G. Nichols in 1838, Field gives a slightly different version of the epitaph: "Thomas Mallere valens miles qui obiit 14 die mensis marcii anno domini 1470 de parochia de monkenkyrkby in comitatu warwicii" (1993: 133). A loose translation of the epitaph might read: "Here lies Sir Thomas Malory | Gallant soldier | Died 14 March 1470 | Of the parish of Monks Kirby in | the county of Warwickshire". Field points out that the year of Malory's death is actually 1471: the epitaph gave the year 1470 "because in the fifteenth century the year began on 25 March", Lady Day (1993: 133). "Was never . . . him": Field 1996: 117. "Ornate . . . Spain": Matthews 1966: 33.

112 "Orgy": Baugh 1933: 4. "Gangster": Bradbrook 1958: 9. "Single grand Paradox": Lewis 1963: 7 (the other paradoxes are that the work strikes the reader as "a rich feast of marvels" but Malory tried "to eliminate the marvellous"; that the *Morte* looks like a case of "interwoven" narrative but Malory "detested this technique"; that the Grail quest is fundamentally spiritual but Malory "evaded the religious significance"; and that Saintsbury's sense of the *Morte* as "one story and one book" is incompatible with Vinaver's conviction that Malory intended to produce a number of separate "works"). "Moral paradox": Matthews 1966: 43; "too absolute": 50.

113 "Not unusual . . . century": Field 1993: 87.

114 "Absurd": Kittredge 1928: viii. "Legal": Hicks 1928: 52. "Knave . . . eyes": Lewis 1963: 10. "Ambiguous": Reiss 1966: 17. "Less offensive": Matthews 1966: 17; "abducted . . . carnally": 44–5. "But": Field 1993: 97; "modern": 106.

115 "To make": Field 1993: 106. Bellamy argues that when charges of

rape and theft were combined, one "may suspect . . . a lack of resistance" to either crime "on the woman's part" (1998: 180).

116 "False": Batt 2004: 799. "Unparalleled . . . Conquest": Webster 1998: 1.

117 "Bloodsucking": Altick 1950: 80. On the complaints against the Abbot of Combe, see Hicks 1928: 45–7. "Discontent": Hicks 1928: 24; "political . . . doctrinal": 40; "fountain-head . . . Lollardy": 22. On Stafford's opposition to Lollardy, see 25. Followers of John Wycliffe (*c.* 1328–84), the Oxford academic and Bible translator, the Lollards disapproved of the Church's involvement in secular affairs and its interest in worldly wealth. They were initially supported by anti-clerical members of the nobility, but this largely ceased when John Ball espoused Lollardy during the Peasants' Revolt of 1381. The term 'Lollard' probably came from Middle Dutch *lollaerd*, a 'mumbler' or 'mutterer' (*OED*).

118 "Personal . . . dissent": Field 1993: 96; "private . . . picture": 103–4. Mortimer's speech: *1 Henry VI*, II. v. 61–92.

119 "Collective . . . lay": Carpenter 1997: 22; "took": 46; "ancient . . . myth": Carpenter 1997: 114; "ancient . . . society": 120; "ins": 107. "Derogation": Keen 1990: 158. "Self-justifying": Carpenter 1997: 102.

120 "Very difficult period": Carpenter 1997: 2. "An affray": Carpenter 1997: 135; "armies": 21.

121 On Blore Heath as the beginning of the Wars, see Carpenter 1997: 116. "Essentially": Webster 1998: 71. The red rose and the white: the scene between Somerset and Warwick occurs in *1 Henry VI*, II. iv. "Madness": *1 Henry VI*, IV. i. 111. "Unite": *Richard III*, V. iv. 32. "Inadequate": Webster 1998: 71. "This is not": Carpenter 1997: 1.

122 "Perfectly": Carpenter 1997: 252. For the argument that long-term social and economic factors do not explain the Wars of the Roses, see Webster 1998: 12–13. 'Over-mighty' barons: for criticism of the Whig account of the Wars of the Roses, see Carpenter 1997: 6–10. "Rooted": Carpenter 1997: 253. Carpenter's account of Henry VI inverts the 'great man' theory of history: here, personal inadequacy determines events. Carpenter much prefers strong leaders: Edward IV's murder of Henry VI in 1471 is "something he should have done long before"; the assassination in 1477 of Edward's brother Clarence makes the King "a man to be reckoned with" (180, 190).

123 "Lack . . . disorder": Carpenter 1997: 112; "by . . . obligation": 52. "Setter up": *3 Henry VI*, II. iii. 37. "Immensely": Carpenter 1997: 131.

124 "Convenience . . . fragmented": Carpenter 1992: 10. "Esquire . . . knight": Field: 1993, 83–4. For the figure of 2,000 armigerous gentry and 74 knights of the shire, see Wolffe 1981: 99, 216. 'Armigerous' means "entitled to bear (heraldic) arms" (*OED*). "23. *H.* 6.": Dugdale

1656: 56. "May well": Field 1993: 34. "By 8 October": Field 2004: 359. "Coal-face": Carpenter 1997: 46. "Something": Carpenter 1992: 39; "specialist": 82. "Less": Field 1993: 84. On Malory's debts, see Field 1993: 108, 117–19. On the £40 figure, see Keen 1990: 8–9.

125 "Property . . . cultivating": Carpenter 1980: 42. "Poor": Carpenter 1992: 60. "Highly probable": Hicks 1928: 10. "From 1439": Carpenter 1980: 33. "May": Field 2004: 359. "Associates": Field 1993: 89. Carpenter prefers to see Malory's election in 1445 as evidence of his connection to Henry Beauchamp, the first Duke of Warwick: according to her, though, Malory was a "none-too-reliable" supporter of Beauchamp (1992: 418). "Provable . . . influence": Field 1993: 95. "Most wealthy": Wolffe 1981: 99.

126 "Belonged . . . York": Field 1993: 98.

127 "Community": Watts 2004: 738. "Beheaded": Carpenter 1997: 114. "Headless . . . sands": Wolffe 1981: 232. "First": Watts 2004: 738.

128 "I cleft": *3 Henry VI*, I. i. 12. "To moderate": Rawcliffe 2004: 53; "ungovernable": 54. "Single . . . sword": Carpenter, 1992: 427; "small . . . devastation": 455. "Confrontational": Carpenter 1997, 135; "bi-partisan": 142.

129 "Beyond": Field 1993: 106. Vinaver would agree: £500 is "an impossible figure" (1947: xvii n. 2). "Mounted . . . occasion": Field 1993: 99.

130 "Over-much . . . stigma": Kittredge 1928: vii. "Mindless": Carpenter 1997: 53. "Appalling . . . violence": Carpenter 1992: 495; "series": 365; "criminal . . . troublemaker": 430; "spectacularly . . . spiral": 432.

131 "Upper class": Bellamy 1998: 180. "Not . . . terrors": Carpenter 1997: 48. "Flagrant . . . of Malory": Field 1993: 105.

132 "Special": Field 1993: 115; "Lancastrian . . . subversion": 117. "Almost": Carpenter 1980: 41. "Record": Field 1993: 117.

133 "To make": Field 1993: 109; "another": 112. "Very probable . . . gratitude": Field 1993: 30; "left": 120. Control of Edward IV's northern campaign was given to Warwick in July 1461, though the Northumbrian castles – Warkworth, Alnwick, Dunstanburgh and Bamburgh – changed hands several times and were only finally taken after the Battles of Hedgeley Moor (25 April 1464) and Hexham (15 May 1464), at which Warwick's brother, John Neville, Lord Montague, was victorious.

134 "His first": Field 1993: 104; "might": 128. "Legendary . . . dagger": Pollard 2004: 534. "Filled": Field 1993: 103. For discussion of when Warwick joined the Yorkists, see Carpenter 1997: 127.

135 "Overlords": Carpenter 1980, 32; "still . . . 1459": 40. On Malory's connections with the Duke of Norfolk, see Field 1993: 108–15, 121. Field points out that the Caludon estate was historically connected to Norfolk – a fact which might have come as "an extremely disagreeable surprise" to Malory in the aftermath of his 1450 vandalism (100).

136 "Most turbulent . . . was": Field 1993: 122; "illicitly": 121. The Battle
    of Blore Heath was fought on 23 September 1459 and may have left
    3,000 dead.
137 "Armour . . . Street": Field 1993: 122. Watling Street, the ancient
    British trackway later paved by the Romans, leads from Dover to
    London, more or less following the route of the A2, and then from
    London to Wroxeter near Shrewsbury, roughly along the present-day
    A5. For the full route, see fig. 9. For the route through London, see
    fig. 10. For the route through Warwickshire see fig. 8 (this also shows
    the route of the Fosse Way, which connects Exeter and Lincoln and
    crosses Watling Street at High Cross, about four miles north of
    Newbold Revel).
138 "Melted": Carpenter 1997: 145. The defection of the Calais contin-
    gent under Sir Andrew Trollope seems to have been the main cause
    of the Yorkist collapse at Ludford Bridge. Warwick subsequently fled
    to Calais. York fled to Ireland after abandoning his wife and three
    children in Ludlow. On Malory's first period of imprisonment and
    possible release dates, see Field 1993: 122–4, 142; "the thick": 126.
    Wakefield: fought on 30 December 1460, the battle resulted in the
    death of York, who during an ill-advised sortie was caught in 'Dickie's
    Meadow' – the open space outside Sandal Castle – by Lancastrian
    forces. The Battle of Mortimer's Cross in Herefordshire (2 February
    1461) was, like Blore Heath, a Yorkist victory – the first for Edward,
    York's son and the future king. It is remembered for the appearance
    of a sun dog – "Three glorious suns, each one a perfect sun", as
    Edward puts it in *3 Henry VI* (II. i. 26). The second Battle of St Albans
    (17 February 1461) was another Lancastrian victory, or rather a defeat
    for Warwick, who may have been a subtle statesman but seems to
    have been rather a poor general: after house to house fighting in the
    town, the Earl was outflanked by the Lancastrian forces and forced to
    retreat at dusk. Shakespeare's Warwick says that he promised his
    troops "high pay, and great rewards: | But all in vain". And so, collec-
    tively, "we fled" (*3 Henry VI*, II. i. 134–7). In Act II, scene iii, Henry
    VI's wife Margaret mocks the "long-tongu'd" Warwick, saying that at
    St Albans, "your legs did better service than your hands" (102–4).
    Until February 1461, the Lancastrian record in the Wars of the Roses
    was the stronger one: the Yorkists had won a major victory at
    Northampton and two minor ones at Blore Heath and Mortimer's
    Cross but the Lancastrians had imposed three thumping defeats at
    Ludford Bridge, Wakefield and St Albans. The Battle of Towton in
    Yorkshire (29 March 1461) turned the balance in favour of the
    Yorkists. Towton is not particularly famous but is almost certainly the
    largest battle ever fought in this country (it may have involved 80,000
    troops) and also the bloodiest: figures of around 28,000 dead have

been quoted. Given what we know of his connections, it's possible to speculate that Malory travelled to the battlefield with Warwick's contingent and was part of a cavalry detachment under Fauconberg which forded the River Aire and engaged Lancastrian forces on 28 March at the Battle of Ferrybridge. Clifford, the Lancastrian commander at this encounter, was shot in the throat and later hacked to pieces. The Battle of Towton took place twelve miles to the north of Ferrybridge the next day. There was hand to hand fighting in driving snow. When the Lancastrian lines gave way early in the afternoon, bridges broke under the weight of fleeing men and streams filled with bodies which then served others for bridges. "Could": Field 1998: 54.

139 "Pouring rain": Pollard 2004: 531. The Battle of Northampton was Warwick's most significant military success after the first Battle of St Albans (he ran away at the Battle of Ludford Bridge and at the second Battle of St Albans). Assisted by treachery in the Lancastrian ranks, the Earl was able in half an hour to break through on the right flank and attack the group around the King, killing Shrewsbury, Percy, Egremont, Beaumont, and also Buckingham, who was "slain near the King's tent" (Rawcliffe 2004: 54).

140 "Overlook": *3 Henry VI*, I. iv. 180; "irks . . . soul": II. ii. 6.

141 "A chill": Horrox 2004: 857.

142 "Something": Field 1993: 131; "unlikely": 144; "royal": 147; "crime": 144; "dangerous": 31; "real": 138.

143 "Natural": Field 1993: 132. "Return": *3 Henry VI*, III. iii. 194. "Obscure": Carpenter 1997: 172. "Was not . . . assumption": Field 1993: 137.

144 "Followed": Field 1993: 103. "reasonable . . . allegiances": Carpenter 1992: 429; "very nominal . . . divisions": 438–9. "Crude choices": Carpenter 1997: 150; "more . . . support": 152; "political": 263.

145 "Lesson . . . politician": Carpenter 1980: 40–3. "Criminal . . . often": Carpenter 1992: 622. "Loser": Carpenter 1980: 42.

146 "Thug": Carpenter 1997: 20. Bastard feudalism tends to be seen as an unstable hierarchy in which the land-based relationships of true feudalism gave way to "a debased dependency resting on money and contract"; Carpenter views affinity groups as a more prevalent and also more stable social arrangement (Carpenter 1997: 8).

147 "Assisted": Wolffe 1981: 27–28. "England . . . sun": *1 Henry VI*, I. i. 7–14. "The most": Wolffe 1981: 3. "Fatal . . . lose all": *1 Henry VI*, III. i. 193–8. "No king": Griffiths 2004: 509.

148 "Destitute": Wolffe 1981: 211. "Limpness": Carpenter 1997: 155; "incapacity . . . inertness": 255–6. "Indecision . . . obstinacy": Webster 1998: 58–9. "Semblance": Carpenter 1997: 93; "no king": 114; "positive . . . rule": 256. "Sillie": Wolffe 1981: 351.

149 "Poor": Carpenter 1997: 154. "Worschipfully . . . kepte": Griffiths 2004: 508; "saddely": 499. The heretic: see Aurner 1933: 385. "Pure": Webster 1998: 31. According to Wolffe, an exhumation conducted in 1910 found hair matted with blood on Henry's skull (see 1981: 347).

150 "To become . . . innocence": Griffiths 2004: 500; "shocked": 502; "more timorous": 508.

151 "Boys . . . rule": Carpenter 1997: 92. "Custodian": Griffiths 2004: 498; "helpless": 507. "Subject": *2 Henry VI*, IV. ix. 6. "Homely": *3 Henry VI*, II. v. 22.

152 "No sense . . . upright": Wolffe 1981: 272. "Catatonia": Carpenter 1997: 129. "Catatonic schizophrenia": Webster 1998: 20.

153 "Shulde": Griffiths 2004: 507; "first": 504.

154 "First . . . realms": Wolffe 1981: 28. "Played": Watts 2004: 734. "Slavish": Wolffe 1981: 145. New College, Oxford and Winchester College were founded by William of Wykeham, Bishop of Winchester, in 1379 and 1382 respectively. "Interested . . . purpose": Carpenter 1997: 108. "Over chargefull": Wolffe 1981: 8.

155 "Of connyng . . . habit": Griffiths 2004: 501–2. "Bookish": *2 Henry VI*, I. i. 260. "My study": *1 Henry VI*, V. i. 22. "*Disguised*": *3 Henry VI*, III. i, stage direction. "*Discovered*": *3 Henry VI*, V. vi, stage direction; "cam'st": V. vi. 54.

156 "Rescues . . . childbirth": Wolffe 1981: 354.

157 The King's Bench was a peripatetic court until 1421, when it was located permanently in Westminster Hall. Malory made numerous appearances here in the 1450s. Malory is known to have been committed to Ludgate Prison between January and April 1452 and spent a second period here between January and May 1457. This prison, housed within the westernmost gate of the old walled city, was rebuilt in 1215 and demolished in 1760. Malory was held in the King's Bench Prison (properly the Marshalsea of the Marshal of the King's Bench, not to be confused with the other and more famous Marshalsea, the nearby Marshalsea of the Marshal of the King's Household) from April 1452 to November 1454, although he was out on bail for two periods of uncertain duration (possibly October 1452 to October 1453 and May–October 1454). There were subsequent spells in the King's Bench Prison in early 1456, between December 1457 and April 1459, and in 1460. According to Bellamy, the King's Bench Prison was mainly used for "prisoners awaiting trial" (1973: 168–9). The building was repaired after Cade's Rebellion in 1450 but demolished in 1761, when the prison moved to another site in Southwark until its closure in 1880. Residents have included Thomas Dekker, Emma, Lady Hamilton, Marc Isambard Brunel and Dickens's Mr Micawber. Malory was moved to the Tower of London in May 1455, shortly before the first Battle of St Albans (possibly to

prevent him being freed if Yorkist forces entered London) and remained there until January 1456, when he returned to the King's Bench Prison. His continued detention was clearly important to the Lancastrian authorities: Dixon notes that the Tower was used for "the most dangerous offenders" (1850: 32). The Tower served as a prison from the earliest times but facilities were extended under the reigns of Henry III (1216–72) and Edward I (1272–1307). Prisoners have included Geoffrey Chaucer, Henry VI, Sir Thomas More, Sir Francis Bacon, Anne Boleyn, Thomas Cromwell, Thomas Cranmer, Lady Jane Grey, Sir Walter Raleigh, Samuel Pepys, Sir Robert Walpole and, more recently, Rudolf Hess. Malory seems to have been moved from the Tower to King's Bench Prison and then to Newgate early in 1456. He also spent part of the year 1460 here. Located on the site of the Central Criminal Court, Newgate was built in 1188 and demolished only in 1904, though it sustained considerable damage during the Great Fire (1666) and the Gordon Riots (1780). In 1862 Mayhew and Binny drew attention to the "stern grandeur" of the architecture (588). Hangings took place on Monday mornings, when, according to Dixon, the nearby ale houses were "gorged with company" (1850, 193). Prisoners have included Thomas Nashe, Ben Jonson, Daniel Defoe – and Defoe's Moll Flanders. Malory may well have spent significant portions of his second period of imprisonment here. The British Library's Archives and Manscripts online catalogue entry for "Sir Thomas Malory, Le Morte Darthur" claims that the *Morte* was "composed in Newgate prison". But Field thinks that Malory was "probably" held in the Tower after June 1468 (2004: 360). Malory also seems to have had some connection with the Fleet Prison in 1452, although it is not clear that he was actually imprisoned here. Described by Brown as "the oldest prison in England", the Fleet was certainly in use from the twelfth century (1996: 1). By the thirteenth century it was being used to hold debtors as well as "those who had trespassed in the King's parks and forests" (Brown 1996: 4). Having been rebuilt after the Peasant's Revolt (1381), the Great Fire of London and the Gordon Riots, the Fleet was demolished in 1846. Inmates have included John Donne, William Wycherley and William Penn, as well as Shakespeare's Falstaff. On Malory's periods of detention in London prisons, see Field 1993: 107–32. "Near": Field 1993: 170.

158 "An horse-litter ... Albans": Malory 1978: I. 4. On Uther at St Albans, see Geoffrey of Monmouth 1984: VIII. 23–24. According to Geoffrey, Arthur is "only fifteen years old" when he becomes King (IX. 1).

159 The location of Joyous Gard: see Malory 1978: XXI. 12. "Great guns": Malory 1978: XXI. 1. The anachronism might tend to confirm

a prevalent perception that the 'medieval mind' was ahistorical. In a letter of 28 January 1959, however, John Steinbeck noticed something which points in a different direction: "in the *Morte* there is no mention of the bow" (1976: 327). This isn't quite right: Merlin uses "a bow and arrows" in one of his disguises; Gawaine feels "wonderly sore" after being shot through the arm by an archer; Tristram is "shot . . . through the shoulder" with an "envenomed" arrow and also "in the thick of the thigh"; in his chamber at the Castle Adventurous, Bors endures a volley of arrows, some of which "hurt him in the bare places"; Launcelot is shot "in the thick of the buttock" by an archeress and his horse is killed by Meliagrance's "thirty archers" (Malory 1978: I. 17; III. 8; VIII. 35; X. 87; XI. 5; XVIII. 21; XIX. 4). But the point is an intriguing one: Malory must have been familiar with the use of the longbow in warfare, but he always refers to it as a weapon of wood and field – ideal equipment for an ambush but not for a pitched battle. Perhaps he wanted to keep so yeomanlike a weapon out of the aristocratic world he was conjuring up in his mind. But I am inclined to see the omission of the bow from the *Morte*'s battle scenes as evidence that he was thinking in historical terms. "An hundred": Malory 1978: XXI. 4. "A view": Field 1993: 126.

160 "Final . . . situation": Archibald and Edwards 1996: xiv. "They": Malory 1978: XXI. 3. "Clear": Aurner 1933: 388 (see also Stewart 1935: 209).

161 "Different": Field 1993: 124; "sympathy": 2. "Great default": Malory 1978: XXI. 1. "National": Field 1993: 146. "Remarkably": Field 1998: 66.

162 "Fair . . . force": Malory 1978: III. 3.

163 "Unto hanging": Malory 1978: XIX. 4. On Malory's experience of Thames river travel, see Field 1993: 107.

164 "That ever": Malory 1978: XX. 13; "love day": X. 15.

165 "Sore . . . breast": Malory 1978: V. 6; "duke": V. 12; "kindness": XX. 1; "overthrown . . . down": XX. 21.

166 Warwick as Mordred: Hales argues that Malory's remarks on the "great default" (Malory 1978: XXI. 1) should be read as "a manifest remonstrance against the re-opening of a war that had already cost England so much blood" (1900: xviii). His point is that Mordred's rebellion against Arthur can be equated with Warwick's rebellion against Edward IV. This is an intriguing suggestion, although the chronology is tight. If Malory wrote all of the *Morte* whilst in prison, around 388 days' work would have been available. He was excluded from Edward IV's pardon in February 1469 and we can assume that he was by then in prison; the *Morte* was completed in the "ix yere" of Edward's reign, which is to say by 3 March 1470 (Malory 1485: XXI. 13). For a manuscript of almost 300,000 words this period of time

implies a composition rate of about 750 words a day. But if Hales is right, we must consider the possibility that Malory only began to write the *Morte* in July 1469, when Warwick's abandonment of Edward became public knowledge. This would increase his rate of composition to around 1,200 words a day – not impossible, but obviously a greater challenge (particularly in the circumstances). Whether or not one takes the connection between Mordred and Warwick seriously it seems more likely that Malory composed a significant part of the *Morte* some time before his final period of imprisonment.

167 "Four hundred": Malory 1978: X. 58; " an hundred": XXI. 4. "More": Chrétien de Troyes 2004: 104–5; "more": 202; "never . . . five hundred": 115; "only . . . gathering": 430. On Malory's "depopulated and ruined countryside" as a portrait of "England after the first plague", see Steinbeck 1976: 358.

168 "Ready . . . country": Field 1993: 144. On Malory's sources, see Vinaver 1929: 128–54; Field 1998; Norris 2008; Windeatt 2009. Vinaver argues that Malory's knowledge of Arthurian sources was comparatively limited: for an alternative view, see Wilson 1950. "Under": Altick 1950: 84. "Hour": Parins 1988: 55. "Faded": Chambers 1922: 3.

169 "Philistines . . . treatises": Carpenter 1992: 205. Malory's familiarity with the Count of Armagnac's library: Matthews initially made the suggestion (1966: 142) but Field discounts it as "untenable" (1993: 25). "Long passages": Norris 2008: 166. "Relatively": Field 1993: 6; "honourable": 144. "Rooms . . . pleasant": Bellamy 1998: 171. Malory's use of Greyfriars library: Hicks raised the possibility (1928: 66–8) and was followed by a number of critics including Altick (1950: 75–6) and Matthews (1966: 33, 52). In his 1967 introduction to the second edition of Malory's *Works*, Vinaver thought that Malory "possibly" used Greyfriars (xxvi). But Meale asserts that the Greyfriars theory is supported by "no convincing argument" (2004: 866).

170 In 1982 Field declared that Malory "probably" knew the library of "the king's brother-in-law, Anthony Wydeville" (455). This suggestion was originally made by Griffith (1981). Field later argued more cautiously that "any such suggestion must be very tentative" (1993: 145). Meale finds the Woodville connection "intriguing" but remains skeptical: as a "gentleman amateur", Malory didn't necessarily need the assistance of an aristocratic patron and might have owned the relevant works himself (2004: 866, 878). "Bibliographical": Matthews 1966: 57.

171 "Hapless . . . shuttlecock": Altick 1950: 74. "Deep . . . sorrow": Malory 1978: VI. 2; "in sunder": VI. 9.

172 "During": Malory 1978: IV. 23; "dureth": X. 56; "endure": XVIII.

25; "duresse": XIII. 12. 'Duresse': *OED* defines this as "hardness, roughness, violence, severity; hardiness of endurance, resistance, etc.; firmness" (sense 1). Sense 2 refers to "harsh or severe treatment, infliction of hardship, oppression, cruelty; harm, injury; affliction". But sense 3 is also relevant: "forcible restraint or restriction; confinement, imprisonment".

173 "Strong . . . pain": Malory 1978: IX. 36. "Most . . . experience": Hicks 1928: 84–5. On the personal quality of the prison passage in Book IX, see also Chambers 1922: 12; Vinaver 1929: 8; Field 1978: 34. "The greatest pain": Malory 1978: IX. 36.

174 Field argues that Vinaver "proved beyond reasonable doubt" that the Winchester and Caxton texts were independently derived from "a common original" and provided "good evidence" that this was itself a copy (1998: 12). "Smudges": Hellinga 1981: 128. In 1975, Hellinga detected oil-based printer's ink on the manuscript (scribes used water-based compounds). In 1977, after the manuscript had been moved from Winchester College to the British Library, Hellinga used an infra-red image converter provided by the Metropolitan Police's Forensic Science Laboratory to show traces of Caxton's type at more than 60 points. She concluded that the manuscript had been in Caxton's office sometime between 1480 and 1483.

175 On the sale of the Winchester manuscript, see Dancy 1995: 292–4. Yeats-Edwards (one of Oakeshott's successors as School Librarian at Winchester College) reports that the proposal to sell the manuscript "split the college in half" (2000: 380). When Yeats-Edwards received the British Library's £150,000 cheque at noon on Friday 26 March 1976, he was startled to see this unique manuscript simply "popped into a knapsack" by the BL official (380–1). Until 1990, the college used the proceeds of the sale to fund two 'Malory scholars' each year. 'Colophon': "the inscription or device . . . formerly placed at the end of a book" (*OED*, sense 2). "Thys . . . al": Malory 1485: XXI. 13 (folio ee62).

176 "Entytled . . . notwythftondinge": Malory 1485: XXI. 13 (folio ee62). "Accidentally . . . *Table*": Field 2004: 360. "The hoole": Malory 1485: XXI. 13 (folios ee61–ee62). In Malory 1889, "hoole" is incorrectly given as "booke" (II, 861). "The noble": Malory 1889: I, 4. "Ignorant": Vinaver 1929: 10.

177 On Spenser's and Shakespeare's knowledge of the *Morte*, see Shepherd 2004: xxix.

178 "Black-letter": from around 1600, "the form of type used by the early printers, as distinguished from the 'Roman' type, which subsequently prevailed" (*OED*).

179 "Piece": A. S. G. Edwards 1996: 242. "Scorned": Merriman 1973: 32. "Standing pool . . . bawdry": Ascham 1909: 83. Thinking, perhaps, of

the reign of Henry VIII, Ascham remembers a time when "God's Bible was banished the Court, and 'Morte D'Arthur' received into the prince's chamber" (83). But he is clear that "ten 'Morte Arthurs' do not the tenth part so much harm" as more recent translations of "books made in Italy" (84). "Vile . . . whoremasters": Parins 1988: 59. "As the author": [Oldys] 1747–8: 1243 (repr. by Parins, who identifies the author as William Oldys). "High . . . door": Girouard 1981: 205. In Dante's "Inferno", Francesca and Paolo are confined to the second circle of Hell for committing adultery. In Francesca's account, the lovers became aroused by reading about Launcelot and his Queen. Just one page is all it takes: they kiss – and "that day we got no further with our reading" (Dante 1998: Canto V, l. 138).

180 "Politically . . . Arthurianism": Higham 2002: 234–5. Henry VII married Elizabeth of York in 1486 and Arthur was born at Winchester in September of that year but the succession passed to Henry when Arthur died in 1502. Oakeshott thought that the Winchester manuscript was brought to the town at the time of Prince Arthur's birth (see Dancy 1995: 85). For an alternative history based on Malory's descendants, see Yeats-Edwards 2000. "English": Higham 2002: 235. "Imperial": Scarisbrick 1968: 271; "foundation . . . empire": 272–3.

181 "There was": Malory 1978: 2. "Ridiculed . . . court cult": Higham 2002: 236–8. "Beyond . . . Saxons": Holinshed 1976: 474. "Royal": Higham 2002: 238.

182 "Recall": Parker 1968: 186; "Igraine . . . such": 189–90; 'monkish': 296. On seventeenth-century Arthurianism, see also Brinkley 1932.

183 "FIB": Higham 2002: 240–1. On Dryden's *King Arthur*, see Shap 2002.

184 "About 1702": the date is my best guess (the Cambridge University Library catalogue gives 1700 and the British Library catalogue suggests 1685 or even 1680). *Great Britain's Glory* is surely a response to the succession crisis which followed the death of Queen Anne's last surviving child in 1700. It also seems to support union between England and Scotland. This was only achieved by the Act of Union in 1707, although the negotiations which led to the Act began in 1702. J. S.'s version of the Arthurian story is anti-Hanoverian and may also serve a Jacobite purpose, harking back to the unification of the realm under James I and VI and holding up James II and his heirs as rightful monarchs of "Great Britain". The *DNB* reports that John Shurley ("*fl.* 1681–1702") "sometimes used the name of J. S. Gent" (Burns 2004: 397). The old *DNB* has it that John Shirley [*sic*] ("*fl.* 1680–1702") was said, "on very doubtful evidence", to be the son of James Shirley the dramatist, a catholic and a royalist (E. I. C. 1897: 134). Both editions of the *DNB* list versions of Amadis the Gaul and the life of Guy of Warwick among Shurley/Shirley's works, but only the old *DNB* mentions his abridgment of the "History of King Arthur". It may be

significant that further editions of *Great Britain's Glory* appeared in 1708 and 1715 – the years, respectively, of the attempted invasion by James Stuart and the first Jacobite Rising. "Pedant": Dryden 1958: IV, 1759. In Pope's "The Dunciad" (1728), Blackmore appears in the 'Argument' of the first book as a citizen of the "great empire of Dulness" (1975: 125). When the goddess visits the "cave of Poverty and Poetry", we are told that Eusden, the former Laureate, here ekes out "Blackmore's endless line" (ll. 34, 104). In the second book, Dulness opens her public games. In a footnote, Pope attributes to Dryden the phrase about the "everlasting" Blackmore (143). "Antient ... Aliens": Shurley *c.* 1702: n. p. "Minor": Higham 2002: 241; "some foundation . . . Arthur": 243.

185 "Lords": Malory 1978: 3. "Young . . . maid": Ascham 1909: 84. "Corrected . . . prophane": A. S. G. Edwards 1996: 242. "Eye": Merriman 1973: 130. "Crept . . . library": Darton 1932: 43.

186 "Cultural": St Clair 2004: 79; "old canon": 121. "Literally": A. S. G. Edwards 1996: 243. "The Discovery of Prince Arthur's Tomb": the title of the painting alludes, not to the *Morte*, but to the legend recounted by Holinshed that in 1191 the corpse of Arthur was discovered at Glastonbury under "a mightie broad stone with a leaden cross . . . conteining this inscription: 'Hic iacet sepultus inclytus rex Arthurius in insula Aualoniae' ['Here lies buried the renowned King Arthur in the Isle of Avalon']". According to Holinshed, Guenever's body lay next to that of Arthur: her hair was "of colour like to the burnished gold" but when touched it "fell to dust" (1976: 577). "Acknowledged": Poulson 1999: 16. The painting was William Bell Scott's "King Arthur Carried to the Land of Enchantment", which was displayed with the "quondam Rex que futurus" quotation from Book XXI, Chapter 7 of the *Morte*. On the abolition of perpetual copyright, see St Clair 2004: 43–54. "Remarkably . . . edited": Pochoda 1971: 142.

187 "Several . . . volume": Lockhart 1902: 228. Irving's reference to the "black-letter volume" suggests that Scott owned Stansby's 1634 edition of the *Morte*. On Wordsworth and Keats reading Malory, see A. S. G. Edwards 1996: 248. "Still strange": Tennyson 1969: 1464. "Monstrous": Girouard 1981: 33. "Stillborn": Merriman 1973: 173. "Without": Parins 1988: 78. "Scrupulous": Southey 1817: xxviii (repr. in Parins 1988). Merriman confirms that Southey's edition is "generally accurate" (1973: 130). "My delight . . . copy": Southey 1817: xxviii. "The 1634": Poulson 1999: 13. "There was": Southey 1817: xxviii; "adventure": xxxi–xxxii.

188 "Much . . . art': Hallam Tennyson 1897: I, 194 (the comment is dated to 1842). "Ill-digested": Benson 1968: 81–2. "Mythical": Higham 2002: 249; "whether": 251.

189 "Compilation": Southey 1817: ii; "French": xxvi. "Compilation": Wright 1858: x. "Author . . . end": Strachey 1868: viii. "Our first": Parins 1988: 323. "One work . . . novel": Lanier 1880: xx. "One of . . . book': Parins 1988: 390–1. "Scattered": Raleigh 1911: 14. "One of": Saintsbury 1913: 25; "mere": 8; "vast . . . book": 25.

190 "Little": Tennyson 1969: 1464; "3 vol.": 585; "haunted . . . subjects": 1462. "Sir Launcelot and Queen Guinevere: A Fragment" was probably completed in 1830 but remained unpublished until the two-volume *Poems* of 1842; "The Lady of Shallott" had been written by May 1832 and was published in *Poems* (1832); "Morte d'Arthur" was completed in 1834 but not issued until 1842; "Sir Galahad" was written by September 1834 but again remained unpublished until 1842. Tennyson did not embark on the "Idylls of the King" until the 1850s. "Enid" was privately printed in *Enid and Nimuë: The True and the False* (1857), as was "Nimuë" (later "Vivien"). The first version of *Idylls of the King* appeared in 1859 and consisted of "Enid", "Vivien" (later "Merlin and Vivien"), "Elaine" (later "Lancelot and Elaine") and "Guinevere". It sold 10,000 copies in one week and, according to Faulkner, marked Tennyson's acceptance as "the great English poet" (2009: 25). Tennyson expanded "Enid" in 1870, divided it into two books in 1873 and came up with final titles – "The Marriage of Geraint" and "Geraint and Enid" – in 1886. After the publication of the first four idylls, Tennyson paused until 1869, when he added "The Coming of Arthur", "The Holy Grail", "Pelleas and Ettarre" and "The Passing of Arthur" to the text (the latter poem included the earlier "Morte d'Arthur"). "The Last Tournament" was included in 1871; "Gareth and Lynette" in 1872. Although it was completed by 1874, "Balin and Balan" wasn't added until 1885, when Tennyson gave the "Idylls" its final form. Ricks observes that the composition of the "Idylls" is "not a record of firm creative decision" (1999: 660–1).

191 "Arthurian revival": Merriman 1973: 127–8. The trailblazers were the nineteenth-century editors of the *Morte*. After Southey and Haslewood, editions were produced by Thomas Wright (*La Mort d'Arthure*, 1858), Edward Strachey (*Morte Darthur*, 1868), Oskar Sommer (*Le Morte Darthur*, 1889), Ernest Rhys (Books I–IX of Malory in *The Noble and Joyous History of King Arthur*, 1893; Books X–XXI in *The Book of Marvellous Adventures, & other Books of the Morte D'Arthur, c.* 1893), F. J. Simmons and John Rhys (*The Birth, Life and Acts of King Arthur*, 1893–4), Israel Gollancz (*Le Morte D'Arthur*, 1897) and A. W. Pollard (*Le Morte Darthur*, 1900). Critical discussions of the Arthurian Revival in general include Chandler 1971, Merriman 1973, Girouard 1981, Mancoff 1992, Archibald and Edwards 1996, Lacy 1996, Mancoff 1998, Lacy 2005, Lupack 2007, Archibald and Putter 2009 and Fulton 2012. On the "forgotten tradition" of Arthurian literature

by women, see Lupack and Lupack 1999b (xi). On Arthurian themes in art, see Mancoff 1990; Mancoff 1995; Whittaker 1990; Poulson 1998 Poulson 1999; Howey and Reimer 2003; Lupack and Lupack 2008; Fox-Friedman 2009. On Arthurian themes in music, see Barber 2002; Nastali 2002; Reel 2002; Howey and Reimer 2003: 529–94.

192 "Essentially . . . unify": Coleridge 1987: 167. "Borrows": McCarthy 1996: 78. "Enchanted": Ker 1905: 150.

193 "Does not . . . fancy": Poulson 1999: 50. "Too": Ricks 1999: 661. "Frequently": Southey 1817: xv; "cruelties . . . ages": xxx; "original": xv. "Touched": Tennyson 1969: 1756.

194 "'Modern": Tennyson 1969: 597; "simple": 1471; "courtesy . . . knighthood": 1581; "zones . . . wings": 1669; "heathen . . . new": 1483; "pure . . . human-hearted": 1464; "first": 585.

195 "Allegorical": Tennyson 1969: 1463; "sublime . . . gone": 1467–8. Albert's Arthurianism: in 1847, as chair of the Fine Arts Commission, the Prince facilitated William Dyce's commission to decorate the Queen's Robing Room in the new Palace of Westminster with a series of frescoes based on the *Morte d'Arthur*. Designed by Charles Barry and Augustus Pugin, the new Palace was "the first civic structure in the medieval mode" (Mancoff 1990: 65). Dyce's work remained uncompleted on his death in 1864, but it installed Malory at the heart of a "national mythology" with a literality that even the "Idylls" could not match (68). "Complacency": Eliot 1932: 336. "Tempest . . . shadows": Tennyson 1969: 1755–6.

196 "Clean . . . season": Tennyson 1969: 1664; "reel": 1708; "stricken . . . world": 1742–3. On Tennyson's interest in Darwinism, see Hill in Tennyson 1999, 449 n. 4, 463 n. 8. On Tennyson's response to "scientific materialism", see Hill in Tennyson 1999, 375, 444 n. 1. According to Hill, Tennyson "misconstrued" Darwin, believing the theory of evolution supported a belief in progress (511 n. 3). If so, Tennyson's "reels back into the beast" may articulate a general loss of faith in human progress without specifically invoking evolution as an amoral process. "The old order": Tennyson 1969: 1752.

197 On Digby and Montgomerie, see Girouard 1981: 56, 87–110. "Eglinton Tomfooleryment": Mancoff 1995: 35. "Noble": Taylor and Brewer 1983: 3. "Stunner": according to Girouard, Burne-Jones's term for such women as Jane Burden. "Heavy": G. Burne-Jones 1904: I, 73. "Not even": Fitzgerald 1975: 13.

198 "General . . . heart": G. Burne-Jones 1904: I, 77; "Edouard": 81; "Crusade . . . age": 84; "exquisitely": 77; "age": 59.

199 "All . . . Tennysonian": Faulkner 2009: 16. "The cause": G. Burne-Jones 1904: I, 86. "Symbolic": Poulson 2000: 504; "ideals": 502. On the religious aspects of Pre-Raphaelite Arthurianism, see Poulson 1999: 62–82; Poulson 2001.

200 On the public and private aspects of the Arthurian revival, see Mancoff 1990: 136–7. "Brotherhood . . . London": G. Burne-Jones 2004: I, 77–8; "exclusive": 121; "first": 123.

201 "Flat . . . gone": G. Burne-Jones 2004: I, 78; "prime": 67; "fiercely . . . wanted": 182.

202 "Feasted": G. Burne-Jones 2004: I, 117; "innumerable cherries": I, 181. "Bowdlerization": Faulkner 2009: 33. "The book . . . birthright": G. Burne-Jones 1904: I, 116. Burne-Jones's love of Malory was expressed in a series of Arthurian works which followed the two drawings of Sir Galadad. The most notable of these were "The Beguiling of Merlin" (1874) and "The Sleep of Arthur in Avalon" (1880–98).

203 "Ideal . . . play": Taylor and Brewer 1983: 3. "Sanctioned": Mancoff 1990: xviii. "Revaluation": Taylor and Brewer 1983: 1.

204 "Tory-Radical": Chandler 1971: 6. On conservative and radical elements in the Arthurian revival, see also Girouard 1981: 70. "Aspiration . . . force": Board 1992: 137; "conscripted": 147. "Symbol": Poulson 1999: 112.

205 "Stirring": *The Manual for Leaders of the Order of Sir Galahad*: 3; "Foursquare": 15; "potted": 75; "Rah!": 182. On the Knights of King Arthur and similar organisations, see Fox-Friedman 1998; Lupack and Lupack 1999a; Lupack 2007: 164–7. On American uses of Arthurian material, see Lupack 1992; Lupack 1998; Lupack and Lupack 1999b; Sklar and Hoffman 2002.

206 "Scandalmongering": Goodman 1984: 252; "jealous . . . *vol-au-vent*": 254; "jingo", 242.

207 On de Liguoro, see Harty 2002a: 9. *Camelot* the musical: lyrics by Alan Jay Lerner and music by Frederick Loewe, with Richard Burton as Arthur, Julie Andrews as Guenever, Robert Goulet as Launcelot and Roddie McDowall as Mordred, 1960. *Camelot* the film: dir. Joshua Logan, with Richard Harris as Arthur, Vanessa Redgrave as Guenever, Franco Nero as Launcelot and David Hemmings as Mordred, Warner Brothers, 1967. Hollywood and Madison Avenue: see Davis 1985: 506. According to Davis, Jacqueline Kennedy told a journalist that, as a boy, her husband used to "dream of performing valiant deeds like . . . King Arthur's knights". In the White House, President Kennedy apparently played tunes from *Camelot* "before going to bed" (504). One imagines him singing along to the big number from Act I: "Don't let it be forgot, that once there was a spot, for one brief shining moment, that was known as Camelot". "First": Harty 2002a: 21.

208 "Explosion": Lacy 2009: 121. Critical discussions of twentieth-century Arthurianism include Taylor and Brewer 1983, Thompson 1985, Archibald and Edwards 1996, Lacy 1996, Mancoff 1998, Howey and Reimer 2003, Lacy 2005, Lupack 2007, Archibald and

Putter 2009 and Fulton 2012. On Arthurian literature by women, see Lupack and Lupack 1999b. On Arthurian themes in radio, see Howey and Reimer 2003: 497–528. On Arthurian movies, see Harty 2002a; Harty 2002b; Howey and Reimer 2003: 497–528; Fulton 2012, 479–542. On Arthurian themes in television, see Lacy 1996: 445–6; Olta 2002; Howey and Reimer 2003: 497–528. "The sun . . . faults": Steinbeck 1976: 303–5.

209 "The adventures": Manguel 1997: 225. David Jones tells the story of the grieving boy in his foreword to Barber's *Arthur of Albion* (see 1961: ix). "Sombre": McCullin 1992: 84; "what . . . ?": 224.

210 *Monty Python and the Holy Grail* (dir. Terry Gilliam and Terry Jones, EMI Films UK, 1974). David Day (2002) sees the film as a satire on academic history; Donald Hoffman argues that it is a "deconstruction of film tradition" (2002: 136).

211 Fielding: *The Tragedy of Tragedies; Or, The Life and Death of Tom Thumb the Great* (play, 1731); Peacock: "The Round Table; Or, King Arthur's Feast" (poem, 1817); *The Misfortunes of Elphin* (novel, 1829); du Maurier: "A Legend of Camelot" (illustration for *Punch*, 17 March 1866, satirizing the Pre-Raphaelite fascination with all things Arthurian). On humorous treatments of the Arthurian story, see Lupack 2007: 159–64. "Mocked": Malory 1978: X. 44. Cooper puts it well when she observes that Dinadan is "the only one of Malory's male characters who consistently understands how to relate to people other than by combat or kinship"; Dinadan "operates by intelligence and sympathy rather than brute force" and is "given a degree of inner life – of motivation and of unspoken thoughts – unusual in the *Morte*" (1996: 194). On Dinadan, see also Pochoda 1971: 111–12; McCarthy 1988: 34–5.

212 "Woman's . . . down": Malory 1978: X. 49; "dureth": X. 56.

213 "Computer-assisted": Pickford and Last 1981: ix.

214 Sponsored by the University of Rochester, the Camelot Project (www.lib.rochester.edu/camelot/cphome.stm) was created in 1995 by Alan Lupack and Barbara Tepa Lupack. The editorial board includes Norris J. Lacy and Bonnie Wheeler.

215 *Sir Galahad* and *Sir Tristram* were Round Table class LSLs (Landing Ship Logistics). *Sir Galahad* was launched in 1966 and destroyed at Bluff Cove in the Falkland Islands on 8 June 1982 with the loss of 48 lives. *Sir Tristram* was launched in the same year as *Sir Galahad* and seriously damaged during the Bluff Cove encounter when two further servicemen were also killed. She was later rebuilt and is now used for training purposes.

216 The most notable examples are Geoffrey Ashe (*The Quest for Arthur's Britain*, 1968) and John Morris (*The Age of Arthur*, 1973).

217 On Arthurian themes in comics, see Lacy 1996: 97–8; Tondro 2002;

Howey and Reimer 2003: 489–96. On games, see Corless 2002; Howey and Reimer 2003: 595–605. On advertising, see Sklar 2002.

218 "Rusted . . . moustache": MacLean 1957: 7; "good . . . lips': 23–4.

219 "Appalled": Dancy 1995: 292; "almost": 297; "representative": 293; "almost": 295; "murdered": 319.

220 "Green . . . readiness": Briggs 1957: 39; "rolling": 40.

221 "Response": Stephens and McCallum 1998: 129. "Suggested": Taylor and Brewer 1983: 180. "A madness": Robinson 1930: 430. On Robinson, see Lupack and Lupack 1999a: 119–22. "Work . . . legend": Eliot 1982: vii.

222 "Were not . . . Malory": Murray 2010: 6. "Relieved": Lawrence 1935: 485. "If": Murray 2010: 222. "A Welshman": Rhys 1978: v. The Welsh Malory: the suggestion was originally made by John Bale in his *Index Britanniae Scriptorum* (1547). "Grimly": Malory 1978: VI. 5. "War landscape . . . voice'": Jones 1937: x–xi. On Jones's use of Malory, see Taylor and Brewer 1983: 265–72.

223 "Probably": Southam 1977: 72. "Bogus": Lacy 1996: 130. Weston's interest in Arthurian literature was originally a literary one: in 1896 her poem "Sir Lancelot" troped Tennyson's *Enid and Nimuë* (1857), which had been subtitled "The True and the False". Matters are not so simple for Weston's Guenever, who asks: "'Are we false? are we true? I know not, | The twain are so wrought in one | No matter what men think'" (Weston 1999: 243). In 1899, Weston's approach to the Grail myth remained somewhat belletristic: the Arthurian narrative opened "the gates of a Fairy-land" (1). But Weston's conviction that the story was "partly, at least, real" indicated that she was already a student of folklore (1). Arthurian narratives were evidence of "the Celtic genius" and of "the spread of culture from one land to another" (4, 10). Some years later, however, Weston abandoned the folklore explanation: in *The Quest of the Holy Grail*, she argued that the theory of the Grail as a Celtic "food-providing talisman" was inadequate (1913: 53). For Weston, the "*Ritual* theory" was the best way to explain "the story as a whole" (74). In particular, "the ritual of the Adonis cult provides us with the only real parallel to the *mise en scène* of the Grail story" (82–3). The Grail quest was an initiation, and the knights of the medieval romances were replaying rituals of seasonal renewal. Weston developed the anthropological approach in *From Ritual to Romance*, tracing nature rituals from Babylon (Tammuz) through Phrygia (Attis) to Phoenicia and Greece (Adonis) and claiming to have discovered modern "survivals" in "remote cantons of the Alps and the Vosges" – and even (see p. 173, this volume) in medieval Warwickshire (1920: 86, 161). Some of this – particularly the reading of the Tarot pack (see 73) – sounds awfully Dan Brownish. Lacy points out that from an academic point of view, Weston's work

has been "thoroughly discredited" and, were it not for Eliot, would have been "an obscure footnote"; nevertheless, Weston's was "a serious and scholarly effort" (2001: 335). And one can see why Eliot was intrigued: for Weston, the Grail narrative is not just "imaginative literature of a high order": it is also the product of "tradition" (1913: 96–7). On Eliot's use of *The Mabinogion*, see Hargrove 1978: 121. "Dissociation": Eliot 1953: 117.

224 "As grand . . . book": Eliot 1934: 278.

225 "Ideal . . . sterilization": Eliot 1934: 278.

226 "Censorious": Staines 1975: 289. "Flawed": Barczewski 2000: 116. "Far": Strachey 1868: viii; "such . . . boys": xviii. "Passing": Malory 1868: X. 24; "wept": XI. 4; "loved": XVIII. 1. "Pleasance": Malory 1978: XIX. 6. "False": Malory 1868: XIX.6.

227 "He": Malory 1868: XXI. 4. "His . . . Mordred": Malory 1978: I. 19. "Sister . . . her": Malory 1868: I. 17 (compare Malory 1978: I. 19).

228 "Skill . . . school": Eliot 1942: 211. On Uther and Ygerna, see Geoffrey of Monmouth 1984: VIII. 19–21. The union leads to the birth of a daughter, Anna, who is subsequently married to Loth. Loth's wife has two sons – Gawaine and Mordred (see IX. 9). But there is some confusion here: the mother of Gawaine and Mordred is not Anna but the sister of Arthur's uncle Aurelius Ambrosius, which would make Mordred Arthur's cousin. Mordred is subsequently described as Arthur's nephew (see X. 2) but is never his son. I don't mean to imply that Geoffrey anticipates Victorian bowdlerizations of the Arthur story. There is no Launcelot in Geoffrey and so no affair with Guenever, but Geoffrey elsewhere has Mordred "living adulterously" with Guenever (X. 13). "My sister's": Tennyson 1969: 1739; "some": 1665; "vague": 1624; "splintering . . . lungs": 1745. "A thousand . . . knight": Malory 1978: XVIII. 19. "Should . . . seas": Tennyson 1969: 1647.

229 "Sprightly": Tennyson 1969: 1600; "lissome": 1602; "harlot": 1620. "Comes in . . . scheme": Ricks 1999: 660. "Breaking": Tennyson 1969: 1687.

230 "Outmoded . . . recoil": Eliot 1932: 331. "Style . . . content": Eliot 2005b: 162. "Seriousness . . . vogue": Eliot 2005a: 145. "Great poet": Eliot 1932: 328; "wholly new": 330; "metrical . . . Milton": 328; "greatest": 331; "for narrative . . . feelings": 331–3.

231 "Original . . . Milton": Eliot 1942: 211. "All": Tennyson 1969: 1683; "wet . . . head": 1708; "greatly care . . . hast sinned": 1736; "grovelled": 1735.

232 "Denouncing": Tennyson 1969: 1735; "new disease": 1737; "kingdom's curse": 1738; "shame . . . colour": 1735; "maiden . . . man": 1737.

233 "Faith . . . interpretation": Tennyson 1969: 1463.

234 "Modern": Tennyson 1969: 597; "spirit . . . institutions": 1460–1.

235 "Message . . . universe": Eliot 1932: 334; "his feelings . . . doubt": 336; "time-conscious . . . depths": 337. "What they wanted": G. Burne-Jones 1904: I, 182. "Looking . . . poets": Eliot 1932: 337.

236 "Vital": White 1958: 323. "I will not": Steinbeck 1976: 297. "Story . . . cinematograph": White 1958: 539; "promiscuous": 497; "film star": 596; "while": 498. Film seems to have lagged behind literature: Harty claims that Cornel Wilde's *Lancelot and Guinevere* (1963) was the first movie "to treat unhesitatingly the adultery between Lancelot and Guinevere" (2002a: 16).

237 'Permissive society': *OED* dates this term to 1968. "May well": A. S. G. Edwards 1996: 250.

238 On Lanier as a Southerner, see Taylor and Brewer 1983: 164.

239 "Foundation . . . edition": Eliot 1934: 278. "Sinful": Lanier 1880: 273; "his uncle's wife": 377.

240 "Rule . . . so": Knowles 1862: iii. "Manners . . . uses": Strachey 1868: xviii.

241 "Great": Knowles 1862: 130; "such . . . evils": 307; "King": 308.

242 "Loyal sister": Tennyson 1969: 1475. "To avoid . . . story": Lupack 2007: 463. "Occasional . . . unjustifiable": Conybeare 1868: iv; "resort . . . before": 308; "bare": 351; "false": 351.

243 "When": Eliot 1934: 278. "Worldly": Macleod 1900: 368; "as hot": 322; "son": 325.

244 "Dreamy": Ackroyd 1984: 25. On the life of Walker, see "Arthur George Walker". "Young": Hales 1900: viii. On the life of Hales, see "John Wesley Hales". On Macleod, see "Mary Macleod". "Forgotten": Lupack and Lupack 1999b: xi.

245 "He would": Sencourt 1971: 18.

246 "Among . . . brain-pan": Macleod 1900: 406; "youngest": 389; "nephew . . . wife": 24; "wife . . . half-sister": 20; "King": 22.

247 "Goodly . . . privily": Malory 1978: X. 26; "all that . . . sleep": X. 27; "great": X. 12; "lay . . . sang": X. 27; "that ever . . . country": X. 31.

248 "Now turn": Malory 1978: X. 32; "now turn . . . Mark": X. 50; "*second*": XII. 14; "*first*": VII. 35; "*followeth*": IX. 43; "*no rehearsal . . . Sangreal*": XII. 14.

249 "Questing": Malory 1978: X. 53; "tents . . . gathering": X. 58; "great buffets . . . sit": X. 78; "unknowingly": X. 79; "sickness": X. 81.

250 "Fairest": Malory 1978: IX. 13; "passing . . . naked": X. 24; "privy . . . back": X. 58. "Ominous": Lupack 2007: 139. "Meddle": Malory 1978: X. 58.

251 "A jousts . . . Listinoise": Malory 1978: X. 52; "feloniously": X. 54. "Bungle": Chambers 1922: 4–5.

252 "Wonderfully": Macleod 1900: 313 (compare Malory 1979: X. 31); "how darest . . . ?": 314.

253 "Sir": Macleod 1900: 314.

254 "Scoffer . . . japer": Malory 1978: X. 47.

255 "Disruptive . . . power": Ellis 2009: 53. "Wild": Lacy 1996: 130. "A few . . . slight": Lupack and Lupack 1999a: 115. "There is no quest": Taylor and Brewer 1983: 238. "Heart . . . silence": Eliot 1977: 64; "cruellest": 63.

256 "What they wanted": G. Burne-Jones 1904: I, 182. "Classicist": Eliot 1928: ix.

257 On the young Eliot being influenced by Tennyson, see Howarth 1965: 95; Sencourt 1971: 29, 31; Bergonzi 1972: 7. "General": Hargrove 1978: 23. "Strange . . . own": Eliot 1932: 334. "Deep": Miller 1977: 3; "surprising": 2; "talking", 5. "On the whole": Taylor and Brewer 1983: 24. A number of other critics have also suggested that parts of the "*In Memoriam*" essay can be applied to Eliot as well as to Tennyson (see Scofield 1988: 3; Ellis 2009: 47–8, 135).

258 "Without bothering": Pratchett 2009: 338. "Clerk": Malory 1978: I. 2; "slain": XXI. 1.

259 "Cowardly": Malory 1978: X. 25.

260 "Great": Grahame 1961: 300. "Joy": Malory 1978: XVIII. 7; "great": XIX. 1.

261 "Terror": Grahame 1961: 124. "Overgrown": McCarthy 1988: 50. "Theft . . . driving": Lambert 1975: 198.

262 "Remotest": Grahame 1961, 143; "chivalry": 166; "growing": 169. "His meat . . . him": Malory 1978: XIX. 8; "maiden's": X. 49. Lerer does not mention the presence of Malory in "Toad's Adventures" although he does identify references to *The Yeomen of the Guard, The Merry Wives of Windsor* and *The Prisoner of Zenda* (see Grahame 2009: 163 n. 1, 164 n. 3, 222 n. 2). But Lerer notes elsewhere that Frederick Furnivall (second editor of the *OED* and founder of the Early English Text Society) introduced Grahame to Malory soon after he started work at the Bank of England in the 1870s (14). According to Winchester, Furnivall "encouraged" Grahame to write *The Wind in the Willows* and was rewarded by being cast as "the Water Rat, a cunning and ever-keen creature" whose "rattish pedantry" is evident in his correction of Toad's insouciant grammar (2003: 64).

263 "Our noble": Malory 1990: I. 209.

264 "Great": Malory 1978: XXI. 2; "when . . . unhap": XX. 1.

265 "Alive": Steinbeck 1976: xiii.

266 My colleague Axel Schäfer informs me that 'lustig' can indeed mean both 'merry' and 'funny'. Although the noun 'Lust' has "shadier connotations" – sexual desire and a more general appetite for something (as in *Wanderlust*) – these "require the Umlaut . . . the translation of 'lustful' would not be 'lustig', but 'lüstern'". It seems that my name is more innocent than I had supposed – or, perhaps, hoped.

267 In the online *OED*, Malory is "the 222nd most frequently quoted source", below Shakespeare (2nd), Scott (3rd), Chaucer (6th) and Milton (7th) but some way above Austen (243rd), Arnold (338th), James (415th) and Faulkner (454th). I relish the fact that Malory comes 260 places above his Elizabethan detractor Roger Ascham, though it's disappointing to see that he is below both Caxton (12th) and Tennyson (26th) – writers who wouldn't have had quite the same prominence without the *Morte*. It's also worth pointing out that *OED* cites a further 322 instances in which Malory gives us the first evidence of a new meaning coming into the language: examples include 'achieve', 'beginner', 'damage', 'deadly', 'errant', 'germane', 'mad', 'natural', 'stability', 'staunch', 'varlet', and 'villainous' as well as such phrases as 'labour in vain' and 'at liberty'.

268 "First": Altick 1950: 78. "Centre": Bradbrook 1958: 7. "Permanent": Benson 1968: 81. "First": Field 1971: 7. "English prose": Parins 1988: 323; Raleigh 1911: 14; Parins 1988: 390–1. "Excellent": Parins 1988: 78. "Written . . . sublime": Scott 1957: 173 n. 1.

269 "No style": Lewis 1963: 24. "Invented": Vinaver 1929: 39. "Great . . . least": Vinaver 1947: xcix–c. "Cultural": Field 1971: 8.

270 "Foundation . . . latecomer": Lynch 2012: 297. On the originality of the tale of Gareth, see Guerin 1964: 106; Reiss 1966: 101. On the healing of Urre, see Lumiansky 1964b; Reiss 1966: 169; Lambert 1975: 56. "Book": Malory 1978: VII. 14; XIX. 4; "French book": XIX. 13; "all England": I. 5. "English world": Reiss 1966: 21. On the use of English place names in Malory, see Aurner 1933: 391; Stewart 1935; Noguchi 1981; Holbrook 1985.

271 "Modern . . . century": Hobsbawm 1992: 3; "sounds": 11. "English enigma": Nairn 1977: 292. "Bitterer . . . mornings": Orwell 1941: 10–11. General studies of nationalism include Gellner 1983, 1994, 1997; Anderson 1991; and Smith 2001. Studies of the development of a more specifically 'British' or 'English' identity include Newman 1987; Kearney 1989; Colley, 1992; Elton 1992; Porter 1992; Weinbrot 1993; Harriss 2005; Pocock 2005; Dentith 2006; Kerrigan 2008; and Featherstone 2009. Historians like Newman and Colley write what might be called centripetal history, emphasizing the factors that create a unified national identity (for Newman, Romanticism; for Colley, Protestantism). Kearney, Pocock and Kerrigan, on the other hand, are centrifugalists: for them, national identity is migratory, diasporic, hybrid or archipelagic. In many ways, this seems the more attractive approach. But centrifugalism brings technical challenges – can one ever be comprehensively archipelagic? – and attendant blindspots: for Kearney, the Wars of the Roses were merely a squabble between "rival factions of the feudal nobility in the north and west" which obscures the emergence of London and the south-

east as a centre of political, economic and cultural power. Studies of contemporary 'British' or 'English' identity appealing to a wider market include Samuel 1998; Gill 2005; Bragg 2006; Scruton 2006; Hitchens 2008; Beckett 2009. Samuel, Bragg and Beckett lean to the left; Gill, Scruton and Hitchens to the right. Examples of discussions in the quality press include Runciman 2010; McKibbin 2010; Ascherson 2011.

272 "English nation": Carpenter 1997: 102. "Proto-nationalist": Hodges 2005: 7; "imagined . . . nation": 78. "Aspect . . . phenomenon": Higham 2002: 43; "national": 38.

273 "Constructed . . . configured": Kerrigan 2008, 40. Finke and Shichtman declare that they are "not quite ready to join the consensus on the emergence of national sentiment in the Middle Ages" (2004: 107). Kerrigan himself is a moderate primordialist, arguing that something like the modern conception of nationhood existed before the Reformation and was fully in place during the seventeenth century. According to Smith, modernism is "strong on theory, but rather weak on history" whilst primordialism can boast only of "a flawed theory or none, and little or no history" (2002: 61). "Great . . . term": Malory 1978: XXI. 1.

274 "Best . . . arrogance": Geoffrey of Monmouth 1984: I. 2–3. Geoffrey's jeremiad against the British is reserved for the closing section of the work: his own people were "foolish", "monstrous" and divided amongst themselves through jealousy and pride; they "gave themselves airs" and indulged in "sexual excesses such as had never been heard of" (XI. 9; XII. 6). The Saxons in contrast "behaved more wisely"; under Adelstan, therefore – as Geoffrey puts it in the last line of his work – they "ruled over the whole of Loegria" (XII. 19). "As great": Malory 1978: X. 58.

275 "Discourse": Eckhardt 2005: 196. On the shift from 'Britain' to 'England' in the *Morte d'Arthur*, see Riddy 1996: 60–4; Barron 2004; Brewer 2004: 273; Kelly 2005: 79–80. On the 'matter of Britain', see Riddy 1996.

276 "King . . . perspective": Riddy 1996: 64; "worst": 55; "larger failure": 66. For the view that the French wars "contributed significantly to the development of a new consciousness of national identity", see Keen 1990: 6.

277 "Sustains": Riddy 1996: 72. "Ideological": Smith 1996: 113. "Advertisement": Pochoda 1971: x; "central": xii; "establishment": 3; "exposé": xii. "Simple": Hodges 2005: 16.

278 "Élite": Hobsbawm 1992: 59; "something close": 75.

279 "Founding . . . state": Higham 2002: 239; "quintessential": 265; "mantra": 262; "entire": 2; "world": 2; "consigned": 32; "European":

30. For a more recent (inconclusive) investigation into the archaeological evidence for Arthur, see Gidlow 2010.

280 "Severely damaged": "John Morris (historian)". "Fair rolling": Briggs 1957: 14; "rolling": 39; "British fleet": 40; "British army": 43.

281 "Specifically": Bennett 1963: vi. "Masculine . . . etiquette": Bradbrook 1958: 18. "Coyness": Elizabeth Edwards 1996: 51. "Sophisticated": McCarthy 1991: 152; "basically": 174; "soldierly": 153.

282 "One": Green 1953: 12. "Perhaps": Brewer 1963: 61. "One": Knight 1969: 95.

283 Guerin sees the tragedy of the *Morte* in eschatological terms as a punishment for the "sins and errors of the characters" (1964: 269). For Sklar, the Christian conception of tragedy does not dictate the *Morte*'s "tragic thrust" (1993: 310). For Pickering, the rise and fall pattern evident in Malory's work more closely resembles that of "English Renaissance tragic drama" (1983: 326). For a majority of commentators, however, the tragic dimensions of Malory's work do indeed relate to "the characters" – if not to their "sins and errors" then to the conflicts of love and loyalty, of private and public duty, that they must undergo. The *Morte* is a "tragedy of character" (Kennedy 1992: 343), a "tragedy of virtue" (Benson 1996: 231) or a "romantic tragedy" (Tolhurst 2005: 136).

284 "Earthly . . . earth': Bradbrook 1958: 31; "taciturnity": 27. "Wordy . . . elemental": Field 1971: 114–5.

285 "Incapacity": Brewer 1963: 62. "Not important": Lambert 1975: ix. "Is not": McCarthy 1988: xiii. "Strikingly": Field 1993: 172.

286 "Greatest": Burrow 2009: 233. "As musical": Lewis 1963: 24. "Conscious . . . feeling": Brewer 1963: 62–3. "Simple . . . primitive": Field 1971: 38; "calls": 86.

287 "Ale . . . writer": Lambert 1975: 68; "particular": 124; "glimpse": 176. "Strange": Vinaver 1929: 111; "mysterious": 114.

288 "My favourite": Eliot 1934: 278.

289 "Sir . . . world": Joyce 1977: 385. On Joyce's use of the *Morte* in 'Oxen of the Sun', see Davison 2009.

290 "And whiles . . . wassailing": Joyce 1977: 384–5.

291 "Would be": Woolf 1978: 203 (the conversation about *Ulysses* took place on Saturday 23 September 1922); "showed": 203. "Latent": Iser 1974: 187; "ideology . . . reality": 190; "naiveté . . . itself": 192.

292 "Ideal . . . procreation": Iser 1974: 188–9; "both": 194 "problem . . . preconditioned": 191–2.

293 "Monster . . . style": James 1984: 1209.

294 "There may . . . Englishmen": Malory 1978: XXI. 1.

295 I spent the morning of 9 April 2013 examining Caxton's *Morte d'Arthur* – or, as the spine has it, in embossed gilt: "LA MORTE D'ARTHUR" – in the Elsevier Reading Room on the fourth floor of

the John Rylands Library in Manchester. It surprised me by its compactness and robustness: the paper is supple, not dusty; the ink is generally as flat and as saturated as lampblack. I could feel the thickness of the pages, which are surprisingly variable, though the edges are crisply cut and gilded. On a number of occasions I needed to remove my spectacles so that I could see details of the text more clearly. It was by doing this that I noticed, with the thrill of the furtive book fetishist, that Caxton's *Morte* smells, first, of leather, then of dried mushrooms, and then, finally and most faintly, of cigar smoke. "Centre": Carpenter 1992: 17. According to Wikipedia, the Ordnance Survey has established that the centre of England is not at Meriden in the West Midlands (as has long been thought) but at "Lindley Hall Farm, Leicestershire (near Fenny Drayton)" ("Centre points of the United Kingdom").

296 For details of Newbold Revel's owners to 1640, see Dugdale 1656: 56. Architectural and historical information in this chapter is drawn from documents by S. M. Stanislaus and Andor Gomme supplied to me by Catherine Fell, Librarian of H. M. Prison Service College at Newbold Revel. Catherine and her colleague Dot Jeffcott provided additional information about the role Newbold Revel played during the Second World War. I am grateful to Andrew Hinett for the guided tour of the house and grounds.

297 "Provincial baroque": Gomme *c.* 1995: 6; "bones . . . mansion": 2. Gomme points out that the "massive stack" of the chimney is "not something an economical builder would replace if he could re-use it" (3).

298 "In": Dugdale 1656: 56.

299 "Hocum slocum . . . thee": from the text of the Newbold-on-Avon Mumming Play, as given by Rouse 1899: 190–2. "Symbolic": Weston 1920: 91.

300 "Widely . . . inward-looking": Samuel 1998: 49. "Ingerland": the George flag has been flown from car windows to support the English football team since the 1996 European Championship.

References

Ackroyd, P. 1984: *T. S. Eliot*. London: Hamish Hamilton.

Allen, J. B. 1985: Malory's diptych *distinctio*: the closing books of his work. In J. W. Spisak (ed.), 237–55.

Altick, R. D. 1950: *The Scholar Adventurers*. New York: Free Press.

Anderson, B. 1991: *Imagined Communities: Reflections on the Origin and Spread of Nationalism* (1983). Rev. ed. London: Verso.

Archibald, E. 1996: Beginnings: "The Tale of King Arthur and King Arthur and the Emperor Lucius". In E. Archibald and A. S. G. Edwards (eds), 133–51.

———, 2012: Malory's Lancelot and Guenevere. In H. Fulton (ed.), 312–25.

———, and Edwards, A. S. G. 1996: Introduction. In E. Archibald and A. S. G. Edwards (eds), xiii–xv.

———, and Edwards, A. S. G. (eds) 1996: *A Companion to Malory*. Cambridge: Brewer.

———, and Putter, A., (eds) 2009: *The Cambridge Companion to the Arthurian Legend*. Cambridge: Cambridge University Press.

Arlott, J. 1954: John Speed and his maps: a note. In J. Arlott (ed.), *John Speed's England: A Coloured Facsimile of the Maps and Text from The Theatre of the Empire of Great Britaine First Edition, 1611*. London: Phoenix House, 7–8.

Armitage, S. 2012: *The Death of King Arthur*. London: Faber.

Arthur George Walker. en.wikipedia.org/wiki/Arthur_George_Walker, accessed 10 May 2013.

Ascham, R. 1909: *The Schoolmaster* (1568). London: Cassell.

Ascherson, N. 2011: Wolves in the drawing room. *London Review of Books* (2 June), 8–9.

Aurner, N. S. 1933: Sir Thomas Malory: historian? *PMLA* 48, 362–91

Barber, R. W. 1961: *Arthur of Albion: An Introduction to the Arthurian Literature and Legends of England*. London: Barrie and Rockliff.

———, (ed.) 2002: *King Arthur in Music*. Cambridge: Brewer.

Barczewski, S. L. 2000: *Myth and National Identity in Nineteenth Century Britain: The Legends of King Arthur and Robin Hood*. New York: Oxford University Press.

Barron, W. R. J. 2004: Arthurian romance. In C. Saunders (ed.), 65–84.

Batt, C. 2004: Malory and rape. In T. Malory, ed. S. H. A. Shepherd, 797–814.

Baugh, A. C. 1933: Documenting Sir Thomas Malory. *Speculum* 8 (1), 3–29.

Beckett, A. 2009: *When the Lights Went Out: What Really Happened to Britain in the Seventies.* London: Faber.

Bellamy, J. 1973: *Crime and Public Order in England in the Later Middle Ages.* London: Routledge.

Bellamy, J. G. 1998: *The Criminal Trial in Later Medieval England: Felony before the Courts from Edward I to the Sixteenth Century.* Stroud: Sutton.

Bennett, J. A. W. 1963: Introduction. In J. A. W. Bennett (ed.), v–vii.

———, (ed.) 1963: *Essays on Malory.* Oxford: Clarendon.

Benson, C. D. 1996: The ending of the *Morte Darthur.* In E. Archibald and A. S. G. Edwards (eds), 221–38.

Benson, L. O. 1968: Sir Thomas Malory's *Le Morte Darthur.* In R. M. Lumiansky and H. Baker (eds), 81–131.

Bergonzi, B. 1972: *T. S. Eliot.* New York: Macmillan.

Board, M. L. 1992: Art's moral mission: reading G. F. Watts's "Sir Galahad". In D. N. Mancoff (ed.), 132–54.

Boron, R. de, see De Boron, R.

Bradbrook, M. C. 1958: *Sir Thomas Malory.* London: Longman's, Green and Co.

Bragg, B. 2006: *The Progressive Patriot: A Search for Belonging* London: Bantam.

Brewer, D. S. 1963: "the hoole book". In J. A. W. Bennett (ed.), 41–63.

———, 1981: Introduction. In T. Takamiya and D. S. Brewer (eds), 1–8.

———, 2004: Personal weapons in Malory's *Le Morte Darthur.* In B. Wheeler (ed.), 271–84.

———, (ed.) 1991: *Studies in Medieval English Romances: Some New Approaches.* Cambridge: Brewer.

Briggs, P. 1957: *King Arthur and the Knights of the Round Table* (1954). London: Dean & Son.

Brinkley, R. F. 1932: *Arthurian Legend in the Seventeenth Century.* Baltimore, Md.: Johns Hopkins.

Brown, R. L. 1996: *A History of the Fleet Prison, London: The Anatomy of the Fleet.* Lampeter: Edwin Mellen.

Bruce, J. D. 1928: *The Evolution of Arthurian Romance: From the Beginnings down to the Year 1300.* 2nd edition, 2 vols. Göttingen: Dandenhoed and Ruprecht.

Bryant, N. 2001: Introduction. In *Merlin and the Grail: Joseph of Arimathea, Merlin, Perceval; the Trilogy of Prose Romances Attributed to Robert de Boron.* Trans. N. Bryant. Cambridge: Brewer, 1–13.

Burne-Jones, G. 1904: *Memorials of Edward Burne-Jones.* 2 vols. London: Lund Humphries, Vol. I.

Burns, F. D. A. 2004: Shirley, John (*bap.* 1648, *d.* 1679). *Oxford Dictionary of National Biography*. Oxford: Oxford University Press.

Burrow, J. 2009: *A History of Histories: Epics, Chronicles, Romances and Inquiries from Herodotus and Thucydides to the Twentieth Century*. London: Penguin.

C., E. I. 1897: Shirley, John (1648–1679). *Oxford Dictionary of National Biography*. Oxford: Oxford University Press.

Carpenter, C. 1980: Sir Thomas Malory and fifteenth-century local politics. *Bulletin of the Institute of Historical Research* 53, 31–43.

———, 1992: *Locality and Polity: A Study of Warwickshire Landed Society, 1401–99*. Cambridge: Cambridge University Press.

———, 1997. *The Wars of the Roses: Politics and the Constitution in England, c. 1437–1509*. Cambridge: Cambridge University Press.

Centre points of the United Kingdom. en.wikipedia.org/wiki/ Centre_points_of_the_United_Kingdom, accessed 10 May 2013.

Chambers, E. K. 1922: *Sir Thomas Malory*. English Association Pamphlet 51 (January).

Chandler, A. 1971: *A Dream of Order: The Medieval Ideal in Nineteenth-Century English Literature*. London: Routledge.

Chrétien de Troyes, see De Troyes, C.

Coleridge, S. T. 1987: *Biographia Literaria: Biographical Sketches of My Literary Life and Opinions* (1817). Ed. G. Watson. London: Dent.

Colley, L. 1992: *Britons: Forging the Nation, 1707–1837*. New Haven: Yale.

Conybeare, E. 1868: *La Morte D'Arthur: The History of King Arthur*. London: Edward Moxon & Co.

Cooper, H. 1996: "The Book of Sir Tristram de Lyones". In E. Archibald and A. S. G. Edwards (eds), 183–201.

———, 2004a: Malory and the early prose romances. In C. Saunders (ed.), 104–20.

———, 2004b: Malory's language of love. In B. Wheeler (ed.), 297–306.

Corless, P. 2002: Knights of imagination: Arthurian games and entertainments. In E. S. Sklar and D. L. Hoffman (eds), 182–96.

Dancy, J. 1995: *Walter Oakeshott: A Diversity of Gifts*. Norwich: Michael Russell.

Dante Alighieri. 1998: *The Divine Comedy*. Ed. D. H. Higgins. Trans. C. H. Sisson. Oxford: Oxford University Press.

Darton, F. J. H. 1932: *Children's Books in England: Five Centuries of Social Life*. Cambridge: Cambridge University Press.

Davis, J. H. 1985: *The Kennedy Clan: Dynasty and Disaster, 1848–1984*. London: Sidgwick and Jackson.

Davison, S. 2009. Joyce's Incorporation of Literary Sources in "Oxen of the Sun". *Genetic Joyce Studies* 9, www.antwerpjamesjoycecenter.com/GJS9.

Day, D. D. 2002: *Monty Python and the Holy Grail*: madness with a definite method. In K. J. Harty (ed.), 127–35.

Delano-Smith, C. and Kain, R. S. P. 1999: *English Maps: A History*. London: British Library.

Dentith, S. 2006: *Epic and Empire in Nineteenth-Century Britain*. Cambridge: Cambridge University Press.

De Boron, R. (attrib.) 2001: *Merlin and the Grail: Joseph of Arimathea, Merlin, Perceval*. Trans. N. Bryant. Cambridge: Brewer.

De Troyes, C. 2004: *Arthurian Romances*. Ed. W. W. Kibler. Trans. W. W. Kibler and C. W. Carroll. London: Penguin.

Dixon, H. 1850: *The London Prisons: with an Account of the more Distinguished Persons who have been Confined in them, to which is added a Description of the Chief Provincial Prisons*. London: Jackson and Walford.

Dryden, J. 1958: Prologue (1700) to F. Beaumont and J. Fletcher's *The Pilgrim*. In J. Kinsley (ed.), *The Poems of John Dryden*, 4 vols. Oxford: Clarendon, IV, 1758–9.

Dugdale, W. 1656: *The Antiquities of Warwickshire Illustrated; From Records, Leiger-Books, Manuscripts, Charters, Evidences, Tombes, and Armes: Beautified With Maps, Prospects and Portraictures*. London: Thomas Warren.

Eckhardt, C. D. 2005: Reconsidering Malory. In N. J. Lacy (ed.), 195–208.

Edwards, E. 1996: The place of women in the *Morte Darthur*. In E. Archibald and A. S. G. Edwards (eds), 37–54.

Edwards, A. S. G. 1996: The reception of Malory's *Morte Darthur*. In E. Archibald and A. S. G. Edwards (eds), 241–52.

Eliot, T. S. 1928: Preface. In *For Lancelot Andrewes: Essays on Style and Order*. London: Faber and Gwyer, ix–x.

———, 1932: *In Memoriam*. In *Selected Essays*. London: Faber, 328–38.

———, 1934: *Le Morte Darthur*. *Spectator* (23 February), 278.

———, 1982: A note of introduction (1937). In David Jones, *In Parenthesis*. London: Faber, vii–xv.

———, 1942: The voice of his time: T. S. Eliot on Tennyson's "In Memoriam". *The Listener* 27 (12 February), 211–12.

———, 1953: The metaphysical poets (1921). In J. Hayward (ed.), *Selected Prose*. London: Penguin, 111–20.

———, 1977: "The Waste Land" (1922). In *Collected Poems 1909–62*. London: Faber.

———, 2005a: The lesson of Baudelaire (1921). In L. Rainey (ed.), *The Annotated Waste Land with Eliot's Contemporary Prose*. New Haven: Yale, 144–45.

———, 2005b: Prose and verse (1921). In L. Rainey (ed.), *The Annotated Waste Land with Eliot's Contemporary Prose*. New Haven: Yale, 158–65.

Ellis, S. 2009: *T. S. Eliot: A Guide for the Perplexed*. London: Continuum.

Evans, M. J. 1985: *Ordinatio* and narrative links: the impact of Malory's tales as a "hoole book". In J. W. Spisak (ed.), 29–52.

Elton, G. 1992: *The English*. Oxford: Blackwell.

Faulkner, P. 2009: Morris and Tennyson. *Journal of William Morris Studies* 18 (2), 15–51.

Featherstone, S. 2009: *Englishness: Twentieth-Century Popular Culture and the Forming of English Identity*. Edinburgh: Edinburgh University Press.

Field, P. J. C. 1971: *Romance and Chronicle: A Study of Malory's Prose Style*. London: Barrie and Jenkins.

———, 1978: Introduction. In P. J. C. Field (ed.), *Le Morte Darthur: The Seventh and Eighth Tales*. London: Hodder, 1–67.

———, 1982: The last years of Sir Thomas Malory. *Bulletin of the John Rylands University Library of Manchester* 64 (2), 433–56.

———, 1985: Time and Elaine of Astolat. In J. W. Spisak (ed.), 231–36.

———, 1993: *The Life and Times of Sir Thomas Malory*. Cambridge: Brewer.

———, 1996: The Malory life-records. In E. Archibald and A. S. G. Edwards (eds), 115–30.

———, 1998: *Malory: Texts and Sources*. Cambridge: Brewer.

———, 2002: Malory and his audience. In A. Lupack (ed.), 21–32.

———, 2004: Malory, Sir Thomas (1415x18–1471). *Oxford Dictionary of National Biography*. Oxford: Oxford University Press.

Finke, L. A., and Shichtman, M. B. 2004: *King Arthur and the Myth of History*. Gainesville, Fla.: University Press of Florida.

Fitzgerald, P. 1975: *Edward Burne-Jones: A Biography*. London: Michael Joseph.

Fox-Friedman, J. 1998: The chivalric order for children: Arthur's return in late nineteenth- and early twentieth-century America. In D. N. Mancoff (ed.), 137–57.

———, 2009: King Arthur in Art. In H. Fulton (ed.), 381–400.

Fries, M. 1985: Indiscreet objects of desire: Malory's "Tristram" and the necessity of deceit. In J. W. Spisak (ed.), 87–108.

Freud, S. 1953–74: *The Standard Edition of the Complete Psychological Works of Sigmund Freud*. Ed. and trans. James Strachey et al. 24 vols. London: Hogarth.

Fulton, H. (ed.) 2012: *Companion to Arthurian Literature*. Chichester: Wiley-Blackwell.

Gellner, E. 1983: *Nations and Nationalism*. Oxford: Blackwell.

———, 1994: *Encounters with Nationalism*. Oxford: Blackwell.

———, 1997: *Nationalism*. London: Weidenfeld and Nicolson.

Geoffrey of Monmouth 1984: *The History of the Kings of Britain*. Ed. and trans. Lewis Thorpe. Harmondsworth: Penguin.

Gidlow, C. 2010: *Revealing King Arthur: Swords, Stones and Digging for Camelot*. Stroud: History Press.

Gill, A. A. 2005: *The Angry Island: Hunting the English*. London: Weidenfeld and Nicolson.

Gillon, E. V., Jr. 1972: *Beardsley's Illustrations for Le Morte Darthur*. New York: Dover.

Girouard, M. 1981: *The Return to Camelot: Chivalry and the English Gentleman.* New Haven, Conn.: Yale.

Gomme, A. *c.* 1995: *Newbold Revel: An Architectural History.* Standford Hill: H. M. Prison Service Training and Development Group.

Goodman, J. R. 1984: The last of Avalon: Henry Irving's *King Arthur* of 1895. *Harvard Library Bulletin* 32 (3), 239–55.

Grahame, K. 1908: *The Wind in the Willows.* London: Methuen.

———, 2009: *The Wind in the Willows: An Annotated Edition.* Ed. Seth Lerer. Cambridge, Mass.: Belknap.

Green, R. L. 1953: *King Arthur and His Knights of the Round Table: Newly Re-Told out of the Old Romances.* London: Faber.

Griffith, R. R. 1981: The authorship question reconsidered. In T. Takamiya and D. S. Brewer (eds), 159–77.

Griffiths, R. A. 2004: Henry VI (1421–71). *Oxford Dictionary of National Biography.* Oxford: Oxford University Press.

Guerin, W. L. 1964: "The Tale of the Death of Arthur". In R. M. Lumiansky (ed.), 233–74.

Hales, J. W. 1900: Introduction. In M. Macleod, vii–xix.

Hargrove, N. D. 1978: *Landscape as Symbol in the Poetry of T. S. Eliot.* Jackson, Miss.: University of Mississippi Press.

Harriss, G. 2005: *Shaping the Nation: England, 1360–1461.* Oxford: Clarendon.

Harty, K. J. 2002a: Cinema Arthuriana: an overview. In K. J. Harty (ed.), 7–33.

———, 2002b: A comprehensive filmography and bibliography. In K. J. Harty (ed.), 252–301.

———, (ed.) 2002: *Cinema Arthuriana: Twenty Essays.* Rev. ed. (Jefferson, NC: McFarland, 2002).

Hellinga, L. 1981: The Malory manuscript and Caxton. In T. Takamiya and D. S. Brewer (eds), 127–41.

Heng, G. 2004: Enchanted ground: the feminine subtext in Malory. In T. Malory, ed. S. H. A. Shepherd, 835–49.

Hicks, E. 1928: *Sir Thomas Malory: His Turbulent Career.* Cambridge, Mass.: Harvard University Press.

Higham, N. J. 2002: *King Arthur: Myth-Making and History.* London: Routledge.

Hitchens, P. 2008: *The Abolition of Britain: From Winston Churchill to Princess Diana.* 2nd edition. London: Continuum.

Hobsbawm, E. 1992: *Nations and Nationalism since 1780: Programme, Myth, Reality.* 2nd edition. Cambridge: Cambridge University Press.

Hodges, K. 2005: *Forging Chivalric Communities in Malory's Le Morte Darthur.* Basingstoke: Palgrave Macmillan.

Hoffman, D. L. 2002. Not dead yet: *Monty Python and the Holy Grail* in the twenty-first century. In K. J. Harty (ed.), 136–48.

References

Holbrook, S. E. 1985: Malory's identification of Camelot as Winchester. In J. W. Spisak (ed.), 13–28.

Holinshed, R. 1976: *Holinshed's Chronicles of England, Scotland and Ireland* (1586). Ed. V. F. Snow. 6 vols. New York: AMS Press. I.

Homer 1975: *The Odyssey*. Trans. E. V. Rieu. Harmondworth: Penguin.

Horrox, R. 2004: Edward IV (1442–1483). *Oxford Dictionary of National Biography*. Oxford: Oxford University Press.

Howarth, H. 1965: *Notes on Some Figures Behind T. S. Eliot*. London: Chatto & Windus.

Howey, A. F. and Reimer, S. R. (eds) 2003: *A Bibliography of Modern Arthuriana, 1500–2000*. Cambridge: Brewer.

Ihle, S. N. 1983: *Malory's Grail Quest: Invention and Adaptation in Medieval Prose Romance*. Madison, Wis.: University of Wisconsin Press.

Iser, W. 1974: *The Implied Reader: Patterns of Communication in Prose Fiction from Bunyan to Beckett*. Baltimore, Md.: Johns Hopkins.

James, H. 1984: Introduction to *The Tempest* (1907). In L. Edel (ed.), *Literary Criticism: Essays in Literature, American Writers, English Writers*. New York: Library of America, 1205–20.

John Morris (historian). en.wikipedia.org/wiki/John_Morris_(historian), accessed 10 May 2013.

John Wesley Hales. en.wikipedia.org/wiki/John_Wesley_Hales, accessed 10 May 2013.

Jones, D. 1937: *In Parenthesis*. London: Faber.

–––, 1961: Foreword. In R. Barber, *Arthur of Albion: An Introduction to the Arthurian Literature and Legends of England*. London: Barrie and Rockliff, vii–ix.

Joyce, J. 1977: *Ulysses* (1922). Harmondsworth: Penguin.

Kearney, H. 1989: *The British Isles: A History of Four Nations*. Cambridge: Cambridge University Press.

Keen, M. 1990: *English Society in the Later Middle Ages, 1348–1500*. London: Penguin.

Kelly, R. L. 1985: Wounds, healing, and knighthood in Malory's "Tale of Lancelot and Guenevere". In J. W. Spisak (ed.), 173–97.

–––, 2005: Malory's "Tale of King Arthur" and the political geography of fifteenth-century England". In K. S. Whetter and R. L. Radulescu (eds), 79–94.

Kennedy, B. 1992: *Knighthood in the Morte Darthur*. 2nd edition. Cambridge: Brewer.

–––, 2001: Malory's Guenevere: a "trew lover". In B. Wheeler and F. Tolhurst (eds), 11–34.

Kennedy, E. D. 1981: Malory and his English sources. In T. Takamiya and D. S. Brewer (eds), 27–55.

–––, 2001: Malory's Guenevere: "a woman who had grown a soul". In B. Wheeler and F. Tolhurst (eds), 35–44.

References

Ker, W. P. 2005: *Essays on Medieval Literature*. London: Macmillan.

Kerrigan, J. 2008: *Archipelagic English: Literature, History, and Politics 1603–1707*. Oxford: Oxford University Press.

Kibler, W. W. 2004: Introduction. In C. de Troyes, *Arthurian Romances*, ed. W. W. Kibler, trans. W. W. Kibler and C. W. Carroll. London: Penguin, 1–22.

Kittredge, G. L. 1928: Preface. In E. Hicks, *Sir Thomas Malory: His Turbulent Career*. Cambridge, Mass.: Harvard University Press, vii–x.

Knight, S. 1969: *The Structure of Sir Thomas Malory's Arthuriad*. Sydney: Sydney University Press.

Knowles, J. T. 1862: *The Story of King Arthur and His Knights of the Round Table*. London: Griffith and Farran.

Lacy, N. J. 2001: Jessie Laidlay Weston (1850–1928). In B. Wheeler and F. Tolhurst (eds), 335–42.

———, 2005: The ambiguous fortunes of Arthur: the Lancelot-Grail and beyond. In N. J. Lacy (ed.), 92–103.

———, 2009: The Arthur of the twentieth and twenty-first centuries. In E. Archibald and A. Putter (eds), 120–35.

———, (ed.) 1996: *The New Arthurian Encyclopaedia*. New York: Garland.

———, (ed.) 2005: *The Fortunes of King Arthur*. Cambridge: Brewer.

Lambert, M. 1975: *Malory: Style and Vision in Le Morte Darthur*. New Haven, Conn.: Yale.

Lanier, S. (ed.) 1880: *The Boy's King Arthur, Being Sir Thomas Malory's History of King Arthur and His Knights of the Round Table*. London: Sampson Low, Marston, Searle and Rivington.

Lawrence, T. E. 1935: *Seven Pillars of Wisdom: A Triumph* (1926). London: Cape.

Lewis, C. S. 1963: The English prose *Morte*. In J. A. W. Bennett (ed.), 7–28.

———, 1979a: *The Allegory of Love: A Study in Medieval Tradition* (1936). Oxford: Oxford University Press.

———, 1979b: *The Discarded Image: An Introduction to Medieval and Renaissance Literature* (1964). Cambridge: Cambridge University Press.

Lockhart, J. G. 1902: *The Life of Sir Walter Scott*. 10 vols. Edinburgh: Constable. V.

Loomis, R. S. 1963: *The Development of Arthurian Romance*. London: Hutchinson.

———, (ed.) 1959: *Arthurian Literature in the Middle Ages: A Collaborative History*. Oxford: Clarendon.

Lumiansky, R. M. 1964a: Introduction. In R. M. Lumiansky (ed.), 1–7.

———, 1964b: "The Tale of Lancelot": prelude to adultery. In R. M. Lumiansky (ed.), 91–8.

———, 1964c: "The Tale of Lancelot and Guenevere". In R. M. Lumiansky (ed.), 205–32.

———, (ed.) 1964: *Malory's Originality: A Critical Study of Le Morte Darthur.* Baltimore, Md.: Johns Hopkins.

———, and H. Baker (eds) 1968: *Critical Approaches to Six Major English Works.* Philadelphia, Pa.: University of Pennsylvania Press.

Lupack, A. 1992: American Arthurian authors: a declaration of independence. In D. N. Mancoff (ed.), 155–73.

———, 1998: The Figure of King Arthur in America. In D. N. Mancoff (ed.), 121–36.

———, 2007: *The Oxford Guide to Arthurian Literature and Legend.* Oxford: Oxford University Press.

———, (ed.) 2002: *New Directions in Arthurian Studies.* Cambridge: Brewer.

———, and Lupack, B. T. 1999a: *King Arthur in America.* Cambridge: Brewer.

———, and Lupack, B. T. 2008: *Illustrating Camelot.* Cambridge: Brewer.

———, and Lupack, B. T. (eds) 1999b: *Arthurian Literature by Women.* New York: Garland, 1999.

Lynam, E. 1947: *British Maps and Map-Makers.* London: Collins.

Lynch, A. 2012: Malory's *Morte Darthur* and history. In H. Fulton (ed.), 297–311.

The Mabinogion 2007: ed. and trans. Sioned Davies. Oxford: Oxford University Press.

MacLean, A. 1961: *The Guns of Navarone* (1957). London: Fontana.

Macleod, M. 1900: *The Book of King Arthur and His Noble Knights: Stories from Sir Thomas Malory's Morte Darthur.* London: Wells Gardner, Darton & Co.

Mahoney, D. B. 2005: Symbolic uses of space in Malory's *Morte Darthur.* In K. S. Whetter and R. L. Radulescu (eds), 95–106.

Malory, T. 1485: *Le morte Darthur* (*the byrth / lyf / and actes of the fayd kynge Arthur / of his noble knyghtes of the rounde table / theyr meruayllous enqueftes and aduentures / thachyeuyng of the fangreal / & in thende the dolorous deth & departyng out of thys world of them al*). Westminster: William Caxton. The John Rylands Library, The University of Manchester, Incunable Collection, 18930.

———, 1817: *The Byrth, Lyf, and Actes of Kyng Arthur; of his Noble Knyghtes of the Rounde Table, Theyr Merveyllous Enquestes and Aduentures, Thachyevyng of the Sanc Greal; and in the end Le Morte Darthur, with the Dolourous Deth and Departyng out of thys Worlde of them al.* Ed. W. Upcott. 2 vols. London: Longman, Hurst, Rees, Orme and Brown.

———, 1858: *La Mort d'Arthure: The History of King Arthur and of the Knights of the Round Table.* Ed. T. Wright. 3 vols. London: John Russell Smith.

———, 1868: *Morte Darthur: Sir Thomas Malory's Book of King Arthur and of His Noble Knights of the Round Table.* Ed. E. Strachey. London: Macmillan.

———, 1889: *Le Morte Darthur by Syr Thomas Malory.* Ed. H. O. Sommer. 2 vols. London: Nutt.

———, 1978: *Le Morte d'Arthur.* Ed. J. Rhys. Everyman edition, 2 vols. London: Dent.

———, 1990: *The Works of Sir Thomas Malory.* Ed. E. Vinaver, 3rd edition, rev. P. J. C. Field, 3 vols. Oxford: Clarendon.

———, 2004: *Le Morte Darthur.* Ed. S. H. A. Shepherd. New York: Norton.

Mancoff, D. N. 1990: *The Arthurian Revival in Victorian Art.* New York: Garland.

———, 1995: *The Return of King Arthur: The Legend through Victorian Eyes.* London: Pavilion.

———, (ed.) 1992: *The Arthurian Revival: Essays on Form, Tradition, and Transformation.* New York: Garland.

———, (ed.) 1998: *King Arthur's Modern Return.* New York: Garland.

Manguel, A. 1997: *A History of Reading.* London: Flamingo.

Mary Macleod. en.wikipedia.org/wiki/Mary_Macleod, accessed 10 May 2013.

Matarasso, P. M. 1969: Introduction. In *The Quest of the Holy Grail.* Ed. P. M. Matarasso. Harmondsworth: Penguin, 9–29.

Matthews, W. 1966: *The Ill-Framed Knight: A Skeptical Inquiry into the Identity of Sir Thomas Malory.* Berkeley, Calif.: University of California Press.

———, 2000: A question of texts. In B. Wheeler *et al.* (eds), 65–108.

Mayhew, H., and Binny, J. 1862: *The Criminal Prisons of London and Scenes of Prison Life.* London: Charles Griffin.

McCarthy, T. 1988: *An Introduction to Malory.* Cambridge: Brewer.

———, 1991: *Le Morte Darthur* and romance. In D. S. Brewer (ed.), 148–75.

———, 1996: Malory and his sources. In E. Archibald and A. S. G. Edwards (eds), 75–95.

McCullin, D. 1992: *Unreasonable Behaviour: An Autobiography.* London: Vintage.

McKibbin, R. 2010: Time to repent. *London Review of Books* (10 June), 11–15.

Meale, C. M. 1996: "The hoole book": editing and the creation of meaning in Malory's text. In E. Archibald and A. S. G. Edwards (eds), 3–17.

———, 2004: Manuscripts, readers, and patrons in fifteenth-century England: Sir Thomas Malory and Arthurian romance. In T. Malory, ed. S. H. A. Shepherd, 865–82.

Merriman, J. D. 1973: *The Flower of Kings: A Study of the Arthurian Legend in England between 1485 and 1835.* Lawrence, Kan.: University Press of Kansas.

Michelsson, E. 1999: *Appropriating King Arthur: The Arthurian Legend in English Drama and Entertainments, 1485–1625.* Uppsala: Acta Universitatis Upsaliensis.

Miller, J. E., Jr. 1977: *T. S. Eliot's Personal Waste Land.* Philadelphia, Pa.: Pennsylvania State University Press.

Moorman, C. 1964: "The Tale of the Sankgreall": human frailty". In R. M. Lumiansky (ed.), 184–204.

———, 1965: *The Book of Kyng Arthur: The Unity of Malory's Morte Darthur.* Lexington, Ky.: University of Kentucky Press.

Murray, N. 2010: *The Red Sweet Wine of Youth: British Poets of the First World War.* London: Little, Brown.

Nairn, T. 1977: *The Break-Up of Britain: Crisis and Neo-Nationalism.* London: NLB.

Nastali, D. 2002: Arthurian pop: the tradition in twentieth century pop music. In E. S. Sklar and D. L. Hoffman (eds), 138–67.

Newman, G. 1987: *The Rise of English Nationalism: A Cultural History, 1740–1830.* London: Weidenfeld and Nicolson.

Noguchi, S. 1981: Englishness in Malory. In T. Takamiya and D. S. Brewer (eds), 17–26.

Nolan, B. 1996: The "Tale of Sir Gareth" and the "Tale of Sir Lancelot". In E. Archibald and A. S. G. Edwards (eds), 153–81.

Norris, R. 2008: *Malory's Library: The Sources of the Morte Darthur.* Cambridge: Brewer.

Oakeshott, W. F. 1934: A Malory MS: the discovery at Winchester. *The Times* (25 August), 11.

———, 1934: "The text of Malory. *The Times Literary Supplement* (27 September), 650.

———, 1963: The finding of the manuscript. In J. A. W. Bennett (ed.), 1–6.

Oldys, W. 1747–48: Caxton (William). In *Biographia Britannica: Or, The Lives of the Most eminent persons who have flourished in Great Britain and Ireland, From the earliest Ages, down to the present Times: Collected from the best Authorities, both Printed and Manuscript, And digested in the Manner of Mr Bayle's Historical and Critical Dictionary.* 7 vols. London. II, 1223–49.

Olta, B. 2002: Was that in the Vulgate? Arthurian legend in TV film and series episodes. In E. S. Sklar and D. L. Hoffman (eds), 87–100.

Orkneyinga Saga: The History of the Earls of Orkney (1981). Trans. Hermann Pálsson and Paul Edwards. London: Penguin.

Orwell, G. 1941: England your England. In *The Lion and the Unicorn: Socialism and the English Genius.* London: Secker and Warburg, 9–55.

Parker, W. R. 1968: *Milton: A Biography.* 2 vols. Oxford: Clarendon.

Parins, M. J. (ed.) 1988: *Malory: The Critical Heritage.* London: Routledge.

Peach, L. Du G. 1965: *Richard the Lion Heart: An Adventure from History.* Ill. John Kenney. A Ladybird History Book, Series 561. Loughborough: Wills and Hepworth.

Pickering, J. D. 1983: Malory's *Morte Darthur*: the shape of tragedy. *Fifteenth Century Studies* 7, 307–28.

Pickford, C. E., and Last, R. 1981: Introduction. In *The Arthurian Bibliography.* Eds C. E. Pickford and R. Last. 2 vols. Cambridge: Brewer. I, vii–xiii.

Plummer, J. F. 1985: *Tunc se coeperunt non intelligere*: the image of language in Malory's last books". In J. W. Spisak (ed.), 153–71.

Pochoda, E. T. 1971: *Arthurian Propaganda: Le Morte Darthur as an Historical Ideal of Life*. Chapel Hill, NC: University of North Carolina Press.

Pocock, J. G. A. 2005: *The Discovery of Islands: Essays in British History*. Cambridge: Cambridge University Press.

Pollard, A. J. 2004. Neville, Richard, sixteenth earl of Warwick and sixth earl of Salisbury [*called* the kingmaker] (1428–71). *Oxford Dictionary of National Biography*. Oxford: Oxford University Press.

Pope, A. 1975: "The Dunciad". In *Collected Poems*. Ed. Bonamy Dobrée. London: Dent, 125–81.

Porter, R. (ed.) 1992: *Myths of the English*. Cambridge: Polity.

Potter, B. 1902: *The Tale of Peter Rabbit*. London: Frederick Warne, n.d.

Poulson, C. 1998: *Morris, Burne-Jones and the Quest for the Holy Grail*. London: William Morris Society.

———, 1999: *The Quest for the Grail: Arthurian Legend in British Art, 1840–1920*. Manchester: Manchester University Press.

———, 2000: Galahad and war memorial imagery of the nineteenth and early twentieth centuries. *Nineteenth-Century Contexts* 21 (4), 493–512.

Pratchett, T., and Simpson, J. 2009: *The Folklore of Discworld*. London: Corgi.

Radulescu, R. L. 2004: "Now I take upon me the adventures to seke of holy thynges": Launcelot and the crisis of Arthurian knighthood. In B. Wheeler (ed.), 285–96.

———, 2005: "Oute of mesure": violence and knighthood in Malory's *Morte Darthur*. In K. S. Whetter and R. L. Radulescu (eds), 119–32.

Raleigh, W. 1911: *The English Novel: A Short Sketch of its History from the Earliest Times to the Appearance of* Waverley. 5th edition. London: John Murray.

Ranking, B. M. n. d. [1871]: *La Mort d'Arthur: The Old Prose Stories whence the "Idylls of the King" have been taken by Alfred Tennyson, D. C. L., Poet Laureate*. London: John Camden Hotten.

Ransome, A. 1970: *Swallows and Amazons* (1930). Harmondsworth: Penguin.

Rawcliffe, C. 2004: Stafford, Humphrey, first duke of Buckingham (1402–60). *Oxford Dictionary of National Biography*. Oxford: Oxford University Press.

Reel, J. V. 2002: Sing a song of Arthur". In E. S. Sklar and D. L. Hoffman (eds), 123–37.

Reiss, E. 1966: *Sir Thomas Malory*. New York: Twayne.

Rhys, J. 1978: Introduction. In T. Malory ed. J. Rhys. I, v–xxiv.

Ricks, C. 1999: *Idylls of the King*, 1859–85. In R. W. Hill (ed.), *Tennyson's Poetry*. New York: Norton, 658–67.

Riddy, F. 1987: *Sir Thomas Malory*. Leiden: Brill.

———, 1996: Contextualizing *Le Morte Darthur*: empire and civil war. In E. Archibald and A. S. G. Edwards (eds), 55–73.

Robinson, E. A. 1930. *Collected Poems*. New York: Macmillan.

Rouse, W. D. H. 1899: Christmas mummers at Rugby. *Folk-lore* 10, 186–94.

Rumble, T. C. 1964: "The Tale of Tristram": development by analogy. In R. M. Lumiansky (ed.), 118–83.

Runciman, D. 2010: Is this the end of the UK? *London Review of Books* (27 May), 3–5.

St Clair, W. 2004: *The Reading Nation in the Romantic Period*. Cambridge: Cambridge University Press.

Saintsbury, G. 1913: *The English Novel*. London: Dent.

Samuel, R. 1998: *Island Stories: Unravelling Britain*. Ed. Alison Light *et al.* London: Verso.

Saunders, C. (ed.) 2004. *A Companion to Romance: from Classical to Contemporary*. Oxford: Blackwell.

Scala, E. 2002: Disarming Lancelot. *Studies in Philology* 99 (4), 380–403.

Scarisbrick, J. J. 1968: *Henry VIII*. London: Eyre and Spottiswoode.

Scofield, M. 1988: *T. S. Eliot: The Poems*. Cambridge: Cambridge University Press.

Scott, W. 1957: *The Poetical Works of Sir Walter Scott*. Ed. J. Logie Robertson. London: Oxford University Press.

Scruton, R. 2006: *England: An Elegy*. London: Continuum.

Sencourt, R. 1971: *T. S. Eliot: A Memoir*. London: Garnstone.

Shakespeare, W. 1947a: *The First Part of King Henry the Sixth*. In W. J. Craig (ed.), *The Complete Works of William Shakespeare*. London: Oxford University Press, 502–30.

———, 1947b: *The Second Part of King Henry the Sixth*. In W. J. Craig (ed.), *The Complete Works of William Shakespeare*. London: Oxford University Press, 531–63.

———, 1947c: *The Third Part of King Henry the Sixth*. In W. J. Craig (ed.), *The Complete Works of William Shakespeare*. London: Oxford University Press, 564–95.

———, 1947d: *The Tragedy of King Richard the Third*. In W. J. Craig (ed.), *The Complete Works of William Shakespeare*. London: Oxford University Press, 596–634.

Shap, R. 2002: Dryden and Purcell's *King Arthur*: legend and politics on the Restoration stage". In R. Barber (ed.), 9–22.

Shaw, S. 1963: Caxton and Malory. In J. A. W. Bennett (ed.), 114–45.

Shepherd, S. H. A. 2004: Reception of *Le Morte Darthur to 1934*. In T. Malory, *Le Morte Darthur*. Ed. S. H. A. Shepherd, xxxii–xxxiv.

Shurley, J. c. 1702: *Great Britain's Glory; Being the History of King Arthur, with the Adventures of the Knights of the Round Table*. London: "Printed by and for W. O."

References

Sir Thomas Malory, Le Morte Darthur. Archives and Manuscripts online catalogue. www.bl.uk, accessed 10 May 2013.

Sklar, E. S. 1993: The undoing of romance in Malory's *Morte Darthur. Fifteenth Century Studies* 20, 309–27.

——, 2001: Malory's other(ed) Elaine. In B. Wheeler and F. Tolhurst (eds), 59–70.

——, 2002: Marketing Arthur: the commodification of Arthurian legend. In E. S. Sklar and D. L. Hoffman (eds), 9–23.

——, and Hoffman, D. L. (eds) 2002: *King Arthur in Popular Culture.* Jefferson, NC: McFarland.

Smith, J. 1996: Language and style in Malory. In E. Archibald and A. S. G. Edwards (eds), 97–113.

Smith, A. D. 2001: *Nationalism: Theory, Ideology, History.* Cambridge: Polity.

Southam, B. C. 1977: *A Student's Guide to the Selected Poems of T. S. Eliot.* London: Faber, 1977.

Southey, R. 1817. Preface. In T. Malory, ed. W. Upcott. I, i–xxxii.

Spenser, E. 1916. *The Poetical Works.* Ed. J. C. Smith and E. De Selincourt. London: Oxford University Press.

Spisak, J. W. 1985a: Introduction: recent trends in Malory studies. In J. W. Spisak (ed.), 1–12.

——, 1985b: Malory's 'Lost' Source. In J. W. Spisak (ed.), 227–30.

——, (ed.) 1985: *Studies in Malory.* Kalamazoo, Mich.: Western Michigan University.

Staines, D. 1975: King Arthur in Victorian fiction. In J. H. Buckley (ed.), *The Worlds of Victorian Fiction.* London: Harvard University Press. 267–93.

Stanislaus, S. M. *c.* 1964: *Newbold Revel: A Warwickshire Manor.* Newbold Revel: St. Paul's College.

Steinbeck, J. 1976: *The Acts of King Arthur and His Noble Knights.* Ed. C. Horton. London: Heinemann.

Stephens, J., and McCallum, R. 1998: *Retelling Stories, Framing Culture: Traditional Story and Metanarratives in Children's Literature.* New York: Garland.

Stewart, G. R. 1935: English geography in Malory's *Morte D'Arthur. Modern Language Review* 30, 204–9.

Strachey, E. 1868: Introduction. In T. Malory, vii–xxxvii.

Takamiya, T., and Brewer, D. S. (eds) 1981: *Aspects of Malory.* Cambridge: Brewer.

Taylor, B., and Brewer, E. 1983: *The Return of King Arthur: British and American Arthurian Literature since 1900.* Cambridge: Brewer.

Tennyson, A. 1969: *The Poems of Tennyson.* Ed. C. Ricks. London: Longmans.

——, 1999: *Tennyson's Poetry.* Ed. R. W. Hill, Jr. New York: Norton.

Taylor, B., and Brewer, E. 1983: *The Return of King Arthur: British and American Arthurian Literature since 1900.* Cambridge: Brewer.

Tennyson, A. 1969: *The Poems of Tennyson.* Ed. C. Ricks. London: Longmans.

———, 1999: *Tennyson's Poetry.* Ed. R. W. Hill, Jr. New York: Norton.

Tennyson, H. 1897: *Alfred Lord Tennyson: A Memoir by His Son.* 2 vols. London: Macmillan.

The Manual for Leaders of the Order of Sir Galahad (1921). 3rd edition. Boston, Mass.: Order of Sir Galahad, Inc.

Thompson, R. H. 1985: *The Return from Avalon: A Study of the Arthurian Legend in Modern Fiction.* Westport, Conn.: Greenwood.

Tolhurst, F. 2005: Why every knight needs his lady. In K. S. Whetter and R. L. Radulescu (eds), 133–47.

Tondro, J. 2002: Camelot in comics. In E. Sklar and D. L. Hoffman (eds), 169–81.

Tooley, R. V. 1979: Introduction. In *Saxton's Atlas 1579–1979: Commissioned by Cambridge University Library in Commemoration of its Publication by Christopher Saxton.* Cambridge: Cambridge University Press, n. p.

Twain, M. 1986: *A Connecticut Yankee at King Arthur's Court* (1889). Ed. J. Kaplan. London: Penguin.

Vinaver, E. 1929: *Malory.* Oxford: Clarendon.

———, 1947. Introduction. In *The Works of Sir Thomas Malory.* Ed. E. Vinaver. 3 vols. Oxford: Clarendon. I, xiii–cix.

———, 1959: Sir Thomas Malory. In R. S. Loomis (ed.), 541–52.

———, 1963: On Art and Nature. In J. A. W. Bennett (ed.), 29–40.

———, 1967: Introduction. In *The Works of Sir Thomas Malory.* Ed. E. Vinaver. 2nd edition, 3 vols. Oxford: Clarendon. I, xix–cxxvi.

———, 1970: Preface. In *Malory* (1929). Repr. Oxford: Clarendon, n. p.

Wace. Roman de Brut. In *Wace and Layamon: Arthurian Chronicles.* Ed. G. Jones. Trans. E. Mason. London: Dent, 1–114.

Walsh, J. M. 1985: Malory's "very mater of la Cheualer du Charyot": characterization and structure. In J. W. Spisak (ed.), 199–226.

Watts, J. 2004: Pole, William de la, first duke of Suffolk (1396–1450). *Oxford Dictionary of National Biography.* Oxford: Oxford University Press.

Webster, B. 1998: *The Wars of the Roses.* London: UCL.

Weinbrot, H. D. 1993: *Britannia's Issue: The Rise of British Literature from Dryden to Ossian.* Cambridge: Cambridge University Press.

Weston, J. L. 1999: Sir Lancelot (1896). In A. Lupack and B. T. Lupack, 243.

———, 1899: *King Arthur and His Knights: A Brief Introduction.* London: Nutt.

———, 1964: *The Quest of the Holy Grail* (1913). London: Cass.

———, 1920: *From Ritual to Romance.* Cambridge: Cambridge University Press.

References

Wheeler, B., and Salda, M. N. 2000: Introduction. In B. Wheeler *et al.* (eds), ix–xiv.

—, (ed.) 2004: *Arthurian Studies in Honour of P. J. C. Field.* Cambridge: Brewer.

—, *et al.* (eds) 2000: *The Malory Debates: Essays on the Texts of Le Morte Darthur.* Cambridge: Brewer.

—, and F. Tolhurst (eds) 2001: *On Arthurian Women: Essays in Memory of Maureen Fries.* Dallas, Tex.: Scriptorium.

Whetter, K. S., and Radulescu, R. L. (eds) 2005: *Re-Viewing Le Morte Darthur: Texts and Contexts, Characters and Themes.* Cambridge: Brewer.

White, T. H. 1958: *The Once and Future King.* London: Collins.

Whittaker, M. 1990: *The Legends of King Arthur in Art.* Cambridge: Brewer.

Wilson, R. H. 1950: Malory's early knowledge of Arthurian romance. *Studies in English* 29, 33–50.

Winchester, S. 2003: *The Meaning of Everything: The Story of the Oxford English Dictionary.* Oxford: Oxford University Press.

Windeatt, B. 2009: The fifteenth-century Arthur". In E. Archibald and A. Putter (eds), 84–102.

Wolffe, J. 1981: *Henry VI.* London: Eyre Methuen.

Woolf, V. 1978: *The Diary of Virginia Woolf, Volume II: 1920–24.* Ed. A. O. Bell and A. McNeillie. London: Hogarth.

Wright, T. 1858: Introduction. In T. Malory. I, v–xvii.

Wright, T. L. 1964: "The Tale of King Arthur": beginnings and foreshadowings". In R. M. Lumiansky (ed.), 9–66.

www.gutenberg.org.

www.internationalarthuriansociety.com.

www.lib.rochester.edu/camelot/cphome.stm.

Yeats-Edwards, P. 2000: The Winchester Malory manuscript: an attempted history. In B. Wheeler *et al.* (eds), 367–90.

Index